The Armada in Ireland

NIALL FALLON

The Armada in Ireland

WESLEYAN UNIVERSITY PRESS

MIDDLETOWN, CONNECTICUT

Published simultaneously in Great Britain by
Stanford Maritime Limited
12 Long Acre, London WC2E 9LP

ISBN: 0–8195–5028–0
Library of Congress Catalog Card Number: 77–95546

Manufactured in Great Britain
First American Edition

Contents

		Page
PREFACE		vii
ACKNOWLEDGEMENTS		ix
A NOTE ON THE DATING SYSTEM		x
I	The Troubled Triangle	1
II	The Coast of Wrecks	17
III	The Flail of Connacht	30
IV	A Ship at Torane	57
V	Disaster in Donegal	74
VI	A Fair Wind for Spain	91
VII	The Escape of Captain Cuellar	106
VIII	The Brothers Hovenden	127
IX	The Sheriff of Clare	140
X	The Drowning of the Saints	154
XI	Myths and Mysteries	179
	Epilogue	206
	APPENDICES	
1	*Composition of the Spanish Armada*	209
2	*Armada Losses in Ireland*	211
3	*Excavated Armada Wrecks in Ireland*	216
4	*Irishmen with the Armada*	221
5	*Those in Ireland Concerned with the Armada*	223
	BIBLIOGRAPHY	225
	INDEX	228

Preface

THIS work is the direct result of a surprising discovery made some years ago: that there existed no comprehensive and definitive work on Armada wrecks around Ireland, and which placed the momentous events surrounding the advent of the Spaniards on Irish shores in a proper historical context.

This is not for one moment to suggest that nothing has been written on the subject; anyone writing of the Armada cannot afford to ignore the Irish aspect of the enterprise of Philip II of Spain, nor indeed has it been ignored. At the same time, however, the role which Ireland played in the campaign has been largely understated, and I suspect more from an understandable reluctance to tackle the daunting research involved than to any other single contributing factor. It is possible to compile a reasonable history of the Armada in Ireland without going to the the extremes of geographical and local-historical research but such a history would skim the surface only. Properly, the writer needs an intimate knowledge of the Irish seaboard with its creeks and bays, its tides and currents, its rocks and reefs and the countless navigational and other natural hazards which this fascinating shoreline presents.

As a non-historian, I have written this work primarily for the general reader and so it is not disfigured or encumbered with footnotes, which do not help the continuity of any narrative work. All the necessary verification is supplied by the bibliography; the bulk of the information comes from the various State Papers, Duro's history, charts of the coast, and an exhaustive study of the works of local historians. Every wreck site has been visited and over two hundred interviews with local people carried out; where possible I have gone to sea and approached the wreck site from the probable path of the doomed Armada ship. It has been an exhilarating experience.

A word here on the value or otherwise of tradition and legend in Armada history. There is as yet a wealth of this extant in Ireland; but its real worth lies not in the intricate details with which it clothes the story of a wreck but where it places the site of that wreck. Time and again I have seen tradition fix on a wreck site with great accuracy, an accuracy which is, however, unfortunately paralleled by a wayward depth of error on other facts such as ships' identification or names of survivors.

There as yet remains much work to be done; while travelling the road towards the completion of this work, many tempting side roads appeared here and there along the way. No doubt there is much to be gained by a journey down their mysterious and potentially rich lengths, but that, regrettably, will have to wait for another day.

Acknowledgements

PERHAPS more is owed to the work of William Spotswood Green than to any other single historian. As Chief Inspector of Irish Fisheries at the turn of the century, he was able to devote much of his time to the solid groundwork needed in compiling an accurate list of Armada ships wrecked around Ireland. The finest tribute to his researches which one can possibly give is to point out that his work of seventy years ago is as valuable today as it was then.

My grateful thanks go out to staffs of museums and libraries who never waned in their courtesy and helpfulness; to the National Library, Dublin; the National Museum, Dublin; the British Museum, London; the National Maritime Museum, London; the Archivo General de Simancas, Spain; the Library of University College, Galway; Trinity College, Dublin; Galway County Library; Mayo County Library; Sligo County Library; Donegal County Library; Kerry County Library; County Museum, Armagh; the Royal Geographical Society; the Royal Irish Academy; the Ulster Museum, Belfast, and to several others my debt is great.

Methuen & Co., London, and David & Charles Ltd, Devon, were kind enough to allow me to quote from their authors; and to the Irish Cruising Club for permitting quotations from their *Sailing Directions* go further thanks. Much constructive help and advice came from the work of later Armada historians and researchers such as Dr John de Courcy Ireland, whose unique researches into Ragusan participation in the Armada helped in the identification of two vessels wrecked in Ireland; Colin Martin of St Andrews University, who knows more about Armada wrecks than any other man alive; Dr Kevin Danaher, whose own work on Irish wrecks deserves a much wider audience; Cyril Falls and Prof. G A Hayes-McCoy whose researches into Ulster military history and affairs have left little else that can be said: to all of these I am deeply grateful.

I recall with particular gratitude the many local people living along the coast of Kerry, Clare, Galway, Mayo, Sligo and Donegal who were only too willing to pass on their tradition and legend, handed down from generation to generation with unfaltering assiduity, a memory of the great ships which came

ix

Acknowledgements

looming from the west out of storm and gale to create their own enduring legend. To be on the wreck sites, to study the waves and tides, the rocks and reefs, to stand on the same sand or grass that shipwrecked Spaniards trod some four centuries ago, brings home with unforgettable clarity the events of four centuries ago.

Finally my thanks to my very good and true companion, Denis Kendrick, whose camera skills accompanied me on my journeyings; and to my wife, who stood up with fortitude and good humour to being companionless and in second place for much of the time it took to research and write this volume.

A Note on the Dating System

Any work on the Armada is bedevilled by the fact that the English and the Gregorian Calendar were in 1588 in violent disagreement. If England (and Ireland) remained stubbornly ten days behind the rest of an impatient Europe it was of their own choice, but it has made matters difficult for later generations who have tried to reconcile events in continental Europe with those in England and Ireland. Like most modern writers, I have elected to use the Gregorian Calendar and so have amended dates by ten days, so that September 10 Old Style becomes September 20 New Style. The days of the week remain unchanged.

The Troubled Triangle

AT one o'clock on the afternoon of September 18, 1558 Governor Sir Richard Bingham of Connacht took a sheet of parchment and in a firm hand wrote from his quarters in Athlone to the Lord Deputy of Ireland:

Even now I received the enclosed letter from the Sheriff of Thomond, by which Your Lordship shall perceive some further news of strange ships; whether they be of the dispersed fleet which are fled from the supposed overthrow in the Narrow Seas, or new forces come from Spain directly, no man is able to advertise otherwise than by guess, which doth rather show their coming from Spain, both by these falling from the west, and the others which coasted along the north parts of Sligo . . . by all likelihoods they mind to land.

For some days before this, a steady stream of reports of sightings of strange ships along the outer Atlantic rim of western Ireland had filtered through to the English authorities in the country; that same day, the Mayor of Waterford heard of eleven ships in the Shannon at Limerick, and that 140 ships of the Armada 'as it is thought, are beaten by stress of weather to the coast.' On the 15th George Bingham wrote to his brother from Sligo describing the movements of 'three Spanish ships which bore down towards the harbour of Calebeg' [Killybegs]; a report from Tralee in Kerry sharpened this ominous news; there, twenty-four Spaniards had come ashore from a small vessel in the bay and had been executed.

Within a week, the reports were flooding in from Donegal to Kerry, bringing scattered but confirmatory news of a great fleet of ships, undoubtedly the remnants of the Invincible Armada, sailing along the coast, sometimes close in, at other times far out on the horizon. From the Sheriff of Clare came the news that 'last night two ships were seen about the islands of Arran [Aran Islands] and it is thought that more sails were seen westward from the islands . . .'. Governor Bingham again wrote that 'seven ships have arrived at Carg-e-colle' (Carrigaholt in Clare); four ships were at Loop Head in Clare, and Spaniards had been captured in Dingle. Towards Galway were seen four more great ships. And so it went on. The entire coast of the western half of the country came alive to the arrival of the Spanish ships; a flood of frightened appeal and entreaty came from almost every county, heightened by reports of landings as the days wore on towards October: Spaniards, armed and hostile, had come ashore in Inishowen in Donegal, Dingle in Kerry, 'ten sail in Sir John O'Dogherty's country' (this last report being later proved false), Burris (Burrishoole) in Clew Bay.

However contradictory and exaggerated many of these reports, one thing was clear. Spanish ships, in large numbers, were off the coast and from them had come ashore soldiers and sailors of Spain. It was an invasion, if an inadvertent one, and the numbers of the invaders were formidable. In the early days, following the first reports of the sighting of Spanish ships, all was confusion; later on, as evidence arrived on the Lord Deputy's desk to show that many ships and men had arrived on the coast and that several thousand Spaniards had landed in different areas of Ireland, a more coherent if still exaggerated picture began to emerge. But the fact remained that for the first time a threateningly sizeable force of Spain had landed on the shores of Ireland, thereby constituting a direct threat to the England which ruled Ireland. It was at first sight the most critical challenge to the authority of England to emerge since the conquest of Ireland in the twelfth century; and it was natural that such a challenge, if it were to emerge at all, should come from Spain.

The growing power and spread of influence, not only throughout Europe but through much of the world then known to western civilization, of the empire of Philip II of Spain had attracted increasing interest from Ireland, particularly during the decades of the 1570s and 80s. As the colonization of Ireland under the energetic Elizabeth began to take greater effect, Ireland turned for help to the mainland of Europe, but particularly to Spain. There were many ties between the two countries, although Spain was much more than just a single nation; ties of common Iberian ancestry, of commerce, and perhaps most of all, of a similar Catholic religion, common to both in its intensity and devotion. Spain's religious relationship with Ireland had grown deep roots, with many Irish ecclesiastics educated in the seminaries of what was the largest empire in the world, an empire on which 'the sun never set'.

During the second half of the sixteenth century, a growing tide of Irish exiles, both voluntary and involuntary, flowed across the seas primarily to Spain but also to Rome and Lisbon. Most those who left their country were soldiers, seamen, religious or students; a few were noblemen, forced from their estates and territories by the tightening of England's grip on Ireland. By the time the Armada was ready to sail from Lisbon at the end of May 1588, the sound of an Irish accent in the capitals of Mediterranean Europe particularly was a common sound to European ears. It was inevitable, too, that the importunities of Irish exiles seeking help to raise rebellion in their home country against English rule should reach deep into the corridors of Philip's court.

On a spring day in 1587, while in Lisbon the Armada was preparing to launch itself against England, one of these Irishmen was brought before the Marquis of Santa Cruz, Don Alvaro de Bazan. Santa Cruz, then ageing and irritable, had been entrusted by Philip II with assembling the fleet in Lisbon; a troublesome and vexing task with a shortage of ships, men, ammunition, guns and provisions, it took up most of the Marquis' attention. Yet he found time to question a lone and apparently minor Irish exile, Myles Brewitt.

Santa Cruz's short interview with the shadowy expatriate Brewitt has a special fascination: Ireland could quite logically have provided a very real target for Philip's ships and men, and a cogent alternative to the clumsy master plan which a year later was to fall dismally on its face as the Armada ploughed up the English Channel. If Santa Cruz's questioning of Brewitt was perfunctory, he nevertheless discovered that Ireland had never been quieter, that while strongly fortified it was at the same time weakly garrisoned and governed, and that Philip, should he choose to make Ireland his objective when his fleet sailed at last from the Tagus, would find on Irish shores a populace sympathetic to Spain and mutinously opposed to England – the ideal springboard, in fact, from which to launch a more ambitious invasion, that of England.

Philip's obvious and continued reluctance to invade Ireland has often puzzled historians, more so regarding the sixteenth century than of later periods. But had he much to gain? To attempt to conquer Ireland before invading England, he would have had to find the troops, equipment and all the vast resources needed not only to govern but also to defend the island, and defence in the face of certain English retaliation from across the Irish seas would be inevitable. Philip was already hard pressed to hold his threatened possessions in the Netherlands, and the numbers of troops which he could spare were negligible. There were other considerations: Philip clearly realized the obvious, that if he invaded and conquered England, Ireland would be his in the natural course of events while he would be spared the necessity of taking on and defeating English forces in Ireland, and what was perhaps more problematical, of maintaining supplies along a sea route dominated by Elizabeth's naval power.

As well as this, however, it may well have been apparent to Philip that Irish appeals for aid in overthrowing English rule were subjective; Ireland had never felt any warmth towards any occupying force, Norman, Danish or English, and it was unlikely that this natural antagonism towards the invader would undergo a radical turnabout simply because the new invader was Spain and its religion Catholic. Ireland would welcome Spain's intervention in its domestic affairs merely as a lever which could be used to expel English influence, but beyond that lay considerable doubt; there was little indication that, once the initial period of euphoria ended and the Irish had begun to wriggle under Philip's rule, the Spanish king would find this naturally rebellious and mutinous nation any easier to govern than had Elizabeth.

Irish arguments urging Spain to invade Ireland and to expel and defeat the

English thus fell on increasingly deaf ears. Philip had once before (if in a peripheral and carefully uninvolved way) tested this theory at Smerwick in 1580, when a Papal force largely comprised of Italians but with a considerable Spanish element had landed in the Kerry port and implored Irish aid, had been ignored, and afterwards suffered the usual fate of being murdered by the English forces. The message had sunk home; after Smerwick the Irish found it increasingly difficult to persuade Philip that if he landed in Ireland the entire native populace would rush to his side as allies against the English. And later events, particularly during the inadvertent Spanish invasion with the Armada men and ships, were to prove the wisdom of Philip's decision to leave Ireland strictly alone.

The problem of what to do about Ireland was clearly not confined to Philip. After all, it was an English possession and had been so since the twelfth century, since Henry II became the first English king to set foot on Irish soil in 1171 (William the Conqueror, though he often threatened to come, never did). It had been colonized, not on a very wide scale, in the twelfth and thirteenth centuries, but until the accession of Elizabeth in 1558 had passed the intervening centuries in an atmosphere of relative peace. It was not until Elizabeth began a determined and systematic attempt to totally subdue, demoralize and fully colonize the entire island that the whole question of Ireland took on an international aspect. Hitherto it had remained largely remote from the mainstream of western European politics, that increasingly troubled arena in which the dominant emerging themes of nationalism, religion and economics had begun to force wide fissures among its nations, dominated by Spain, France and England. Ireland simply did not count, had not counted for many centuries, in the shifting power struggle of western Europe; since Henry II's annexation of the country, it had sunk into a misty oblivion.

Henry had accomplished his takeover of Ireland with the aid of the only Englishman ever to become Pope of the Roman Catholic Church; it was Adrian IV who gave his blessing to the famous Papal Bull which said '. . . you desire to enter the island of Ireland to subject that people to laws and to root out therefrom the weeds of vice . . . we . . . deem it pleasing and acceptable that . . . you should enter that island and execute whatever shall be conducive to the honour of God and the salvation of that land.'

Later English monarchs seemingly cared as little about their remote western colony as did Henry (no doubt much of this ignorance was due to the inadequacies of pre-Elizabethan cartography, it being difficult to find any interest in something never seen or whose very shape was obscure). For four hundred years after the first English king had stepped onto the shores of Ireland, the country had remained by and large in a dormant state, ostensibly controlled by England but in truth relatively unfettered, with its colonists mostly huddled protectively within the confines of the Pale (the eastern counties in and around Dublin and the east Midlands), while outside this

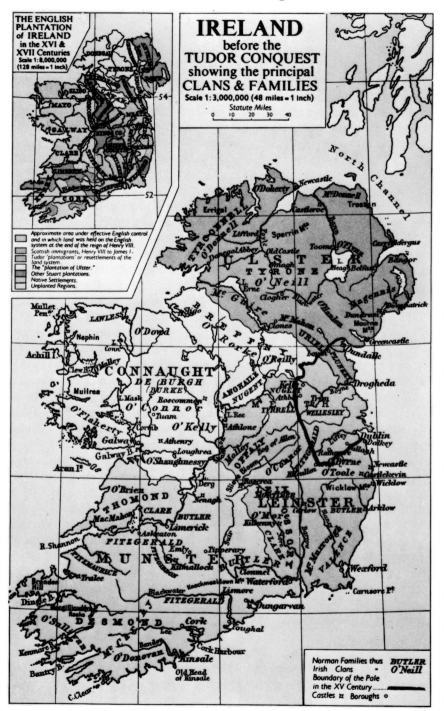

THE ENGLISH
PLANTATION
of IRELAND
in the XVI &
XVII Centuries
Scale 1:8,000,000
(128 miles = 1 inch)

Approximate area under effective English control
and in which land was held on the English
system at the end of the reign of Henry VIII.
Scottish immigrants, Henry VIII to James I.
Tudor 'plantations' or resettlements of the
land system.
The "plantation of Ulster."
Other Stuart plantations.
Native Settlements.
Unplanted Regions.

IRELAND
before the
TUDOR CONQUEST
showing the principal
CLANS & FAMILIES
Scale 1:3,000,000 (48 miles = 1 inch)
Statute Miles
0 10 20 30 40

Norman Families thus *BUTLER*
Irish Clans ▪ *O'Neill*
Boundary of the Pale
in the XV Century ▬▬▬▬▬
Castles ⌗ Boroughs ○

The provinces of Ireland as they were c. 1580, and the principal clans. (Reproduced from Muir's Historical Atlas, Ancient, Medieval and Modern courtesy Geo. Philip & Son Ltd) sphere of English control the great native lords and clans remained relatively untouched, ruling very much the way they had done for centuries, almost untroubled in the vast spaces of bog and forest.

The years under Elizabeth were to change all this. An Irish historian has written of his country that it was a 'unique example of a territory which was colonized in the twelfth and thirteenth centuries in a feudal setting and which was re-colonized in the sixteenth and seventeenth centuries in a post-feudal setting.' And only in the sixteenth century did the ancient Gaelic way of life which had hitherto dominated Irish life and culture come into direct conflict with that of western Europe. This 'dissolution of a Celtic community in contact with a Teutonic influenced by Roman laws and ideas' is largely the story of Elizabethan Ireland. On a different level, the deep divergence of religion and culture underlies all the events in Ireland during the sixteenth and seventeenth centuries and is essential for a clearer understanding of its course during that period, as England gradually and inexorably tightened its grip on the country. By the end of the seventeenth century, the second colonization of Ireland by England had been completed and the country's ancient and indigenous culture destroyed beyond repair; the Battle of Kinsale at the turn of the century heralded the end of the old Ireland and ushered in a new and debasing era of colonial suppression not to be broken for another three and a half centuries.

During the reign of Elizabeth, as indeed at any period during English rule, Ireland assumed a strategic and religious importance: 'Ireland represented an almost classic case of the new problems posed for governments by the clash of competing creeds . . . although Irish society was infinitely less sophisticated than that of the Netherlands, its struggle against English domination was characterized by many of the same features as the Dutch struggle against the domination of Spain. In both societies a religious cause enhanced, and was enhanced by, a sense of national identity. In both, the affiliation of national leaders to an international religious movement provided new opportunities for securing international assistance.'

The intense and unwavering Catholicism of the native Irish, allied with the national cause of its fight against colonial suppression, caused a constant threat to England, a threat given added weight by the growing European might of Spain, sympathetic in religion to Ireland and allied with it in its hatred of Protestant England, now consolidating that Protestantism under Elizabeth's energetic hand. During this period Ireland came to be examined more closely by both England and Spain. Its position on the main sea routes to and from the new, rich lands of the Americas to the west made it of considerable strategic importance for both countries, but there were other factors, such as its closeness to England, its easy accessibility to Spanish ships, and its possible danger as a springboard from which Philip could launch an invasion of England.

This latter prospect was quite feasible. The southeastern tip of Ireland is visible from the hills of Wales on a clear day, while the extreme northeast corner is a bare dozen miles from the coast of Scotland (a geographical neighbourliness availed of by the Scots who peopled Antrim in their thousands). But apart altogether from this closeness, there were other physical advantages as far as Philip was concerned. Ireland was readily accessible by sea from the ports along the Iberian coast, as the winds which circled the earth and blew across the unknown great oceans were the same winds that steered ships along their courses – and from the direction of the south and southwest, steady trade winds could carry Spanish ships quickly to the shores of Ireland. The whole western half of the island's coastline was at the mercy of any fleet homing in on the wings of the prevailing sou'westerlies, winds that would at the same time hamper English ships beating out of southern ports in any attempt to stop such an invasion.

Once Philip had organized, equipped and dispatched an invasion fleet towards Ireland, it was a relatively simple matter for his ships to reach its coasts. It would be equally simple for his forces to land in the extreme northwest corner, where English control was negligible and which formed the territory of the last great independent Irish chiefs, controlling vast areas of land and thousands of fighting men basically hostile to England. Once landed, an alliance of Spanish and Irish power could have been achieved, and had this occurred Ireland could have been re-conquered from the English.

All this was not supposition: it could have happened, and easily enough. Elizabeth and her advisers were painfully aware of its possibilities and the threat to their domination of Ireland. They were acutely sensitive to every possible danger, but their hands were tied financially and physically by the demands of Elizabeth's war efforts in the Low Countries which at this time were providing a constant drain on her scanty exchequer. England quite simply could not afford to govern Ireland permanently on a large scale – her purse and other resources would not permit it. Only in times of extreme threat could large reinforcements be hurried across the Irish Sea, and otherwise the English authorities in Ireland had to rely on a wholly inadequate, poorly equipped and scattered force.

England achieved, with this minuscule force, what by any standards was a remarkable grip on Ireland. Immediate and effective rule was confined to the Pale, the east midlands, and to the larger towns and cities throughout the country. Beyond that was wilderness, in which the English were understandably reluctant to dwell except in considerable strength, and that was available but rarely. Outside its civilized centres of population, Ireland was wild, remote and difficult of access, with huge mountain ranges, vast bogs and thousands of square miles of indigenous forest, into whose close shelter the natives melted at the first sign of any enemy approach. To comb out every pocket of resistance and entirely subdue the entire population, and afterwards to garrison the conquered areas strongly enough to ensure continued subjection, was out of the question for Elizabeth. At a pinch, but only by retracting her forces from the Low Countries and leaving England's own defences much reduced, she could have achieved this; but there was little point.

By the decade of 1580–90 much of the country, especially in Munster, had been ravaged by war and waste, the results of a deliberate policy of Elizabeth's to ruthlessly subdue and colonize Ireland. Only by total warfare could the country be reduced to the impoverished, starving and demoralized state which needed only the bare minimum of occupying forces to keep it in order, with a threat of further reinforcements if fresh trouble arose. Elizabeth beat the Irish to their knees and when they knelt, kicked their legs from beneath them; only when this was achieved could she rest assured that the few troops she could spare to look after her affairs in Ireland were sufficient.

English forces held all the bigger towns and sea ports; the Irish, even the most independent and furthest removed from English control such as the clans in Donegal, retained not one centre of population which could have any real or useful strategic value. There were garrisons where they were needed, even if these were often understrength and nominal. Add to this the efficiency of the English spying network and the quality of the men whom Elizabeth sent to govern the colony, and the picture of intimidation and subjection is clearer; some of the greatest soldiers of the day were placed in charge of Ireland during Elizabeth's reign – Perrott, Fitzwilliam, Essex, Sidney, Sussex and of course Mountjoy. As well there were famous names such as Raleigh and Grenville, Pelham, Bingham and the Norris brothers; the list of those who served their queen in Elizabethan Ireland reads as a roll of the great Englishmen of their day and a clear indication that the Queen did not neglect the dangers which lay under the surface of her western colony; she was too able and too shrewd a ruler not to recognize that the possession and subjection of Ireland was a matter of moment to the security of her country.

In the spring of 1587, when the threat of the Armada was overshadowing events in the rest of Europe and there existed a strong body of opinion that Philip II planned to invade Ireland rather than England, there were under 1800 English troops in the whole of Ireland, and even then there were 'guns rusty and carriages rotting for want of men to maintain them, supplies of powder and shot deficient.' In June of the following year, just a few short weeks before the first of the Spaniards from the fleeing Armada was to land on Irish soil, a tract (possibly by Sir William Herbert) warned that Munster would be in some danger if an invasion took place, and added 'I think it very necessary that the English forces of horsemen and footmen here were in time looked into. I fear me they will be found very defective; that the garrisons also, the storehouses and the munition, were carefully viewed; I think they will be found but in bad plight.'

Limerick was considered then to be the strongest held city in Munster, yet the munition there consisted only of 'four demi-cannons, one culverin, and a demi-culverin, a minion, and a "fawlkon", all out of reparations.' The state of these weapons was ominous, with their 'lying upon the ground' and their carriages 'broken and rotted'. As well, there were 'over two or three hundred calivers all in decay and unserviceable, sundry sheaves of arrows, the feathers gone through the moisture that hath spoiled them; some other weapon and armour there are, but all in very evil case.' This bleak picture, it must be

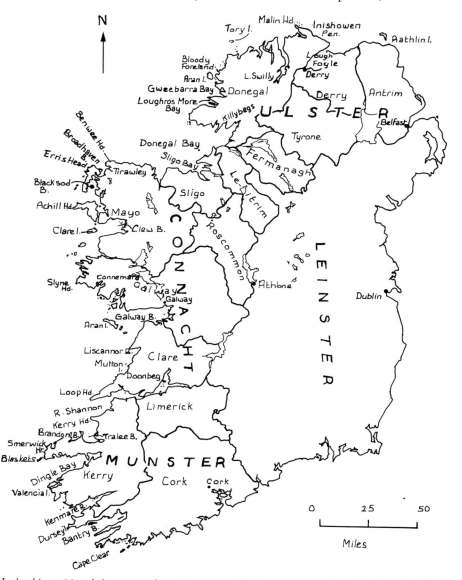

Ireland in 1588 and the areas and counties connected with events surrounding the Armada. Ships were wrecked in Antrim, Donegal, Sligo, Mayo, Galway, Clare (Thomond) and Kerry, and the survivors trekked through or were hidden in the other counties shown.

remembered, showed a city which the English considered one of their strong points; its inadequacies must therefore have found even wider echoes in garrisons throughout the country, building up an overall picture of a tiny, badly trained and equipped occupying force, hardly suited to put up any real resistance to an invasion of highly professional and disciplined troops.

The ultimate failure of the Irish was that they failed to persuade the Spaniards to act as they might have hoped, and at the same time failed to grasp the slim opportunities which came their way whenever Spain showed signs of relenting in its almost constant refusal to aid the Irish. This is a broad argument and must be qualified; at Smerwick in 1580, although the landing force was properly Italian, it could be regarded as having Philip's tacit approval. It was big enough (eight hundred soldiers) to have caused a great deal of concern to the English authorities, as indeed it did until Lord Deputy Grey entered the scene; it is known that Irish aid had been promised: the force would never have landed in the country unless and until it had had sound assurances of such aid. Yet not an Irishman raised a serious hand to help the Papal force, which very soon lost heart sufficiently to surrender. On that occasion, when they had promised to help and when their duty to do so was very clearly defined, the native Irish failed dismally to honour their promise.

There were many reasons for this, which are outside the scope of this book, but it must be said that Smerwick was to be paralleled in the years to come to both a greater and a lesser degree. The Battle of Kinsale in 1601 is a case in point, where the two great Irish chieftains on whom Spain had placed so much faith delayed their advance from the north to Kinsale until they arrived in effect too late to prevent Mountjoy from gathering sufficient forces to win a signal victory, perhaps the most important victory over the Irish throughout the country's history.

It is clear that then as now, the Irish rarely co-operated to the extent where their combined forces made up a fighting unit strong enough to worry the English. Their clan structure with its internecine feuds and jealousies, its strictly defined boundaries, and the innate reluctance of the Gael towards organization and discipline all made the setting up of a cohesive and disciplined force unlikely. Elizabeth knew this, and gambled on it. As in so many instances throughout her long reign, she was to be proved right. It was her shrewdness in reading the mood of the clans, and the vigilance of her officials who ruled Ireland, which were her trump cards; and she played them well.

It is difficult to blame either Spain or Philip for their continued reluctance to commit themselves fully towards wresting Ireland from England, more so as a question of either economics or politics. There were many roads on which the two countries met. From Mesolithic times both had traded flourishingly in fish, hides, furs, timber, linen and wine. Spain's wine exports to Ireland constituted one of her biggest export businesses and there are traces yet of this influence in some of the sea ports of Ireland, particularly Galway, Dingle and

Killybegs. Galway more perhaps than any other city throughout the country hinged its economy almost solely on the importation of Spanish wines, and became a renowned wine centre.

Trade of another and quite different sort also brought the two countries closer together. Atlantic seas off western Ireland offered rich fishing grounds for Iberian fishermen intrepid enough to make the long voyage, a trade which still exists today, although now much reduced. In the sixteenth century the volume of Spanish fishing boats on the rich banks off Ireland was formidable, so much so that Francis Drake was at one time hatching a plan to capture them. Most of these boats were quite large, around 100 tons, and in 1572 Sir Humphrey Gilbert reported from Munster to his queen that there were no less than six hundred or more fishing off Ireland.

The strong religious affiliations between Ireland and Spain were reflected by the extent to which Irish clerics fled to Spain to escape the harshness of the English persecution of Catholics in Ireland. Christopher Arthur, a Limerick merchant, left on a voyage for ports in Spain and Portugal in the summer of 1588, during the time when the Armada had been defeated in the battle of Gravelines, and on his return in February the following year noted that there were many Irish bishops in Spain particularly but also in Portugal. Among those who he claimed were in exile in the two countries were the Bishop of Kildare, Conor O'Mulryan, who was in Lisbon; the Bishop of Limerick, Conor O'Bayll, who was in Spain; the Bishop of Ross, Philip Naghten, who was in Seville; the Bishop of Ossory, 'a man of Waterford', was in St James' in Gallizia (Galicia); while 'there is a Bishop of Dublin in the Groyne [Corunna].' This total of five bishops was in all probability an underestimate; at least one Irish bishop, that of Killaloe, was drowned off an Armada ship in Antrim.

And yet, for all the wine trade, the fishing, the furs and linen, the interchanging of religions, the flood of Irish exiles to the larger cities of the Spanish empire in Europe, each country knew little of the other. The fishermen knew the grounds wherein they could reap their own harvest; the wine merchants knew their colleagues, the linen manufacturers their markets; but beyond these specialized fields remarkably little knowledge appears to have been acquired by one side of the other. Philip had an ideal opportunity of setting up a formidable spy network through his country's trade with Ireland – yet he appears not to have done so to more than a marginal extent. And the lack of knowledge which most of the Armada sailors had of the Irish coastline and its many dangers suggests strongly that aboard those unfortunate vessels there were few of the experienced Spanish fishermen who every year made their landfall along the Irish coastline.

If Philip's lack of detailed knowledge of the Irish and Ireland appears paradoxical, then Ireland itself was equally so. At a time when the Protestantism of England and the Catholicism of Spain were drawing nearer to open conflict, Ireland was in a state of flux and vacillating between sporadic war and peace. Cyril Falls (in *Elizabeth's Irish Wars*) puts the anomaly succinctly.

In the time of Queen Elizabeth, Ireland differed sharply from the England to which it was united by the person of its sovereign and which provided its administrators. Irish civilization lagged behind that of England, yet this fact is far from sufficing to explain the gulf between the two countries. This gulf was wider than the distance by which English civilization was ahead of Irish because Irish was moving along different lines. There were elements of strength and beauty, with here and there the touch of genius, in Irish civilization, but they bore no relation to the magnificent blossom of English civilization in the Elizabethan age. The two stood on different planes . . . a strong antipathy existed between the two cultures because there was scarcely a point of contact between their traditions, their ideals, their art, their jurisprudence or their social life. . . .

The basic differences of religion, ancestry, race and temperament were never better illuminated than during the Elizabethan era, when England brought in its own laws to replace the existing Brehon laws of ancient Ireland. Sir John Perrott shired the country in 1584 and the English system of local government was gradually introduced throughout, with Ireland being governed by an English-chosen Council which included a Lord Chancellor, Chief Justice, Treasurer at Wars, Marshal of the Army, and normally either one or two members of the Irish nobility. The Council was under the Viceroy who bore the title of Lord Deputy (on two occasions, Sussex, and Essex received the more prestigious but no more powerful title of Lord Lieutenant). Outside this, local government was in the shape of sheriffs and mayors together with a plethora of minor figures, buttressed by a formidable array of spies.

This system was totally foreign to the traditions of the Irish. Their clan structure and its rights of succession were based on tanistry, in which clan leaders were replaced by those considered most likely to be a success – this ancient Brehon system being utterly alien to the English system of father-and-son succession. It seems a small point, but was just one fragment of a whole which changed the face of Irish society; there were many other regulations which the English introduced into Ireland, and if they differed substantially from the existing native laws, so much the better: it suited the English to erode and eliminate all that was Irish and synonymous with its ancient culture, as part of the process of total subjection and demoralization.

The administration of English rule in Ireland, during seven centuries of occupation, has never been benevolent nor was it so in the sixteenth century. At the same time, however, its severity was more occasional than constant during the first part of that century; only when Elizabeth began to turn the screw in earnest did it begin to reach dark depths of terror and degradation, particularly during Bingham's long reign as Connacht's Governor when his perverse nature led to every sort of cruel atrocity. This is not to say that the others were milder – Fitzwilliam's ruthless and iron destruction of the

*Sir William Fitzwilliam, Lord Deputy of Ireland 1588–94.
Having previously been Lord Deputy during the period
1571–5, he succeeded Sir John Perrott in 1588. From an effigy
in Marholm church.*

Spaniards down to the last unfortunate impressed boy is an object lesson in total tyranny, and Perrott was known to perform some finely calculated acts of barbarous torture. But cruelty was a feature of the age: human life was cheap, often worthless; and the acts of the Elizabethan era must be judged by its own standards.

England's methods of keeping peace in Ireland were simple, brutal and effective; a final judgment must take seriously into account the latter attribute. The standard treatment of prisoners was to murder them, preferably as publicly as possible so that the message was brought home to the widest possible audience. It was callous, brutal and constant, but it worked.

While at first sight . . . the maintenance of English power in Ireland appears to have been accompanied by indecision, waste and corruption, policies were in fact worked out, though they were not always steadily pursued . . . the qualifications, the doubts, the moral qualms, the generosity of modern England in similar circumstances did not trouble Elizabethan heads. It was enough for them to accept the principles of authority without question and to meet opposition to them as they appeared.

These tactics were successful in keeping Ireland and its people quiet, so much so that 'Elizabeth handed over to her successor an Ireland in part depopulated, hungry, devastated and sullen, but pacified, and constituting no further danger for long years to come.'

That was at the end of her reign, but before that she had had problems in keeping Ireland quiet. By the time of the arrival of Armada ships off the Irish coast she had much to be concerned about, mostly centred around the sensitive area of Ulster in the northwest. Leinster, apart from the irrepressible O'Byrnes of Wicklow, was quiet; Munster, devastated and still barren in the aftermath of the Desmond Rebellion, was equally quiescent; and Connacht, under the ruthless Bingham, was under full control.

Sir John Perrott, who relinquished his post as Lord Deputy shortly before the Armada arrived off Ireland, outlined with close detail the state of the country whose administration he was then handing over. In June, in the presence of the Council, he had run through the condition of every part of the country; Leinster 'stands in reasonable good terms for quietness, save for stealths and robberies which are sometimes committed', while in Munster 'most of the doubtful men there are in hand, so as the state of that province is reasonably well assured, *unless it be disturbed by some foreign attempt*' (author's italics). Of Connacht he was more doubtful, which must have irritated the pride of Bingham (Perrott, as will be seen in a later chapter, detested Bingham, a feeling thoroughly reciprocated): 'the quiet of the province is doubtful,' said the Lord Deputy, 'for that they are men disposed to stir and disturbance, and ill affected to the state of the time.'

Perrott in his later years as Viceroy was unpopular with his Council and towards the end of his period as chief administrator of Ireland his relations with most of his colleagues were strained to say the least (at one meeting of the Council, he and the Marshal of the Army, Bagenal, had come to blows and exchanged insults) but for all that he had a wider friendship and closer feelings with the Irish than almost any other Viceroy had achieved or would later achieve. And he knew his Ireland and the dangers that were an ever-present threat to its administration: 'it is not meet to diminish any part of the forces of the realm,' he told the Council, 'but rather to increase them' – an evident plea to the Queen to send much-needed reinforcements should the Spaniards decide to land in Ireland.

Perrott's laconic and brief dismissal of Munster in a few words, while correct, is misleading. The province had been the particular target of the Lord Deputy's systematic laying to waste of perhaps the best and most fertile land in Ireland, partly in carrying out English policy in Ireland but partly also in revenge for the Desmond Rebellion, which at one time had seemed a distinct threat to English domination of the province. Perrott effectively destroyed it. Of this period (the early years of the 1580–90 decade) an Irish historian has written of Munster:

Villages and towns were gone; the church and the castle were alike unsightly ruins; the poor man's cottage was but a heap of ashes; there was no corn in the haggard, nor crops in the fields, nor cattle, nor sheep; the streets were deserted and silent, where, but late, the little children laughed and played; and the unburied corpses by the wayside told their own mournful tale. In the wake of war, famine and pestilence followed, and struck down those whom the rope, or the sword, or the torch, had spared; in Cork, a small town of only one street, and less than a quarter of a mile in length, the daily death-roll was seventy . . . and in that province, within six months, there died of famine alone thirty thousand human beings . . . Here and there the English saw creeping out of the woods, what could hardly be called living human beings; they were better described by Spenser as anatomies of death, 'ghosts crying from their graves', They were unable to walk, but only crept on their hands and feet. Their faces were pallid, their lips bloodless, their eyes sunken, their bones without flesh, their voices a hoarse whisper . . . they pulled the carcasses out of their graves and scraped the bones; and when one of themselves died the survivors greedily fell upon him and devoured him. Amid such scenes of horror the voice of humanity was silenced, and the instincts of the brute had become supreme.

This was Munster: what of Ulster?

It is perhaps simplifying the state of Ulster to say that by and large it was out of English control: this is far from the truth, but at the same time it was certainly remote from such control and deeply resentful and suspicious of any attempt to apply to it the same treatment meted out to the other provinces. Ulster harboured the last of the great clans, the O'Neills and the O'Donnells, both of which conducted a tortuous and uneasy peace with Elizabeth but evaded every attempt at total subjection. They were still powerful, both as allies or foes, and she was well aware of this. And the area over which they held almost undisputed sway was perhaps the most inaccessible and remote in the entire country. Perrott, as a man who had dealt for many years with the Ulster clans, knew their ways: 'some of the potentates there have put in pledges [to the Crown], and some not; yet they are not to be accounted as men assured indeed, but rather a demonstration and show of assurance, for that they are people light and inconstant.' Clearly the evasiveness of the northwest Ulster clans in Tirconnell was a source of much concern to the country's administrators and was to assume a special significance when the news of landings of large forces of Spaniards there began to filter through. An alliance of clan and invader spelled great danger, but as had happened and was to happen later to every Spanish attempt to help Ireland, the threat would pass away.

In the meantime, Perrott had left the stage open for Sir William Fitzwilliam who late that summer took over for his second term of office. Scarcely had he settled in when alarming reports of great ships and thousands of men arriving off the Atlantic coast began to flood in. What he most feared had come to pass: the Spaniards, after years of prevarication and persuasion, were at last landing on the shores of Ireland.

II

The Coast of Wrecks

SIR JOHN PERROTT accepted his Sword of Office and thus became Elizabeth's sixth Irish Viceroy and Lord Deputy on June 21, 1584. As a former President of Munster, having been closely involved in the Desmond Rebellion and its wars and waste, Perrott knew Ireland and the Irish as well as any previous English administrator. This knowledge was to stand by him in the four years to follow.

Perrott's term as Lord Deputy is notable for many reasons but perhaps most for his extreme sensitivity to the threat of Spanish invasion of Ireland. It became an obsession; he worried over every scrap of information which reached him through his chain of 'spials', and every Irish merchant returning from a business voyage to Cadiz or Lisbon brought back yet another snippet of gossip to further aggravate Perrott's worsening temper and add to his burden of woes.

By the early months of 1586 his concern was spilling over into a stream of worried letters to England. On January 12 he advised Sir Francis Walsingham, Elizabeth's principal secretary, that 'the King of Spain threatenth much, and, as they say, prepareth greatly to annoy England and Ireland', while a fortnight later, in describing an interview with 'one Chalice' (probably Captain John Challis), he wrote of 'the news he giveth forth that King Philip doth prepare one of the greatest armies that ever he made, the most part of them to be landed this next spring in England, and twenty thousand of them to be for Ireland.' Two weeks later he was again fretting that 'the Irishry here do hearken greedily for the coming over of foreign forces, sending for one to another, whereof I have secret and certain intelligences by my spials . . . that part of this Spanish invasion is for this island.'

Hampered by the characteristic shortage of soldiers, equipment and money, Perrott's hands were largely tied; events were to prove his fears unfounded, but this cannot lessen their validity. Clearly the Lord Deputy realized the dangers Spain threatened, and the ease with which Philip could conquer Ireland should he take that path.

Perrott hung onto his post for a further two years, increasingly more ill, and embittered by illness (he suffered from gallstones) and political events (which led to his being incarcerated in the Tower of London where he died in 1592, having been cleared of treason charges). In his last years he became more and more embittered towards his Queen, feelings which erupted in his classic answer to her request of October 1588, to raise two thousand English troops to be sent to Ireland to counter the Spaniards there; he had been at the receiving end of her capricious nature for years and when an opportunity of revenge came, he took it, remarking sourly that 'now the Queen is ready to bepiss herself for fear of the Spaniard, I am become her white boy again.'

When Perrott relinquished the title of Lord Deputy, he was succeeded by Sir William Fitzwilliam. It was the latter's second term, his first covering the years 1571 to 1575; almost ten years later, at the advanced age of sixty-two (very old indeed in Elizabethan terms), he was to take office at yet another period of crisis in the administration of Ireland. Just under three weeks after he received his Sword of Office, Philip's Armada came in sight of the shores of England and Fitzwilliam was plunged into an immediate state of emergency.

For six weeks reports filtered through to Ireland of the naval events to the east. The Spaniards threatened Plymouth, word came of a battle off the Isle of Wight, and then the astounding news of the Spanish fleet's dispersal by fire at Calais and the subsequent resounding victory under Lord Howard of Effingham at Gravelines, north of Calais, where the Armada, its formation disrupted at last, had been hunted and harried by the swifter and handier English vessels in the course of a victory whose echoes would reverberate around the world. And now the Spanish Armada, its morale shattered, its ships damaged, its crews weakening from illness and the scars of war, was on its way home. England was saved.

As the Armada sailed up towards northern waters, its senior officers had decided that the most advisable route home to Spain was to sail up through the North Sea past Scotland, round it to the north, bear west to clear Ireland and Scotland's outlying islands, and then to sail right out into the Atlantic and down towards Spain, thus clearing Ireland and all its potent dangers with room to spare. The Duke of Medina Sidonia, the Armada's commander-in-chief, issued sailing orders from the great cabin of his flagship, the *San Martin*:

The course that is to be followed first is to the north northeast, up to the latitude of $61\frac{1}{2}°$; you will take great care lest you fall upon the coast of Ireland, for fear of the harm that may befall you upon that coast. Then parting from these islands and rounding the Cape in $61\frac{1}{2}°$ you will run west southwest until you are in latitude $58°$ and then southwest until $53°$; then south southwest to Cape Finisterre and so you will procure your entrance into the Groyne [Corunna] or to Ferrol, or to any other port of the coast of Galicia.

The wisdom of this route is shown by the inescapable facts of the return trip to Spain. Not one single ship which faithfully followed that course was wrecked – many must have sunk out in the Atlantic, small tenders and dispatch ships

A map of western Europe showing the route which the Armada took from Lisbon, which it left in May 1588. It had to put into Corunna to refit and replenish stores, etc; while there, some of the ships were dispersed by a gale, further delaying the voyage towards England. Eventually they sighted the English coast on July 29, and from then until August 9 fought a series of running battles with the English fleet led by Lord Howard of Effingham. After the final and decisive battle off Gravelines, north of Calais, the Armada was forced to sail north and rounded Scotland and Ireland into the Atlantic on its way home to Spain. West of Scotland a series of gales scattered the fleet and forced many ships to run for northwest Ireland. Of about sixty which probably sighted Ireland, half were wrecked or foundered at sea. Of 130 vessels which had left Lisbon, some fifty or more failed to return.

whose frail hulls could not withstand the wild gales of the great ocean, but none was wrecked. Only when the course was departed from, for reasons ranging through the dangers of foundering, lack of food and water, diseased and dying crews, or navigational error, did the ultimate disasters of death and shipwreck strike.

Every ship of the Armada got a copy of those sailing orders while at sea off Scotland, and the fleet held on its northwards course; running up towards Norway, it took its first and last departure from the orders of Medina Sidonia, turning northwest to bisect the dangerous channel between the Orkneys and Shetlands. Once past Fair Isle (which was later to claim its only Armada wreck, *El Gran Grifon*), the bulk of the ships held on into the latitude of the 60s and then, and only then, gradually bore westwards to clear Ireland.

Around this time the inherent weaknesses of many ships in the fleet, combined with the battle damage, began to be crucial. They were a mixed bag of vessels, ranging from galleons to humble cargo carriers, with crews of variable ability; during the years when first Philip and Santa Cruz and later, after the latter's death, Medina Sidonia had attempted to gather together a fleet big and well equipped enough to fulfil Philip's design, the quality of the ships mustering at Lisbon was questionable, to put it mildly. Ideally the Armada should have consisted almost entirely of galleons, together with store ships and tenders, but when the fleet finally left the Tagus on May 28 to start for England this aim was far from being accomplished. Philip had had to requisition (and often blatantly steal) ships from virtually every sizeable harbour throughout his empire and from many which were not. Warships were few and far between, and he had to be content with merchant ships, big grain carriers many of them, which were converted and fitted out as warships.

The build of these ships provides a key to their destruction. The Levant Squadron, a fleet of ten vessels under Don Martin de Bertendona in the gigantic *Regazzona* (at 1249 tons the biggest in the entire Armada), gives us a valid example. All of these ten ships were merchantmen, ranging from the *Regazzona* to the 666 ton *Santa Maria de la Vison*, the baby of the squadron. Some were Ragusan ships; all were of either Adriatic or Mediterranean origin and development, designed and built for trading in those more sheltered seas.

There were in the late sixteenth century two distinct schools of shipbuilding and design in Europe: the Scandinavian or northern type of vessel was then clinker built, with planks overlapping each other to give additional strength in the rough northern waters; the southern or Mediterranean ships were carvel built, with planking fitted edge-to-edge over frames or ribs in much the same manner as a wooden floor is laid. The carvel-built ship of the period was smoother finished and sound enough for the waters in which it sailed; in the rough and wild ocean off Ireland, however, it was a different question. The biggest drawbacks of the southern type were the difficulties presented by edge-to-edge planking and by the length of the typical Mediterranean merchantman's mast, which was far taller than was then normal for most Atlantic vessels. Carvel planking was easily strained and its seams were rarely watertight, and these difficulties were further compounded by the overall frailty with which the southern vessel was often constructed. This surprising aspect of the typical southern ship of the period, which is typified by the vessels of the Levant Squadron, has been clearly illustrated by the recent discovery and excavation of two Levant ships which sank in Irish waters – the *Trinidad Valencera* and the *Santa Maria de la Rosa*, examination of whose hull remains show clearly that they were flimsily built and eminently unsuited to northern Atlantic conditions and prolonged gales.

Frail ships had, moreover, other drawbacks; they were easily holed by shot, and that this happened to many of the southern-built vessels off the Irish coast is clear from the State Papers, wherein constant reference is made to the damage done by English guns. The more stoutly built ship could take even a sizeable cannon ball in its timbers and remain unaffected once the danger of

20

fire was averted; the ball would remain embedded in the ship's side as visible evidence of its strength and durability. For a merchant vessel, designed to carry cargo and not to shrug off the effects of concentrated gunfire, matters were dramatically different; one shot could – and did – sink a ship if it hit a vital underwater area.

There is no doubt that many of the ships of the Armada which left the preordained course which Medina Sidonia and his officers had laid down were in serious physical straits, quite apart from being short of food and water and with their crews greatly weakened. The preponderance of southern ships in the lists of those wrecked on and around Ireland is significant and has been underlined by the information yielded by the remains of the *Trinidad* and *Santa Maria*. The Levant Squadron of ten ships lost eight of those between the North Sea and Kerry, at least six (and possibly seven) of those in Ireland, and one in Scotland. The remaining two were strong enough to follow Medina Sidonia wide out into the Atlantic, far off Ireland; and they reached home. Apart altogether from the structural weaknesses of many eventual Armada casualties off Ireland, there were many other contributory factors; the terrible destruction suffered by the fleet on its homeward journey cannot be attributed to any one factor. A complex and often obscure net was drawn around those ships which came down on the coast, from whose meshes many found they could not escape.

Among these factors was the weather. It is a legend that the Armada was destroyed by a wind, a wind that 'blew from God'. Like all legends it is mostly untrue, but there is more than grains of truth in it. The weather had gone against the Armada from the very moment the ships weighed anchor in the Tagus, upriver at Lisbon – even their departure from the mouth of the river where it entered the Atlantic was delayed by contrary winds. And this pattern of headwinds was to be followed for much of the next five months.

Headwinds in sixteenth century navigation offered an almost insoluble problem to the sailor. Most ships were square-rigged (the Mediterranean carracks, on which most of the merchantmen were based, carried a lateen sail, but were on the whole square-rigged, in other words with squaresails placed *before* the mast). Because of the position of the square sail in relation to the mast and rigging, a wind coming from ahead blew the sail back into the mast; the sail itself, due to the rigging behind it which hindered its free movement, could not be manoeuvred so as to spill out the wind and thus nullify its strength. Because of their shape, square sails are inefficient to windward and most square-riggers could sail only within about 67° of the wind; in other words, they could only make headway against a stiff headwind by making long tacks to either wing of their course at at least that angle to their intended direction. A headwind, therefore, was every sailor's nightmare. In some instances, where the wind was not too strong, ships could tack and thus make headway, although this was laborious and time-consuming, and they made a great deal of leeway. If the wind was of gale force the only thing to do was to furl sail and let the vessel drift wherever she would; for this reason, most ships tended to seek plenty of sea-room to avoid being trapped on a lee shore; Medina Sidonia's wide track out into the Atlantic may seem exaggerated by modern standards but in sixteenth century ships off an unknown foreign lee shore, he was being no more than careful.

Once the fleet had turned around Scotland and headed for Spain in a wide curve far out to the west of Ireland, it had battled a series of headwinds. Worse than that were the gales, of which the fleet met more than its share; 1588 by any meteorological standards was not a settled year, and the Atlantic was unusually uneasy in the face of repeated strong winds, many of them of gale force. Off the west coast of Ireland the winds are predominantly westerly, mostly southwesterly, and this was the very worst direction for the fleet. Much worse, however, was the fact that the headwinds were consistently strong, often gales and sometimes close to hurricane force. This is not supposition; by early September, the Duke was complaining to Philip (in messages sent off in dispatch vessels) that 'the winds on this coast are always more tempestuous than elsewhere'; previously he had called the weather 'bad and contrary', his ships having met with 'heavy gales with strong winds, thick fog and rain'. Purser Pedro Coco Calderon lamented the 'constant storms, fogs and squalls' through which the fleet sailed; his ship, he wrote was 'always working to windward, breaking our tackle and taking a great deal of water . . . the coast is rough, the seas heavy, and the winds are strong from the seaward [westward] . . .'.

Later evidence brings strong corroboration of these winds and the bad weather in general. The first Spanish prisoners to land in Ireland testified in Tralee to the 'contrary winds' and 'tempestuous weather'; the Mayor of Waterford heard of Spanish ships 'beaten by the weather'; the Sheriff of Clare told of Spaniards unable to land in Ireland 'by reason of weather'; a report from Cork in the latter half of September speaks of the fleet being 'severed by a late tempest'; seven hundred Spaniards were driven ashore in Donegal 'by force of weather'; Sir Henry Wallop (a member of the Council) wrote that some ships were 'turned back by the wind', and other reports in the State Papers speak of the tempest of the 17th and 18th of September (O.S.). We read of Sir Richard Bingham's description of 'very stormy and foul weather', of 'great floods', while in the detailed sea log of a Castilian Squadron ship off Kerry there are contained perhaps the most closely observed and analytical descriptions of weather in the entire records of the Armada.

A Castilian, Marcos de Aramburu, was Paymaster General of that squadron and in command of the *San Juan Bautista*, a galleon. His description of the weather met in the Atlantic shows clearly the sort of conditions under which they were forced to sail; he speaks of a 'stormy sea, with heavy sky and rain', of a 'southerly gale', 'heavy seas and strong wind', 'a most violent storm with a very wild sea', and so on *ad infinitum*. Rarely was there any day on which the wind was absent and Aramburu's account is sprinkled with reports of gales,

The Kerry mainland at Blasket Sound during a September gale gives a graphic impression of the sort of weather which the Armada met off the Irish coast. (Pat Langan)

high seas, heavy spray and overcast skies. It is a grim picture.

Every contemporary report which mentions the weather of that late summer and early autumn on the Atlantic coast of Ireland reads unanimously on that one point: the weather was abysmal, with gales, storms, strong winds and rain with scarcely a respite. This was not the sort of weather which many of the Spaniards were used to, neither was it helpful to their ships. More than anything else, the adverse conditions brought to a point the many deficiencies in the Armada vessels; it was a very potent factor in their destruction. Again, however, we must sheer away from attributing to one comprehensive reason the fleet's disasters in Ireland. The ships were weak, the storms were strong: but again this is not the full story, for along with these two agents of destruction was a third, equally potent – the question of navigation.

There seems little doubt that the Spaniards sailing in the Armada knew little of the coast of Ireland; again and again this is brought out by the reports in the State Papers, where survivors often showed in their depositions a quite astonishing ignorance of their whereabouts when their ships foundered or were wrecked. Often they were a hundred miles in error, and there are several instances where the north coast was mistaken for the southwest coast; only rarely did they know their position with any precision, and almost without exception their accuracy in those cases was due to the presence on board of Irish pilots.

A glance at any or all of the contemporary charts on which the Spanish based their navigational knowledge of Ireland and its coastal waters shows the extent of their ignorance. Mercator's maps were on the whole reasonably accurate, but there was a wide gap thereafter; most late sixteenth century charts of Ireland showed an acceptable and often close awareness of the shape of the east and south coasts; but in the case of the west and north coasts, all was darkness. Often it appears that to fill in the gaps which knowledge could not, Elizabethan cartographers resorted to their imaginations; in many cases these extended no further than drawing a gentle curve to illustrate the west coast. Nothing could be more wildly in error. Most contemporary maps of Ireland show the west coast as presenting a continuous and even coastline to the Atlantic waters, where in reality the coast is widely varied, with precipitous headlands, huge indented bays and estuaries, outlying islands and rocks; a glance at the two contrasting maps here reveals the disparity between what the Spaniards were led to expect of the shape of Ireland and the reality itself.

Medina Sidonia showed a wariness of his charts when he took a course that would bring him wide of any possible danger, with sufficient sea room for additional safety. It was just as well that he did. It is clear that the ships which did come down on the coast of Ireland did so primarily from the northwest, falling in towards the more northerly parts of Sligo and Donegal. The Atlantic

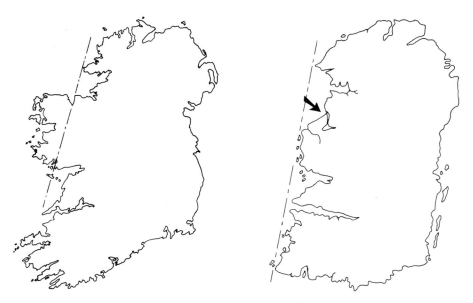

A modern map of Ireland (left) : the line marks the westward bulge of north Mayo, which on the Spanish charts was not shown as such. A contemporary map (right) shows the fatal error which caused so much damage to the Armada : the area around the Erris Peninsula in Mayo is completely distorted. This map was probably drawn between 1577 and 1585 ; Ortelius visited Ireland in 1577 but his map was not published until the spring of 1588. It probably formed the basis for many of the Spanish charts.

coastline of those two counties presents an impressive navigational hazard, but even the complex difficulties of those coasts paled into insignificance when the Spaniards encountered the western bastion of Mayo.

Mayo was unknown to them, and cannot have entered into even the most detailed consideration. Their charts showed a steady curve linking Donegal with Kerry, whereas in fact the most westerly point of Mayo – the huge bulk of Erris and its inland bogs and great sea cliffs – juts a good forty miles seaward of where the Spaniards expected to find open water. More than any other single factor, the intimidating physical presence of Erris Head was to cause the most destruction, direct and indirect, to those Armada ships which sailed down upon it. Any ships which had sighted the coast north of Erris, i.e. Donegal and Sligo, would probably have followed it down towards the south, keeping a safe distance off. This may have appeared the safest course, but to follow it would have led the ships into the deceptive Donegal Bay, whose fifty mile wide mouth offers an apparently troublefree sail to the south. Following the coast round to port (east), the Spaniards would have crossed the bay and then found themselves confronted by the westward thrust of Erris, from Killala Bay right out to Eagle Island, an impenetrable bastion of sheer cliffs, strong currents and heavy seas. Ships which followed this pattern were in fact embayed, caught in Donegal Bay by a combination of wind and land barrier. Few, if any, ships surmounted that twin obstacle.

The real difficulty was that they found themselves, quite suddenly and unexpectedly, in a perilous situation. Crossing Donegal Bay, land would have been out of sight for much of the way until the cliffs of north Mayo appeared on the southern horizon. Often by that time it would have been too late for the ships to alter course westwards in an attempt to weather the projecting coast to the west; the winds were constantly strong and from a westerly quarter – the worst possible wind for a square-rigger sailing into it. To make westing of perhaps fifty miles under such conditions was asking the impossible; it would be almost as difficult to clear the northern shore of the bay, if they turned back and tried to escape to the northeast. Most of the ships which found themselves in this situation were lost.

A look at the map showing Irish wrecks disposes of the objection that this is supposition; north of Eagle Island, beginning with Broadhaven Bay just east of that, the line of wrecks is graphically clear. Two in Broadhaven Bay, one between that and Killala, three in Sligo, one in Donegal, two in Killybegs, one north of Slieve League: most if not all of those ten Armada ships were doomed by the great bulk of Erris, and it is possible that several more northerly wrecks were caused by the same barrier. It can be argued that the presence of Erris, looming out of the mist and rain from the dim horizon, led to the destruction of between a third and half of the total number of Armada ships wrecked in and around Ireland.

But this perhaps underlines the mystery of the Spanish knowledge – or the lack of it – of the Irish coast. There is no apparent reason for this dismal state of affairs; after all, Spanish fishermen by the thousand were thoroughly at home in these very waters and must therefore have known their way along the coast. Trade would have brought further Spaniards to learn the intricacies and dangers of the western coastal waters. And the hundreds of Irish exiles who thronged Lisbon during the build up of the Armada would have included many with a detailed knowledge of some part of the coast. There was, in fact, no clear reason (and many to the contrary) why the ships of the fleet should not carry one knowledgeable and experienced pilot, fisherman or Irish exile on board each vessel of accountable size; yet this was not the case.

That there were Irish pilots with the Armada is proven, but they appear to have been few. Most of the rare instances of fine pilotage during which a close and detailed knowledge of the coast was displayed came in fact from the Spaniards themselves, possibly aided by others. In the case of most of the wrecks, it is clear that the ships were more or less lost, and that those aboard were mystified and puzzled as to their precise location. The lack of good charts augmented this area of doubt, and the combination of poor navigational aids and a shortage of pilots very effectively applied the *coup de grace* in many instances.

On the face of it, the Spaniards appear guilty of an elementary error. It would have been a simple (and obvious) course to have enlisted or impressed Spanish fishermen familiar with Irish coastal waters and used them as pilots. This was not done. Equally, it should have been possible to enlist a sizeable number of Irishmen who knew their own coast equally well. Neither was this done, to any significant extent. Philip, Santa Cruz and Medina Sidonia had admittedly much more to consider than the outside possibility of navigating along a coast which was not their objective to begin with, but this does not excuse them.

It is clear, therefore, that the reasons for, the causes of, most if not all of the wrecks of Armada ships in Irish waters were not any single factor but a combination of factors. There were frail ships, not built for those wild seas and strong winds but for warmer and more temperate weather conditions; often those ships were damaged by wind and wave, or perhaps by gunfire; sometimes their seams were strained by the whipping of top-heavy masts in huge ocean swells. The Spaniards had charts which gave a distorted and dangerously misleading description of the Irish coast; their knowledgeable pilots were few and scattered. And the weather was at its worst, with constant headwinds and frequent gales and wild storms. The combined effects of all these physical enemies was to prove too much for at least twenty-five and possibly thirty or more Armada ships which foundered, were wrecked, or burned to the waterline on and around the coast of Ireland.

The daunting task of enumerating all these wrecks is one which has occupied the minds and energies of many naval historians, archaeologists, divers and others for centuries. They have had mixed success since the contemporary records, while numerous, are contradictory, skimpy in detail, and often in error. For all that, recent research, particularly within the last century or so, has uncovered much and laid bare many facts hitherto hidden. The overall picture is clearer, although still dim in many respects.

Perhaps most of the credit for clearing away the shrouds of mystery which have enveloped the Irish aspects of the Armada should go to a retired clergyman who made the task almost a life work, if that term could contain the disparate energies of an extraordinary man. The Reverend William Spotswood Green, who died in 1919, was the forerunner of all investigators of the broader spectrum centreing around the Armada wrecks in Irish waters and his work has formed the very sound basis for many later investigations.

By any standards except probably his own exacting ones, William Spotswood Green was a remarkable man. Educated in Trinity College, Dublin, at the time the bastion of higher Protestant education in Ireland, he was appointed Protestant rector of the small village of Carrigaline in Co. Cork in 1878; his health was never good and he was ordered by his doctors to spend the winter of 1881 in, of all places, New Zealand 'in order to improve his health.' He went there, and to prove the effectiveness of his new cure climbed the 12,349 foot Mount Cook, the highest peak in the New Zealand Alps, and was the first man to do so. He later put this particular episode between the pages of a book and it makes diverting reading, clearly hinting at the terrible privations and hardships of that arduous ascent, particularly during the final sixty-two hour climb to the summit and down again.

Recovered with the aid of this eccentric convalescence, Spotswood Green came home to Cork once more and threw his frail constitution and indomitable energies into marine investigation, leading several deep-sea dredging and exploratory expeditions in Irish waters. He took some time off to go to British Columbia, leaving behind a parish mystified by such unrectorly conduct, and once there, surveyed and mapped several mountains in the Selkirk ranges. In his absence, it may have been that his neglected parishioners finally rebelled; whatever happened, Spotswood Green retired from his clerical duties, and succumbing to the insistent call of the sea that was evident in everything he did, became Chief Inspector of Irish Fisheries in 1890.

It was for him the ideal post. He was devoted to and interested in anything and everything to do with the sea, and threw himself into the duties of his new job with all his boundless will and energy. 'In 1890 and 1891,' he wrote,

it became my duty to make a special Fishery Survey of the west coast of Ireland. I had to navigate all harbours, channels and creeks on that coast, and while primarily interested in the present conditions of the inhabitants, the traditions of the past that still linger aroused my interest in the history of the places we frequented, and to which I have many times returned in succeeding years.

There proved to be many interesting events associated with those wild western bays, but none probably of so much general interest as the wrecks of the Armada. Twenty-five ships appear to have been wrecked on the Irish coast, while others reached safe anchorages on that coast, and were among those that ultimately returned to Spain.

Perhaps the greatest compliment any Armada historian or investigator can pay to the work of Spotswood Green would be to say that the list of wrecks which he compiled, and the general tone of his commentary allied to the description of those wrecks, remains substantially valid and unalterable to this day: a remarkable tribute when the lack of proper research facilities and other drawbacks are taken into account. Subsequent research has in some instances proven him wrong or, more correctly, slightly in error, but some of his assumptions have been proved astoundingly accurate. A case in point is the finding of the wreck of the *Santa Maria de la Rosa* at the bottom of the Blasket Sound off Kerry in almost exactly the very spot where Spotswood Green suggested her remains would lie. Sidney Wignall, the British naval archaeologist who led the expedition which found the *Santa Maria* in 1968, had paid Spotswood Green this tribute: 'when he ventured the opinion that the *Santa Maria* struck Stromboli Rock he was very, very right . . . the members of the 1968 Spanish Armada expedition take off every hat they own to the memory of the Reverend William Spotswood Green.'

The prime sources for all Armada investigators lie in the various State Papers, the most productive being the Irish State Papers. These give a wealth of information, but it must be handled with caution; Elizabethan standards of accuracy in naming ships and chronicling events related to their wrecking are highly suspect. In addition, place names and geographical locations have suffered the passage of time. More often than not the exact location of a wreck, obviously well known to those who reported it, has to be painfully extracted from contradictory and puzzling reports.

To any fresh mind looking at all this it stands to reason that it is to the contemporary sources that one must go, such as the State Papers. There is another source, contemporary now as then: tradition is repeatedly accurate in placing the sites of Armada wrecks, and while it too should be treated with caution, the combination of written sources and surviving or recorded tradition is a potent one. Through it most if not all of the possible sites of Armada wrecks in and around Ireland have been identified with varying degrees of success. Occasionally tradition is absent, an absence apparently unaccountable until the passage of four centuries is recalled. Ireland in 1588 was wild, remote, with few roads and vast areas of untravelled bog that were undrained and virtually impenetrable. Drainage and improving standards of agricultural husbandry have changed the face of the country and have brought with them an increasing population which has spread into almost every corner of the island. But four hundred years ago there were parts of Ireland, particularly in the west and northwest, where none except a handful of pitiful peasants existed and where tradition withered on stony ground. But by and large a surprisingly healthy body of tradition is still extant, valuable here in that it is usually accurate in pinpointing the site of a wreck. This is not to suggest that its value is limited to only that, but very often the researcher will find it to be the case.

The numbers of Armada ships which finished their lives on the rocks and reefs of Ireland are formidable and provide an almost endless source for the historian and the archaeologist. As archaeological treasures pure and simple, their value is incalculable; it is strange, therefore, to find their history as largely neglected as it has been. There is absolutely no doubt that this situation will in the years ahead change completely as the rapidly climbing standards of marine research in all its aspects are increasingly applied to the fascinating subject of Armada wrecks.

III

The Flail of Connacht

CONNEMARA and Mayo were by no means the first locations in Ireland to witness the murder of Spanish prisoners taken from wrecked Armada ships, and neither was the number of such killings remarkable when compared with similar slaughters elsewhere. Yet the area provided the scene for a wide range of cruelty and misdeed, on the part of both the English administrators, whom exigency might well excuse, and the native Irish themselves, who could find no excuse whatever.

Three ships at least were wrecked in this area, in Galway and south Mayo, and from those three it is a reasonable assumption that scarcely a man or even a boy survived. Some Spaniards were taken instantly by the English forces or by Irishmen in English pay; others were held captive by Irish natives perhaps sympathetic to these unfortunate half-drowned wretches but whose finer feelings gave way to fear of reprisal and thus led to their prisoners being handed over to English custody; others again were butchered without mercy by Irish and English alike, a policy pursued with relentless cruelty by both the Governor of the Province, Sir Richard Bingham, and the Lord Deputy Fitzwilliam even long after all threat to Ireland from the Spanish fleet had passed.

Bingham was appointed Governor of Connacht in 1584, his area of responsibility covering the entire western coast from Mayo right down to the River Shannon at Limerick. He had seemed a good choice: a veteran soldier and seaman with varied and wide experience, he had served both with and against the Spanish (at a time when England and Spain were allies, and later at Lepanto and perhaps at St Quentin) and had also been involved in English naval manoeuvres during the abortive landing of the Papal force at Smerwick in 1580.

Perrott was in the final year of his term as Viceroy when Bingham took over the administration of the western province, and as a breaking-in exercise for the new Governor, took Bingham with him on a tour of Munster shortly before the latter was to take up his new post. Perrott's objectives in Munster were twofold: the consideration of how Munster was to be repopulated following the Desmond wars and the subsequent laying to waste of some of the finest land in Ireland, and second, to arrange to have that land distributed to the many claimants, the bulk of them being Elizabethan adventurers and colonists from England. Bingham probably learned much from this tour; certainly he was to make later use of Perrott's own distinctive style of justice, of which the joint tour brought forth a typical example when Perrott indulged in a ghastly torturing of a local nobleman, Donough O'Brien, who was related to the Earl of Thomond: 'By Perrott's order, he was led forth, hanged from a car, then taken down alive, his bones broken with the back of a heavy axe, and in this mangled condition, though he still lived, he was tied with ropes at the top of the steeple of Quin church, and left there to die.' This savage treatment was meted out to the unfortunate O'Brien as a punishment for several acts of disturbance in the area.

Bingham took over Connacht when the province was relatively quiet, a situation largely due to Perrott. Whatever his methods of justice, the latter was a shrewd and able administrator, an excellent negotiator, and a man who preferred the processes of diplomacy to those of violence in settling disputes. Connacht had a few blots on its general lassitude, however, mostly caused by the rebellious Burkes of Mayo, a wild and unruly clan who were almost untouched in their mountain and bog fastnesses in the north of Mayo. For some time Perrott had been painstakingly evolving his own plan for ensuring a relative peace in Connacht, a peace which would see the native chiefs achieve a certain amount of autonomy while at the same time swearing allegiance to the Crown. In 1585 the Lord Deputy had summoned all the great Connacht clan chiefs to Dublin for a series of constitutional talks in pursuance of this policy; from these meetings he hoped that a formula would emerge whereby Connacht would be governed by its own self-imposed peace rather than an uneasy peace forced on it by war.

Perrott's diplomacy was successful, and from the talks emerged the Composition of Connacht, the principal effects of which were that the chiefs would give up their lands to the Crown but would receive them back through a complicated system known as 'Knight's Service'. Broadly, each chief would be given a certain amount of land rent free, and for the remainder he paid a penny an acre to the Crown in rent and was liable to military service. The chiefs lost all rights to levy contributions on their people or to use them in war. Brehon law, the ancient laws which governed the clan system, was replaced by English laws; tanistry (the rule of succession which decreed that when a chief died, he was replaced by that member of the ruling household considered most likely to succeed as a new chief) went forever, its place taken by the succession of father and son.

It was Bingham's duty as Governor to see to the implementation of this new agreement, and Perrott could be forgiven if he had sat back and congratulated himself on achieving a highly satisfactory solution in Connacht. However, there were some reservations; not all of the Connacht chieftains had agreed on the compositionary terms, and Bingham set off through the province to persuade them. Instead of emulating Perrott's proven methods of diplomacy, however, the new Governor used his own unique mixture of cruelty, impetuosity and arrogance, a policy which ran directly against the wishes of the body of Commissioners whose duty, under Bingham, was to hear the various claims by the chieftains and to adjudicate on their validity.

Bingham would not be controlled. Arrogant, overbearing, arbitrary, he flouted the Commissioners or intimidated them; his nature was cruel, and even bloodthirsty; he scorned to show kindness to the natives, and placed more reliance on severity, on hangings, confiscations and breaches of faith ... when Mahon O'Brien of Clare showed some reluctance to accept the Composition, Bingham attacked him and captured his castle, and when the garrison surrendered, expecting at least that their lives would be spared, Bingham put every man of them to death, and, at a sessions in Galway he had seventy persons hanged, some of them women and children. In Mayo he held sessions at Donamona, and when one of the Burkes refused to come there and submit he had him attacked in his fortified castle on Lough Mask. He failed at first to capture it, and raised the siege, and the Burkes escaped. In revenge Bingham returned and destroyed the castle, pursued the Burkes with fire and sword, executed all of them he could lay his hands on, and desolated the lands of all their followers.

Increasingly concerned by the adverse reports of Bingham's behaviour, Perrott tried to keep this demonic weapon of destruction in check, but could not. Bingham went on his vengeful way, killing, burning and looting. He trapped another of the Burkes and had him hanged; he slew another 120 of the family elsewhere; at a pitched battle on the River Moy in north Mayo he killed over 1500 of a 2000-strong force of Scots who had come to Connacht through Ulster to fight with the Burkes. Bingham, it was said later, took as much pleasure from the killings of well over a thousand women and children in this battle as he had taken from his victory.

Despite all entreaty, and later threats, Bingham went on as he had started. Finally Perrott could stand no more; his commands to Bingham had been repeatedly ignored and eventually he turned to London for help. Bingham was dismissed in some disgrace and sent to the Netherlands on what was clearly a pretext to keep him out of the way for such time until he had cooled down. Scarcely was he gone when he was reinstated, and shortly afterwards the disgusted Perrott resigned, partly in protest. Bingham came back to Connacht and took up where he had left off; soon he again

had the province in a blaze. Those who offered the least resistance to anything he suggested he hunted down, wasted their lands and crops, drove away their cattle, murdered any of their relatives who might be sureties in his hands; and even the chiefs who submitted and professed their loyalty he cast into prison and left there.

This was the man who in the late summer of 1588 stood on the shores of Connacht to await the Spanish Armada; if the Spaniards had hoped for mercy from a man who had once fought by their side, they were to be disappointed.

The first Spaniards to fall into his hands from an Armada ship were

A portrait of Sir Richard Bingham, Governor of Connacht in 1588, by an unknown artist and dated 1564. Familiarly known as the 'Flail of Connacht', Bingham meted out summary justice to the survivors of at least half a dozen Armada vessels which ended up on the rocky shores of the western province. (Courtesy National Portrait Gallery, London)

probably those from a vessel which made her way into Galway Bay and came right into the eastern end of the bay towards the city itself, obviously seeking food and fresh water. This ship, like so many others nameless in all contemporary sources, came to anchor quite close to the city, on the northern side of the bay near Barna. From her seventy men came ashore to seek help, bringing with them food and wine with which to barter. It is possible that among this landing party were Irishmen, or at the very least Spaniards who knew the coast well – the accuracy of their navigation proves that; however, if there were Irishmen aboard, their names do not appear on subsequent lists. In any event, Galway was the centre of the wine trade with the Continent and was well known to those Spaniards who came to the west coast to fish the rich grounds off Connemara.

What happened next is unclear, but the most coherent and logical account is that the Spaniards were met on landing by a force composed of townspeople (Galway being loyal to the Crown) and English troops. There may have been

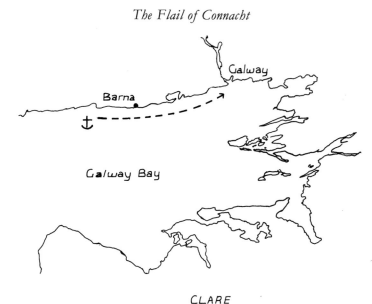

CLARE

Galway Bay and Galway City, near where an Armada ship anchored at Barna, west of Galway. A party of seventy men came ashore but were captured; the ship, however, escaped.

some discussion before the Spaniards agreed to lay down their arms, but surrender they did, possibly on the undertaking that their lives would be spared – an error which other shipwrecked Spaniards were also to commit. Edward Whyte, Bingham's reliable right-hand man throughout his governorship, and Clerk of the Connacht Council, records merely that the Spanish landing party was 'taken by the townsmen'. (Whyte himself spoke Spanish which undoubtedly would have been useful at this stage.) With the landing party taken, there was little point in the ship staying where she had anchored near Barna; she weighed anchor and sailed out of the bay, a wise move in the circumstances and one the wisdom of which was to be underlined by the fate of those who stayed behind.

There is still a tradition attached to this ship: until quite recently a large projecting ship's timber in the sand at Barna represented her wreck, but this is disproved both by the failure of Edward Whyte to record a wreck at Galway and the statement of Sir Geoffrey Fenton, Secretary to the Irish Council, that this mysterious vessel 'escaped and left prisoners seventy.' Investigations of the fabled baulks of timber at Barna in more recent years appear to confirm another and possibly more likely theory, that these scattered remains are those of a French trading barque lost at Barna some three hundred years ago. Nowhere in the State Papers is there anything to suggest that a ship was lost near Galway, despite the tradition to the contrary. Fenton and Whyte were exact and meticulous observers; they were on the spot (at least Whyte was), and theirs were official reports. Above all, they have the additional weight of being contemporary, and in the absence of contrary evidence we must assume that they are correct and that no Armada ship was wrecked near Barna.

Leaving Galway for the moment, we move northwest to the inhospitable coast of Connemara and Mayo, a wild, largely ungoverned area, whose remoteness and comparative lack of English control were largely owing to its barren and desolate land. Colonists however hungry for land baulked when it came to Connemara; they found it difficult to see any value in what was little more than a wrinkled expanse of bog and mountain, dotted with innumerable lakes and laced with tumbling rivers, a dreary country from whose miry depths rose rugged mountains, bleak and barren. Clearly this infertile and inhospitable land bore no welcome for colonists and so it was ignored for many centuries. Bingham kept a watchful eye on it from his stronghold in Galway, and when he felt the need enforced his own unique brand of discipline with ruthless forays to assert his authority.

It is perhaps due to Connemara's remoteness and difficulties of communication that it represents possibly the most misty and vague chapter in the entire history of Armada wrecks. It is known that in this sixty mile stretch of wild and indented coastline, with its treacherously merging sea and lake, its outlying rocks, reefs, shoals and islands, its fierce currents and strong gales, at least three and possibly four Armada ships were lost. The question is which and where.

Taking the area from the northern tip of Galway Bay up along the coast through Connemara and north to Clew Bay in Mayo, there is a wealth of tradition and legend to point to four specific locations as being the sites of wrecks of Armada ships. At least three of these locations are consistent with the reports in the State Papers, which provides the most reliable contemporary source; on the frail evidence offered by those two sources rests a theory incomplete but nevertheless coherent.

First the State Papers, which are less than specific. Fenton, perhaps the most reliable and trustworthy of sources on the wrecks around Connemara, says of Spanish ships lost here that there were wrecked 'in Clear Island, one shipp, 300 men; in Fynglasse, O'Male's country, one shipp, 400 men; in O'Fflaertie's country, one shipp, 200 men.' This gives a total of three, whereas tradition claims four – and even then, there is some evidence to support a theory that the 'Clear Island' and 'Fynglasse' wrecks were one and the same. But there is equal evidence to suggest that Fenton (who was largely relying on Edward Whyte for his information) was by and large more right than wrong. That we are now in an area of utter complexity is becoming self-evident; clearly little can be expected from the State Papers apart from an incomplete confirmation that at least some of the wrecks actually took place. For the moment the wrecks in Clew Bay, Co. Mayo may be left aside and concentration centred on Connemara.

The area covered by Connemara could broadly be said to include the entire seacoast from Galway itself right up to Leenane in the north of the county,

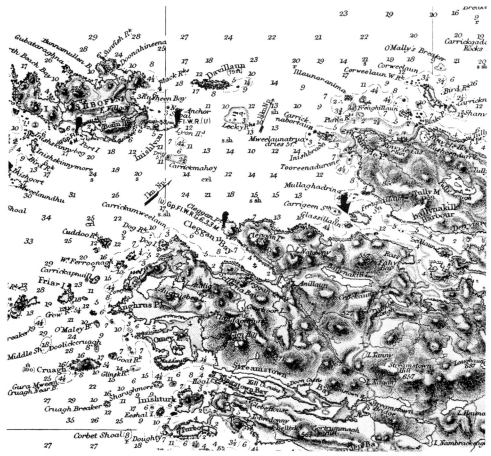

The island of Freaghillaun South is in the entrance to Ballynakill Harbour, Co. Galway. The Falco Blanco Mediano was wrecked on a reef WNW of the island and her survivors were first handed over to the O'Flahertys and later to the Governor of Connacht, who had them executed in Galway. (Produced from portion of BA chart 2420 with the sanction of the Controller, HM Stationery Office and of the Hydrographer of the Navy)

and where Co. Mayo begins. A look at the map will indicate the extent and complexity of this coastline; but if the mystery of the Connemara wrecks is to be unravelled, then this indented stretch provides the key. From Galway to Leenane as the crow flies is less than forty miles, but if one takes into account every channel, bay, estuary, creek, headland and tortuous twisting of land and sea by the coast, there is well over two hundred miles of actual coastline to be dealt with.

Starting furthest to the north of this stretch, it has long been accepted that an Armada ship was wrecked at the island of Davillaun, east of the larger island of Inishbofin, both of these being some miles out to sea off the northwest tip of Co. Galway at Renvyle. From what I have been able to gather, this springs from a further acceptance of the suggestion by William Spotswood Green that tradition holds that a ship was wrecked there; but I can find no corroboration of this nor indeed of any extant tradition to that effect.

Instead, there is a very strong tradition, still adhered to in the area, that an Armada ship was wrecked at the mouth of Ballynakill Harbour, between Clifden and Renvyle, and much further to the southeast than Davillaun. The narrow neck of Ballynakill, perhaps the safest harbour in this area, is blocked by a low island called Freaghillaun (literally, heathy island); to the northwest of the island is a reef, several hundred yards off. This is where the ship struck. It is a logical site for a wreck. Ballynakill has always been known as a safe harbour and doubtless was so even in the late sixteenth century. Whether or not the Spaniards had decided to try to enter on their own or whether a pilot had helped them is not known, but it is evident that they were attempting the passage between Bundouglas on the south and Braadillaun on the north into the inner recesses of Ballynakill. There was probably bad weather; the tides and currents in the sound are strong and need local knowledge to be read correctly. Whatever happened, the ship struck the reef northwest of Freaghillaun. (There are in fact two Freaghillauns; the one with which we are now concerned is Freaghillaun (pronounced *Frake-ill-yawn*) South, the northern island of the same name being on the northern side of Tully Mountain, which forms the northern boundary of Ballynakill.)

Freaghillaun South, Ballynakill, near Clifden, Co. Galway. On the reef to the right of the island the Falco Blanco Mediano *foundered; her survivors were later killed in Galway on the orders of Sir Richard Bingham.*

This part of Connemara was more or less outside the immediate grasp of Bingham; it was likely that there were no English soldiers or agents on hand to murder the survivors as they came ashore. That some did come ashore is indisputable, but their numbers can only be guessed at. From the fact that a fair proportion of the higher officers among them survived, it is fair to assume that the number of other survivors was not insignificant, perhaps a hundred or even more. They made the shore either in small boats or by swimming; many would have drifted from the reef to the island and have been picked up from there by the local natives and brought to the mainland. According to local tradition the men from the Armada ship were looked after by several families called Conneely (still a familiar name in the area), but word had already reached even this remote corner of Ireland of Governor Bingham's proclamation that all Spanish prisoners must be delivered into English hands within four hours of capture under pain of death. And all Connemara had good reason to know that when Bingham made such a threat, he meant it.

It is easy to sympathize with the natives in this case. They probably had little food for a further hundred or so mouths, and indeed little enough inclination to help such a large number of strangers; they would have been interested in the spoils of plunder but little else, and with Bingham's threat hanging over them decided that the only course lay in passing the Spaniards on to someone in authority. It is likely that they would not have risked an open confrontation with such a considerable force and so methods of persuasion may have been used. Whatever happened, the party of shipwrecked men was brought southwest from Ballynakill and placed in the custody of another clan, the O'Flahertys of Ballynahinch, some miles south of Clifden.

The O'Flahertys were the most notable clan in Connemara and held sway over a vast area in western Galway. Originally they had occupied the eastern side of Galway on the other side of Loch Corrib, the long meandering strip of fresh water which splits the county into two distinct geographical and ethnographic entities. Forced westwards by the growing strength of the O'Conor clan (one of whom, Rory, was the last High King of Ireland), the O'Flahertys had settled in the wilds of undisturbed Connemara, gradually annexing vast tracts of bog and mountain in the process of building up a huge land empire which had, however, declined to a mere five hundred acres by the seventeenth century. There were many septs of the O'Flahertys and by the late sixteenth century the clan had been greatly fragmented. The hereditary chieftain at this time was Murrough ne Doe (actually *ne d-tuadh*, or Murrough of the Battle Axes), who ruled over a huge territory known as Gnomore, which ran northward from quite close to Galway up beyond the mountains of Maam. Murrough had his principal residence at Fuathaidh (now Aughnanure) Castle, a mile or so southeast of Oughterard, and some fifteen miles from Galway. It still stands today in a remarkable state of preservation.

Murrough, like many men of the Elizabethan age in Ireland, was a remarkable man with an equally remarkable instinct for self-preservation. He was one of the hereditary Gaelic chieftains who had taken part in the Composition of Connacht initiated by and carried out initially under the close supervision of the former Lord Deputy Perrott, and had even attained the dubious favour of Elizabeth to the extent of being granted, at one time or another, no less than five general pardons for such offences as treason, murder and other pleasantries.

Murrough had been knighted in 1585, just before the talks of the Composition, doubtless as a conciliatory gesture by Elizabeth. Although his territories lay close to Galway at their southern end, and were as a consequence vulnerable to English rule, Sir Murrough's allegiance to Elizabeth, consolidated after the Composition, was a notable scalp on the English belt, ensuring at least a modicum of peace to the northwest of Galway and the removal of a further thorn in Elizabeth's side. The subjugation (for that was what it amounted to) of the hereditary chieftain of one of the most powerful and feared of the native clans was further proof of Perrott's powers of diplomacy and underlined the beneficial effects of the Composition towards a peaceful Ireland – at least from the English point of view.

Perrott's good work, however, was soon undone by the irrepressible Bingham. The Governor had long regarded Sir Murrough with the distaste which he reserved in particular for the heads of native clans, and the newly attained allegiance of O'Flaherty, due solely to Perrott's persuasion, was not allowed to change this attitude. Despite Perrott's orders Bingham continued to harass Sir Murrough, gradually stepping up a campaign against him which culminated in the murder of two of Sir Murrough's twelve sons and several of his grandchildren. By that time Sir Murrough had risen in revolt, a rash action taken in a white fury, and had thrown aside his allegiance vows under the pressure of these latest outrages. The deaths of his sons brought him to his senses, perhaps combined with the cold realization that Bingham would not stop until every O'Flaherty lay dead; he repented, was pardoned by Elizabeth, and forced to surrender all his titles and possessions.

It was to Sir Murrough that the Spaniards from the wreck at Freaghillaun South were brought, passed on from the sept of the O'Flahertys at Ballynahinch. The old chieftain was too sanguine to believe that he could get away with aiding the Spaniards unnoticed, and so it proved, the information that he had fugitives from the Armada within his walls quickly reaching the ears of Edward Whyte. Mindful of Bingham's proclamation, Sir Murrough reluctantly brought the Spaniards to Galway and handed them over to the Crown forces, not without drawing the censure of Whyte who denounced him for his sympathetic treatment, accusing the O'Flaherty chieftain of giving them 'more favour than the Council thought meet.'

The men from the Freaghillaun South wreck joined the seventy already taken prisoner from the nameless ship which by this time had escaped from Galway Bay. Among the new arrivals were several noblemen and a captain; the noblemen included Don Luis de Cordoba and his nephew, Don Gonzalo de Cordoba, and the captain was Pedro de Arechaga. It is from these three names in particular that identification of the Freaghillaun wreck is made comparatively simple. Pedro de Arechaga is listed as being the captain of the 300 ton hulk *Falco Blanco Mediano* of the *Urcas* Squadron, carrying 103 men and sixteen guns, while both de Cordobas were also listed as being aboard the same vessel.

Don Luis in particular was a valuable captive. He commanded a company of seventy-six soldiers aboard the *Falco Blanco*, but more important, came from a notable Spanish family, being a brother of the Marquis of Ayamonte. At Lisbon he had been aboard the Duke of Medina Sidonia's own galleon but had transferred to the *Falco Blanco* shortly afterwards, his nephew accompanying him. It was somewhat unusual to find a man of his standing serving in a storeship, but the *Falco Blanco*, with three parts of her entire complement soldiers, appears to have been almost an auxiliary warship rather than a mere carrier. Don Luis was not examined by his captors until October 10. His deposition tells us little of how the *Falco Blanco* was wrecked save that she was 'driven in upon O'Flaherty's country.'

The second Galway wreck followed a somewhat similar pattern to that of the *Falco Blanco* in that once more it involved the O'Flahertys; but this was a very different branch of the clan and far removed from the gentler and more humane qualities of Sir Murrough, involving as it did the notorious Tadgh na Buile (literally, 'the furious') O'Flaherty.

Tadgh na Buile was the natural successor to Sir Murrough as head of the clan. By this time he was an old man; a deposition of the Patent Rolls dated August 20, 1588 shows him to be then 'of Adge three-score yeares or there-aboutes'. His reputation was at once fascinating and repelling, that of an impetuous warlike man, with mixed traits of bravery, cunning and deceit. Though the natural choice under the system of tanist succession as the next head of the O'Flahertys, he in fact never assumed this title. Tadgh's territory was western Connemara – the Atlantic seaboard – with his headquarters at Ards, near Carna, where he had built a large castle at the head of a small natural harbour. Today just one fragment of a wall still stands to show that he had chosen both site and harbour well; the castle stood on a little knoll looking out to sea, while in front of it was the harbour in which his clan's boats were kept, sheltered by the headlands at either side of the narrow entrance from the full fury of the Atlantic gales.

Tadgh's sept was unusual among Irish clans in that it possessed (like the O'Malleys of Clew Bay) a notable seafaring tradition; they were born seamen and navigators, qualities lacking in most other Irish clans who dwelt near the sea. Much of Tadgh's considerable power and influence stemmed from a mastery of the seas around his lands. Like Sir Murrough, Tadgh owed allegiance to the Crown, but by and large Bingham appears to have left him in comparative peace; doubtless Tadgh had had to pay dearly for this unusual circumstance and from later evidence it is reasonable to suggest that Tadgh maintained links of information with Bingham, looking more to the preservation of his own skin than to that of others. He was, after all, in his sixties and hanging on to his territories by the frailest of threads and then only due to Bingham's comparative benevolence. In return for such an unusual dispensation, the Governor likely sought and received an exacting interest.

In the Atlantic off Carna at least two Spanish ships were sighted around September 22; perhaps they were the same two reported two days earlier as 'there is seen within ten leagues of Galway two ships and are at anchor these three days seaward the island of Arran [Aran Islands, at the mouth of Galway Bay].' The ships, one large and one small, lay for several days near Carna, in the vicinity of the islands off there and in a sort of sound which separates these islands from the mainland at Mace Head, northwest of Carna. There are four

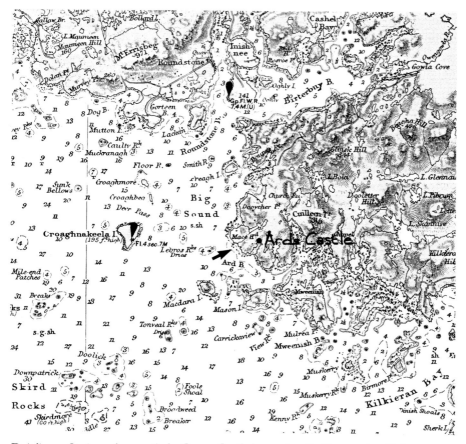

Duirling na Spainneach, near Ards, Carna, Co. Galway, where the Concepcion Delcano *came ashore. Her survivors were handed over to the Governor of Connacht by Tadgh na Buile O'Flaherty and later executed. (Reproduced from portion of BA chart 2173 with the sanction of the Controller, HM Stationery Office and of the Hydrographer of the Navy)*

main islands here; Mweenish, which is connected to the mainland by a present-day bridge; Mason Island, due west of that; St MacDara's Island, west southwest of Mason; and finally, Croaghnakeela Island, almost due west of Mace Head itself. The sound offers many hazards, most of them invisible to the unwary. It is almost totally exposed to onshore winds – the prevailing winds on this coast – and to the unceasing surge of the Atlantic. It is littered with underwater reefs and shallows over which the waves break in rough weather – a classic feature of western ocean shores. The two ships lay in this maelstrom of rocks, islands and tidal currents, possibly having got there with the aid of someone who knew the coastline, one familiar enough to Spanish fishermen.

That Tadgh na Buile knew of their presence is undeniable; Ards Castle was just south around the corner from Mace Head and by striding just a couple of hundred yards from his courtyard and mounting the nearest headland he could have seen the two ships at anchor. But for the moment he held his hand.

For what happened next we must rely totally on tradition, as there is no extant evidence to show how these two ships were wrecked. In the kitchen of a house on Mace Head, within sound of the Atlantic surf booming on the headland, I listened to an old man, who spoke little English but instead the purest of Gaelic, describe with great clarity and utter conviction the story of that event. He himself had heard the story at his father's knee and his father from his grandfather and so on through at least twelve generations. Cosgrave's story (for that was his name) bears the classic stamp of traditional authenticity, a tale bounded firmly by facts and names. Here it is as I heard it.

That night a fire was lit on the land to bring the Spanish ships in, to pretend that there was a safe way in to harbour for them. A family called MacDonagh it was who lit this fire, but whether it was the English or Tadgh na Buile who paid them to do it I couldn't say. The ships saw the light and came in, thinking they would be saved, for the night was bad; but they struck the land down on the shore we call *Duirling Beag* and *Mor* [the place of the stones, small and big]. They were army boats, for they had soldiers aboard them. Not a man in them was saved but a young boy and all the bodies that came ashore that night are buried below on the shore.

The young man was taken in by a family called Lee and was reared to manhood by them in their home. When he grew up, he left them and went back to Spain in a boat that came to the islands. But afterwards he came back and stayed out on MacDara's Island where some of the people he had known went out to him to greet him and make him welcome. There were MacDonaghs who went with them and he gave them drink and hospitality. The MacDonaghs he kept and the rest he sent ashore. And when that was done, in revenge for their having lit the fire he brought off the MacDonaghs in the boat back to Spain and neither hide nor hair of any man of them was heard to this day.

It is instinctive to dismiss this as mere fable. Yet to do so would be a grave error, since there are many threads running through this four hundred year old legend which are common both to tradition and to the few known facts about this wreck. Using both, one can reconstruct the event more or less as

Cosgrave told it before his kitchen fire, with the additional information from more accepted sources shedding extra illumination.

The *two* ships of which tradition speaks, for instance. The presence of an additional ship, which also was wrecked, is easily enough explained; this smaller vessel could be any one of the many tenders which accompanied the ships which reached Ireland's shores. That the tender was wrecked is suggested by the traditional version of the event, and the fact that the State Papers make no mention of a second wreck at Carna is not significant; because she was small, her loss was negligible and therefore scarcely worth reporting. And we have other instances, such as that involving the barque at Tralee, where no word of what happened to the barque herself appears in any contemporary records.

Tradition mentions 'army' boats – clearly this is not an invention of imagination. Almost every single vessel in the Armada carried soldiers, of which the fleet had with her no less than 18,973; the squadrons of Portugal, Andalusia, Castile, Biscay, Guipuzcoa, Levant, *urcas*, and the galleasses all without exception numbered more soldiers than sailors aboard each ship, and only among the *pataches* and *zabras* were some ships able to boast of carrying more sailors than soldiers. The Armada ships were 'army' boats in that they carried an army of soldiers. The bodies of these heavily armed men coming ashore at Carna and being described as soldiers by the natives is not merely coincidence.

The method by which the ships were wrecked may appear unlikely, if dramatic; and yet there is ample evidence to show that the lighting of fires as a lure to bring ships in close to land was a familiar practice among the more lawless clans along the seaboard, and known in other parts of the British Isles. Piracy was an accepted way of life and salvage equally so; sometimes the two were combined, as in the case of the Carna wreck. There are plenty of precedents, even up to the latter years of the last century, to show that the events surrounding this wreck were of classic familiarity.

On the question of survivors, there appears to be a clear discrepancy between what tradition states (one survivor only) and what can be extracted from the State Papers, where no figures are given. However, the number of survivors must have been fairly substantial, since by the time that those from this vessel, the *Falco Blanco*, the unnamed ship at Galway which had landed seventy men and then escaped, and the two(?) wrecks in Clew Bay had been assembled in Galway there were around three hundred. Probably at least fifty men survived the Carna wreck, which would appear to throw the traditional figure for the number of survivors into doubt.

But does it? An analysis of the legend merely confirms one factor, namely that just one Spaniard survived *in the area*. There may well have been others (in fact, undoubtedly were) who did survive but were taken prisoner immediately and taken to Galway the next morning, while the young man or boy was hidden by the local clan, the Lees. The brief presence of the other prisoners in the area was of such short duration that the memory of their coming would have faded fast. Much more enduring, however, was the story of the young boy who was hidden and then reared as one of themselves by the Lees.

Tadgh na Buile brought the prisoners to Galway, a fact confirmed by Bingham. They had been handed over to his custody by the MacDonaghs, who may have been bribed initially by him; this is not proven but is likely. Tadgh undoubtedly would have kept for himself any arms, guns, valuables and other articles which came ashore.

Duirling na Spainneach cannot have changed much, if at all, in four centuries. It is a geological oddity, a heaped mound (for all the world like a macabre mass grave) of conglomerate and granite rocks, rolled smooth by centuries of sea wear. The ships evidently struck in deepish water (thirty feet or so) just offshore, where the water deepens suddenly out from the rocky ledges. The wrecks occurred at night and in the darkness and confusion, a confusion worsened by the heavy seas, many must have been battered to death before they could swim the short distance to land.

The identity of the larger ship is easily proven. Among the list of men whom Tadgh na Buile brought into Galway and delivered into the tender arms of Bingham was a Don Diego Sarmiento, who is listed in the Spanish State Papers as having commanded a company of soldiers (variously numbered as both thirty-eight and sixty-six) aboard a Biscayan ship, the *Concepcion*. There is little doubt therefore that this was the ship wrecked at Carna.

The *Concepcion* was a member of Recalde's Biscayan Squadron; her captain was Juan Delcano (otherwise called Juanes del Cano) and his name was often appended to the *Concepcion*'s to distinguish her from another *Concepcion* (Zubelzu) in the same squadron. Some 418 tons, she carried eighteen guns and some 225 men, most of whom were drowned at Carna, the remainder suffering the fate of all Armada prisoners to fall into Bingham's hands. The *Concepcion* clearly tallies with Geoffrey Fenton's estimate of 'in O'Fflaertie's country, one shipp, 200 men'; she is the source however, of considerable confusion over the years since she is listed by Duro as both lost *and* returned home. In listing her as returned, however, he appears to have been wrong – a not infrequent event.

Sarmiento was the only notable member of the ship's survivors brought to Galway; Delcano himself appears to have been drowned. There still exist faint traditions of wreckage salvaged and various artifacts from the ship being in use by local people up to the last century; today, however, not one relic remains except the strong tradition. Only Tadgh na Buile's walled castle still struggles to keep its few remaining stones standing, brooding silently on its low knoll over the Atlantic.

The number of prisoners in Galway was now growing. But the jails were not yet full; more Spaniards, this time from wrecks further north, were to join

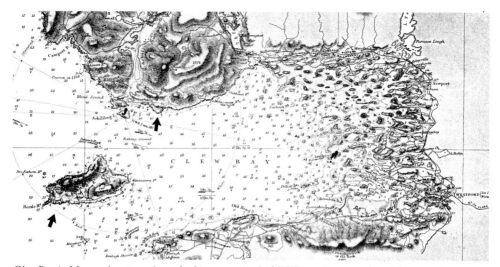

Clew Bay in Mayo, where two Armada ships were wrecked. El Gran Grin was lost either on or close to Clare Island in the mouth of the bay; the San Nicolas Prodaneli went aground at Toorglass on the Corraun Peninsula, between Achillbeg Island and Mulrany (Mallaranny) to the east of the peninsula. Burrishoole is at the northeast corner of the bay and above Newport; Westport at the southeast corner. (Produced from portion of BA chart 2420 with the sanction of the Controller, HM Stationery Office and of the Hydrographer of the Navy)

their countrymen in Bingham's prison.

The coast of Mayo around Clew Bay, although geographically close to that of Connemara, is nevertheless very different. It is here that the voyager begins to view from seaward the soaring cliffs which are so much a feature of the coast of Mayo from Achill round to Killala. Much of Achill and the Corraun peninsula features high cliffs, and from Erris almost without interruption as far eastwards as Killala are similar and even more imposing cliffs. From seaward, sailing into Clew Bay is magnificent but awesome; the innumerable islands and islets (drumlins) in the inner bay present a false front to the little harbours of Newport and Westport, a facade which conceals as treacherous and tricky a navigational hazard as one could weave nightmares around. To the north, the great cliffs of Achill rear above the waters of the bay, bastion against the swell of three thousand miles of open ocean to the west.

At the mouth of the bay Clare Island, dominated by the towering peak of Knockmore, rises to five hundred feet, with beneath it a barren landscape split by valleys; this bare and grim island is a fitting sentinel for the bay and its hinterland, a commanding height set in a position of strategic importance. Such was its importance that for many years during the sixteenth century it served as a base from which an Irish chieftain sent forth a fleet of ships which controlled all the shipping lanes along this wild coast.

That chieftain was Grace O'Malley, head of the O'Malley clan, which still lives on on Clare Island; today there is hardly an islander who is not an O'Malley, but the warlike disposition of their sixteenth century leader has been softened in her descendants over the passing centuries. Grace O'Malley, more fondly and commonly known as Granuaile, was a figure of the period, a typical Elizabethan; using the remote fastnesses of her island as a base of operations, she had built up what amounted to an independent republic on Clare Island, and with it a small navy which was so powerful that its domination of the entire coastline of Mayo and further afield was unquestioned, a state of affairs which caused severe embarrassment to an England whose own fleet was then the world's principal maritime power. Granuaile's impudence extended even to exacting tolls on all vessels – including English ones – using what she properly regarded as her waters.

Granuaile's life was remarkable in most ways. She married twice, once to one of the warlike Burkes of Mayo, that family which caused Bingham so much trouble and brought upon its head his terrible revenge. Her first marriage was to one of the O'Flahertys thus forming a powerful alliance covering both land and sea; on several occasions Granuaile successfully defended her castle on the mainland against English attacks. Her second marriage to Burke provided an eccentric finale to her filial career; she had wed on the condition that both or either of the partners could dissolve the marriage at the end of a year. During that year Granuaile made full and stealthy use of her chance, and when the twelve months ended she had replaced her husband's men with her own picked forces so cleverly that she was able to evict her husband and claim his castle and some of his territory.

She was, moreover, of much more than local importance. Her constant disruption of English shipping off the west coast brought her eventually to the attention of Elizabeth, who perhaps sensing a kindred spirit, invited her to London. True to form, Granuaile went, creating a sensation at Court by appearing, a tall and towering figure, bare-breasted before the Queen. She chatted informally and even pleasantly to Elizabeth but refused her offer to be created a countess, her reason, she said, being that to accept such an offer inferred that Elizabeth was her superior. Such an answer was too typical of the Clare Islander to be questioned; Elizabeth had doubtless felt that by conferring a favour on Granuaile, the western chieftain would be persuaded to slacken off her harassment of English shipping. Granuaile returned to Clare Island and remained there until her death some years later. She is buried on the island, where her tomb may be seen to this day.

Granuaile appears to have been absent on a day in September when there came drifting on the wind towards Clew Bay the Armada ship *El Gran Grin*, vice-flagship or *almiranta* of Recalde's Biscayan Squadron, a huge vessel of 1160 tons and carrying 329 men and twenty-eight guns when she had left Lisbon with the rest of the fleet in May. This was an important ship; although Recalde was the Biscayan commander, the *Gran Grin*, as understudy, nevertheless occupied a high position in the hierarchy of Armada ships. She

Achill Island and Sound, on the northwestern side of Clew Bay in Mayo. The castle is characteristic of many which are connected with the Spaniards in Ireland. It is reputed to have belonged to Grace O'Malley, head of the O'Malley clan of Clare Island on which was wrecked El Gran Grin. *The* Rata Encoronada *was lost north of here. (Peter Baker)*

was a merchantman converted from grain carrying among the ports of Europe to the uses of war, a big, clumsy vessel which was nevertheless very much to the forefront of the Channel battles, during which she had been damaged by gunfire.

The *Gran Grin* was evidently caught in the same gale that had brought the *Falco Blanco* and the *Concepcion* to the rocks along the coast. She was badly damaged and leaking, and like all square-riggers before a strong gale, almost helpless. In coming in too close to the Irish coastline she had allowed herself insufficient searoom in which to run before a gale, and now, with the cliffs of Achill and the maze of rocky islands in Clew Bay opening before her as she wallowed slowly in towards the land, she was in desperate straits. Once in the bay, her chances of escape were non-existent, the bulk of Achill Island blocking off the northern exit and the mainland looming to the east and south. And right in the mouth stood the great mass of Clare Island.

The *Gran Grin* drifted slowly down onto the island. The men on board, watching as the waves beat at the foot of the high cliffs, may have seen tiny figures ashore, running and gesticulating. Like all warlike clans, the O'Malleys gained much of their livelihood from piracy and the sight of the biggest ship that any of those wild clansmen had ever seen must have caused a blaze of excitement on the island. They prepared to meet her in their own way.

There are two distinct and almost equally valid theories as to what then happened. One suggests that the Biscayan *almiranta* struck rock close to the island, probably at the southwestern tip, and sank quickly. Pedro de Mendoza, together with other senior officers including the captain, Gaspar de los Reyes, Don Diego de Mieres and Don Alonso Ladron de Guevara, managed to get a pinnace off with about a hundred men before the *Gran Grin* was finally swallowed by the waters; the rest of those aboard tried to swim or clambered onto floating timbers and wreckage. Most of them were drowned or battered to death by the surf; some got ashore, but it seems certain that about two hundred Spaniards died when the ship struck.

Mendoza was luckier, at least temporarily. The pinnace, though battered and overladen, just made the island, and the hundred or so survivors struggled ashore, wet and shivering. They were met by a horde of armed clansmen but were spared their lives; the O'Malleys were, it seems, unsure as to what to do with their prisoners. In Granuaile's absence the acting chieftain was Dowdarra Roe O'Malley, and on his orders they were sheltered and given food, although technically they were prisoners. At this stage apparently no harm was done to the Spaniards, although it is probable that, in line with the experiences of other Armada survivors elsewhere along the Irish coast, their valuables were taken and their clothes stolen; the State Papers confirm that their arms were taken. But they were alive, and for the moment Dowdarra Roe seemed disinclined to kill them.

We do not know how long Mendoza stayed on the island with his men. In the end, growing restless with enforced inactivity, he led an escape attempt; the Spaniards evidently bursting from their prison and taking the islanders by surprise, tried to get away in their boats (the pinnace had either sunk or was so badly battered that it was now useless). But the O'Malleys were equal to the challenge: a fight ensued and in the words of Edward Whyte, 'sixty-eight Spaniards [were] drowned and slain at the Island of Cleere in Irris.' Among them was Mendoza.

Bingham already was aware of what was happening on Clare Island. He was writing to Fitzwilliam on September 24 from Donmore (Dunmore) that he would gladly recover Mendoza from Clare Island if he could; and a day later, from Castle M'Garratt in Mayo, was reiterating in another letter to the Lord Deputy much the same thing: 'I will send into Dowdarraugh O'Malie to recover Don Pedro de Modosa [sic] if I may.' Evidently he knew just how difficult it would be to get Mendoza off the island, but he need not have worried, since by this time it seems probable that Mendoza was dead. Edward Whyte knew of the massacre three days before this last letter from Bingham, but he may not have been aware that among the dead was Pedro de Mendoza. Clare Island was, after all, sixty miles or more from Galway where the Clerk of the Connacht Council sat collating the scattered scraps of often wrong information which came his way. He cannot have been expected to know everything.

We must look now to Fenton. It is essential at this stage to recognize the diverse sources on which these English officials relied for their reports and

*Clare Island, seen from the west. El Gran Grin was probably wrecked on the south shore in the left foreground of the picture. Dowdarra Roe O'Malley later executed some survivors and may have handed others over to the Governor of Connacht. (*Irish Times*)*

records. Both Whyte and Fenton, in the context of factual records, appear painstaking and meticulous chroniclers and it is basically on what they said in their official reports that we must rely for the bulk of our information. Whyte to a greater degree than Fenton was relying on a variety of reports, some from sheriffs, others from travelling merchants, some from the network of English spies and Irish informers. It was his unenviable task to separate these and to try to decide which were fact and which fiction. That he succeeded admirably is evident in almost everything he wrote; his word, therefore, while not necessarily final, is nevertheless authoritative. Fenton likewise is reliable; to an even greater degree than Whyte he was making an official estimate and report to what amounted to the Government of Ireland. Never one to exaggerate, it is clear that he went to some pains to assure the accuracy of his findings. He is brief on the Clare Island incident, and in a report to the Irish Council (of which, it will be recalled, he was Secretary) mentions merely that there was wrecked 'in Clear Island, one shipp, 300 men.' It is significant that the *Gran Grin* carried about that number; Fenton does not differentiate between those drowned and killed by the O'Malleys, but this does not prove or disprove anything. His 'Note of ships, 16, and men, 5394, drowned, killed, and taken upon the coast of Ireland' was sent to Burghley from Dublin on September 29, having presumably been seen beforehand by the Council.

We are on very unsure ground for all of this; so scarce are the reports concerning Clare Island and the massacre of the *Gran Grin* survivors that it is with a purely tentative confidence that we may surmise that the Biscayan was wrecked there. Tradition confirms it, but not so thoroughly as one would expect or wish. Certainly Mendoza and a party of roughly a hundred men landed there, stayed for some time, and were executed or killed by Dowdarra Roe O'Malley and his men. We have only the official confirmation of the accurate Fenton, allied with two or three other scattered inferences, to support a theory that the *Gran Grin* was in fact wrecked on the island. And there it must rest.

Complications now begin to arise: on September 23 the Mayor of Waterford, Alexander Brywer, was writing to Sir Francis Walsingham enclosing a letter from a merchant called George Wodloke, in which was described the wreck of a huge Spanish ship in Clew Bay. Wodloke, writing from Galway on September 20, wrote to Brywer:

My duty remembered. I have thought good to certify your worship that I have seen a letter bearing date the 6th [16th] of September being the present month of the arrival of one of the Spanish ships at a place called Borreis, which is to the northwards of Galway twenty leagues, which place belongs to the Earl of Ormond. The same ship is cast upon the shore and past recovery, so as the most part of the men are lost and cast away. There is come ashore of them sixteen persons alive, with their chains of gold, and apprehended in the hands of a tenant of my Lord of Ormond, who dwells upon the same land, they report of certain that the ship was of the burthen of 1000 tons, and had in her fifty pieces of brass, besides four great cannon, so as the ship is past recovery.

'Borreis' was in fact Borris or Burris, the Mayo townland whose western boundaries fronted onto the sea at Clew Bay. The name lives on today in the much smaller and more southerly area now defined as Burrishoole (Borris of Owle, the Barony of Owle: Burrishoole), but in the sixteenth century applied to a much wider area than it does today. In later reports, the exact site of the wreck of this very large ship is given as 'Fynglasse'; today there is no such name and the nearest one can find is the modern Toorglass, halfway along the Corraun Peninsula by way of the coast road between Mulrany and Achillbeg Island. Tradition, extant to the present day, gives Toorglass as the location where an Armada ship was, and I had pointed out to me by a local person the very strip of rock where, it is said, the great ship was wrecked. This, however, is not offered as proof.

The barony of Owle was owned in part by the Earl of Ormond, and as Wodloke first reported, the sixteen survivors from the Fynglasse wreck were in the hands of one of Ormond's tenants, which immediately brought the absent earl into the picture. On September 28 he was writing to Gerald Comerford, one of Bingham's sheriffs in the area, that he was 'to save the Spanish wreck at Burrishoole to Her Majesty's use, taking a perfect inventory of the goods' and that any prisoners taken 'are to be safely kept at Galway, Clonmel, Kilkenny and Waterford.' And last of all, following the evident rumour that one of the prisoners was none other than the Duke of Medina Sidonia, that he was 'to be kept without irons and was to have my [Ormond's] horse to ride on.' Later, on October 17, Ormond's official from Clonmel, Mr Henry Shee, was reported by Comerford as having come to Burrishoole to claim the wreck; presumably everything of value aboard the ship had by then been removed and was in the custody of Ormond's tenant. The sixteen prisoners had evidently been brought to Galway.

By October 10, it was clear that any threat which the Spanish landing on Clare Island may have posed for Bingham was long past; Edward Whyte, in a long report to Walsingham, said that Don Pedro de Mendoza and seven hundred men were drowned off the 'Isle of Clear' and that 'Dowdary Roe O'Maly has put one hundred to the sword.' By then, Bingham knew the exact sequence of events on Clare Island; and Whyte's report, scanty though it is on precise detail, seems to confirm that a large number of Spaniards were drowned off Clare Island and that a smaller number were murdered by the O'Malleys. No mention is made of the wreck of *Gran Grin* but the inference that she was indeed wrecked on Clare Island is clear enough.

It has long been held (and a very plausible theory it is) that the wrecks on Clare Island and Fynglasse are one and the same – in other words that the *Gran Grin* was not wrecked on Clare Island but on Fynglasse. The presence of a hundred Spaniards on the island under Mendoza is explained by the theory that they left the *Gran Grin* as she drifted towards the island, fearing that they might strike it and hoping that by taking to the pinnace they might save themselves. Then, according to this theory, the Biscayan missed the island and drifted on until she struck the mainland at Fynglasse.

There is a good deal to be said for this idea, and but for several misconceptions it could be said to satisfy the apparent anomaly existing over the identification of the Fynglasse wreck. For one thing, there were similarities between the two ships: the *Gran Grin* we know was well over 1000 tons and there is evidence that the Fynglasse wreck was of a similar size – '1000 tons burthen'. There were few enough ships in the Armada of that size to make the apparent wrecking of two such leviathans within a few miles of each other appear much more than a coincidence. Then there is the inescapable fact that at least three officers listed among the *Gran Grin*'s complement, Gaspar de los Reyes, Don Diego de Mieres and Don Alonso Ladron de Guevara, were later among the list of Spanish prisoners in Galway. It has been claimed that they were taken from the Fynglasse wreck, but there is no proof whatsoever that this is so.

The presence of los Reyes, Mieres and Guevara in Galway can be explained in several ways; we know that Bingham intended and was anxious to go to Clare Island and 'recover Don Pedro de Mendosa [sic]' – he said so twice on successive days to Fitzwilliam. He was not to know that at the time of writing Mendoza in all probability was dead. But there is a strong possibility that Bingham did eventually send a boat to Clare Island to bring back to the mainland any Spaniards left there, including Mendoza, and that this is how los Reyes, Mieres and Guevara came to be in Galway. It is equally possible that O'Malley himself brought the survivors to the mainland following the massacre and delivered them into Bingham's hands. Even, though highly improbable, that the two escaped from Clare Island and were later captured.

While it is difficult to prove satisfactorily either theory, the balance of the scanty evidence does point to there being two separate wrecks of two separate ships. Both Whyte and Fenton appear to confirm this, and theirs is the most trustworthy evidence in contemporary sources. All else is guesswork. The facts that the two ships were of similar sizes and that two men from the *Gran Grin* appeared in Galway later on cannot be taken as real evidence to support the theory that the *Gran Grin* was the Fynglasse wreck.

One of the most puzzling problems, however, comes in attempting to identify the same Fynglasse wreck. An immediate clue is her size, given in one report as 1000 tons. this need not be taken as exact, but it bears some investigation. Taking all the ships in the Armada from the heaviest (the Levantine flagship *La Regazzona* of 1249 tons) to those of around 900 tons, we can account for them one by one; there were fourteen, of which six were sunk (four of these around Ireland), one taken by the English in the Channel, one stranded in France, and the remaining six returned safely to Spain. The next section of the fleet which might offer a clue is that containing vessels of between 800 and 900 tons, but here again we draw a blank. There were ten in that category and of these six were sunk (five around Ireland) and the remaining four got home safely. This seems to account for every possible vessel of a roughly equivalent size, but at the same time we must remember that this figure of 1000 tons is a guess, and probably not a particularly educated one at that. Ships of that size were rare along the west of Ireland, where the average trading barque was between one and two hundred tons; there was, therefore, no common yardstick reliable enough locally to identify a ship weighing in the range of 800 to 1000 tons.

There is one further possibility, that the Fynglasse wreck may be that of one of two Levant ships from Bertendona's squadron which it appears may have been wrecked in Ireland, the *San Nicolas Prodaneli* (834 tons) and the *Juliana*

(860 tons). Of these, much the firmest evidence revolves around the *Juliana*, since survivors from her wreck were still living in Ballyshannon in Donegal in 1596. It seems unlikely, however, were she the vessel wrecked at Fynglasse, that her survivors would be able to make their way as far north as Donegal. And we know that all sixteen men who scrambled ashore from the Clew Bay wreck were taken prisoner by a tenant of the Earl of Ormond.

This leaves us with the *San Nicolas Prodaneli*, one of the many Ragusan ships in the Armada. That this vessel never returned to Spain is about the one aspect of her disappearance on which there is general agreement. It has been suggested (to my mind without anything like sufficient proof) that she foundered in the North Sea – an assertion frequently used by Armada historians on the slender evidence of Medina Sidonia's diary, in which he noted several Levantine ships gradually falling behind the fleet at that point in the campaign, and which apparently were not seen again. These ships may have been damaged by gunfire and weather, but they were poor sailors at the best of times, overladen and overmasted as many of them were, and the fact that they could not keep up with the fleet is far from proof that they actually foundered there and then. There is at least a strong possibility that the *San Nicolas* reached Ireland and was wrecked there, and this will be dealt with in Chapter XI. We are left, therefore, with an apparently insoluble mystery.

One final point may be of interest: we do know from the State Papers that there were at least two survivors of the Clare Island massacre, which may or may not add to either theory of the Clew Bay wrecks. They were named by Edward Whyte, in a lengthy letter to his brother Alderman Stephen Whyte in Limerick, as 'one poor Spaniard and an Irishman of the County of Wexford.' In another report (October 10) Whyte says that Dowdarra O'Malley took possession of the massacred Spaniard's valuables. There is no mention in either of these reports of any further survivors, least of all Mieres and Guevara, nor indeed of Gaspar de los Reyes, whom Duro confirms as the master of the *Gran Grin*, and who also was a prisoner in Galway.

A pretty problem indeed, in which the scales are nicely balanced. But it is more likely, if narrowly so, that Fenton and Whyte can be relied upon to a greater extent than can almost any other observer or reporter. Whyte was closer and probably knew more than any single man of what went on in Connacht in relation to the Armada wrecks; his evidence, backed by the scrupulous Fenton, appears to confirm the existence of two wrecks in Clew Bay, but against that there is the mystery of how los Reyes, Mieres and Guevara came to be in Galway and where they came from: was it Clare Island or Fynglasse? If we knew that, we would know all – or nearly all.

In Galway the prisoners were being assembled, a growing problem for Bingham. There were at least 300 and possibly 350 Spaniards in prison there, in a city ill-equipped with jails in which to hold this unusual number of captives. But Fitzwilliam had already settled the matter in his edict to Bingham 'to make by all good means, both of oaths and otherwise, to take all hulls of ships, treasures, etc. into your hands, and to apprehend and execute all Spaniards of what quality soever . . . torture may be used in prosecuting this enquiry.'

There it was, unequivocal and brutal. No Spaniard, nobleman or otherwise, was to be spared: all were to be killed. Bingham had ensured by threat of execution and proclamation that virtually every Spaniard who had landed either in Galway or Mayo had been captured or handed over by the natives to the Crown forces. He came to Galway from Athlone to oversee the executions himself and appointed Robert Fowley, Captain Nathaniel Smythe and John Byrte along with several others as his assistants. 'With warrant and commission to put them all to the sword', the grisly work began: three hundred Spaniards were taken to St Augustine's monastery (now Fort Hill) on the hill outside the then much smaller town of Galway and there executed, watched by a stricken crowd of Galway people. Later, after the English forces had left, the Galway townspeople made shrouds for the dead and helped to bury many of the bodies; it is said that two of the Spaniards who survived were hidden in the town and later smuggled to safety along the escape route to the Continent via the Aran Islands at the mouth of Galway Bay. The Pope later sent his forgiveness to the natives in Galway for the Spaniards' execution, but even this has failed to erase the memory of a terrible day in the city's history. Spanish fishermen still come to Fort Hill Cemetery to kneel in prayer on the mass grave of the Armada men, of whom thirty-seven are said to be buried in one corner of the graveyard.

Despite its horror and revulsion at Bingham's treatment of the Spaniards, Galway does not come well out of the period of the Armada. It must be said, whether in its favour or not, that as a town it was loyal to the Crown – indeed it had to be, with a strong garrison of soldiery and within the reach of Bingham's iron arm. Allowing for this, however, the almost indecent speed with which the Spanish fugitives were handed over to the English hardly speaks of western courage and resolution, particularly as in the more remote areas of the province, such as Connemara, the natives had an excellent opportunity of secretly shipping survivors back to the Continent on foreign fishing vessels. Nowhere do the State Papers throw any light on whether or not this was done, except in the city of Galway itself, where it is known that several Spaniards were aided. Of the hundreds of shipwrecked survivors who came ashore along the coast, some probably got back to Spain; but on the whole the fate which they met was grim.

Not all the Spaniards held in Galway died on Fort Hill. Bingham had set aside about fifty, all possible ransom subjects, among them Mieres, Guevara and los Reyes from the *Gran Grin*, Diego Sarmiento of the *Concepcion*, Pedro de Arechaga from the *Falco Blanco*, and from the same ship Don Luis de Cordoba and his nephew Don Gonzalo de Cordoba. They were spared for the time

O'Flaherty's Castle near Renvyle, Co. Galway, which may have housed the survivors from the Falco Blanco, *wrecked several miles away at Ballynakill. From here they were handed over to the English forces and executed.*

The castle of Tadgh na Buile O'Flaherty at Ards, Carna, Co. Galway; the wall is all that remains of what was once an extensive dwelling, from which this western sept of the great clan O'Flaherty ruled a wild and remote area. Tadgh na Buile is commonly supposed to have handed over the prisoners from the Concepcion Delcano *to the English forces in Galway, where they were executed.*

being while Bingham decided what he would do with them. By thus not executing every Spanish prisoner as Fitzwilliam had so expressly ordered, Bingham disobeyed the Lord Deputy. He was not to get away with this impertinence. In a temper, Fitzwilliam denounced Bingham for his failure to carry out his orders and the Governor was forced to execute most of those left, with a reluctance that owed, one feels, more to its mercenary potential than its human element. And so died Mieres, Guevara, los Reyes, Arechaga, Sarmiento and many others: thirteen dons, captains, noblemen and prominent soldiers and seamen. Only two were spared, Don Luis de Cordoba and his nephew Gonzalo, who were sent to Athlone and imprisoned there.

Even then Fitzwilliam was not yet finished. In the meantime, more Spanish prisoners had been handed over to Bingham; these came apparently from a north Mayo wreck (possibly in Tirawley) and were taken to Galway by Bingham's brother George, then Sheriff of Sligo, in whose custody they had been. Bingham, surprisingly, spared them; one of them was a

Don Graveillo de Swasso and another gentleman by licence, and some five or six Dutch boys and young men, who coming after the fury and heat of justice was past, by entreaty I spared them, in respect that they were pressed into the fleet against their wills, and did dispose them into several Englishmen's hands upon good assurance that they should be forthcoming at all times.

But if Bingham could spare these unfortunates, Fitzwilliam would not. On one of his periodic trips through the province (this time to survey Bingham's territory and report on how the Governor had coped with the Spanish 'invasion'), he came to Athlone and there heard of Bingham's act of mercy. Once more he found himself having to order Bingham to execute prisoners: this was unique in that normally Bingham's tendencies had to be curbed rather than encouraged, as Perrott had found to his cost some years back. And once more the sword fell, this time on 'Don Graveillo de Swasso' and the Dutch boys and young men with him. This still left Don Luis and his nephew, and even Fitzwilliam's ruthlessness gave way to avarice when he came to consider their case. Clearly they were suitable for ransom; Don Luis had made no secret of his wealth – it was, after all, the sole reason why he and his nephew still lived and well he must have known that.

While Fitzwilliam postponed the problem of what to do with the two remaining Spaniards and continued on his tour of Connacht, Bingham made no secret of his anger over what he obviously considered as the Lord Deputy's arrogant disregard. In a letter to none other than the Queen, Bingham told Elizabeth that

thus was all the province quickly rid of those distressed enemies, and the service done and ended without any other forces than the garrison bands, or yet any extraordinary charge to Your Majesty [that would have pleased Elizabeth's mercenary streak]. But the Lord Deputy Fytzwilliam having further advertisements from the north of the state of things in those parts, took occasion to make a journey thither and made his way through this province, and in his passing along caused both these two Spaniards which my brother had to be executed, and the Dutch men and boys who had been before spared by me, reserving none but Don Luis de Cordoba and his nephew, whom I have here. I was glad in one respect that his Lordship should take his way through Connaught, for that thereby he might the better satisfy himself of what we had before performed here, and accordingly had written of.

De Cordoba and his nephew were eventually ransomed and returned to Spain, for what exchange we do not know. De Cordoba harboured a deep sense of grievance towards the Irish, particularly to the natives who had handed him over to Bingham (probably Tadgh na Buile O'Flaherty), and he blamed them 'for letting the Spaniards range up and down the country after they had stripped them of their apparral and robbed them of their money and jewels.' He might have contained his bitterness, although his evident anger and contempt are excusable; he was after all, one of the very few to fall into English hands, live through the experience, and return safely home to Spain.

And so ended Galway's role in the Armada. It is a sad and grim tale, hardly relieved by any act of kindness or bravery and dominated by the relentless and ruthless Bingham. Despite all one can say of him, he had done his job supremely well. The Spanish threat afforded by the landing of survivors from at least three and possibly five ships (including the nameless vessel which had escaped from Galway Bay) had been utterly quelled by quick and decisive action on the Governor's part. Fitzwilliam, for all his quarrels with Bingham, must in all honesty have raised his hat in acknowledgement of the job done for him and for England by the man who was truly the Flail of Connacht.

IV

A Ship at Torane

BY the end of the first week of September, the weather off the northwest
of Ireland had scattered the Armada hopelessly. It had fought for many
weeks to keep formation, since to stay together meant survival for some of the
weaker ships; however the increasing severity of the winds demolished that
hope, and while the main body of the fleet doggedly followed Medina Sidonia
on his wide sweep out into the Atlantic, stubbornly battling their way into
the winds, the remainder began to fall away to the southeast, many making
deliberately towards the Irish coast in the hope of succour, whether in the
shape of fresh food and water or of repairing their ships.

The state of some ships and crews is in itself enough to support a theory that
in turning towards Ireland much of the fleet acted on a predetermined
decision. Somewhere in the waters off Rockall, northwest of Ireland, it was
decided that the only way to save ships and lives was to make for the nearest
coast; that that coast represented Ireland, a country Catholic, sympathetic to
Spain and hostile to England, was an additional lure. Nor was this body of
ships (some of them acted independently, of course) inconsiderable; as many as
sixty may have sighted Ireland or come down along its coasts seeking aid. And
that was half of the fleet.

These ships and the men aboard them were by no means the lesser lights of
the Armada. Juan Martinez de Recalde, the Biscayan Admiral and second in
command of the entire Armada, was one; so was Alonso de Luzon, one of the
camp-masters and also one of the most experienced and highly regarded
soldiers in the fleet; also Pedro de Mendoza, of the *Gran Grin*; and many
others. Even these, however, are forced to step back in the face of perhaps the
most noteworthy Spaniard to step on Irish soil, Don Alonso Martinez de
Leiva, Knight of Santiago, Commander of Alcuescar, and designated by
Philip II as commander-in-chief of the land forces of the Armada and, if
Medina Sidonia should die during the campaign, to replace the Duke.

De Leiva occupied a curious but unmistakable position of authority in the
Spanish hierarchy of power. He was well bred (thus fulfilling a prerequisite
condition), his family being the Castilian branch of the de Leivas – 'senor de la
Casa de Leiva de Rioja'. His father, Don Sancho, had been Viceroy of Naples

and, like his son, a Knight of Santiago, and was one of Spain's best known commanders of galleys as well as an experienced soldier. Alonso had followed his father's footsteps in taking up a military/naval career (at that time, this natural tendency also had a political bent). He started with the army, serving as a lieutenant under his father in a number of minor battles. Later he fought in the Grenada Wars in 1568 against the Moors (Moriscos), and after that in the Low Countries under Don John of Austria, who had been sent there by Philip to replace Don Luis de Requesens as Governor in 1576. In 1578 de Leiva returned to Italy.

He had served his military apprenticeship by then and had attracted favourable notice from the Spanish court. It may have been this which spurred him to leave Italy a year after he had returned there and to come closer to Spain, where he took a commission as Captain-General of the Sicilian Galleys, a much favoured political appointment. Later, having taken part in some minor naval encounters, he became Captain-General of the Milanese Cavalry at a salary of three hundred escudos a month – a fair sum in those days. His career was now prospering and he had become a familiar sight at Philip's court, rapidly establishing himself as something of a favourite with the King; possibly he was now beginning to find Milan too distant from Rome and Philip, and so after Drake's raid on Cadiz in the spring of 1587 he resigned his commission, decided to join the Armada, and took up permanent residence at Philip's court. He was rewarded with the titles of Knight of Santiago and Commander of Alcuescar, and his star seemed increasingly in ascendance.

It is at this point that an unsavoury element appears to stain his career: I say 'appears' since there is no proof that he behaved improperly. But it may be that his ambition, of which he had already given ample proof, over-rode his undoubted humanity and good taste. Philip had asked Santa Cruz to form the Armada and at this time the ailing Marquis, then past sixty, was slaving away at the impossible task down south in Lisbon. Philip was growing irritated with the unforeseen and constant delays in getting the Armada out to sea, and with de Leiva present at his elbow, decided to send him down to Lisbon to see what was going on and to report back.

Santa Cruz, as a sailor and a public figure, was immeasurably more important than de Leiva. He was the best known admiral in Philip's Empire, an empire which he had played a considerable part in establishing, with victories over the Ottoman naval forces at Lepanto in 1572 and over Portugal at the island of Terceira in the Azores in 1581 and 1582, the latter victories gaining Portugal and its enormous European and American territories for Spain. But by 1587 Santa Cruz was an old man in poor health, grown crotchety and grumpy, and clearly unable for the task ahead of him.

De Leiva's trip to Lisbon revealed all this, and he reported back to Philip that 'it would be wise to have someone go to Lisbon so as to quicken the Marquis's work'. Philip may have expected to hear this, but the question must be asked: did de Leiva feel that he might himself prove a possible replacement for Santa Cruz if the King should decide that the Marquis was unable to get the Armada on its feet? There is at least a strong possibility that de Leiva used this opportunity of furthering his own career, but in the event Santa Cruz precipitated the problem by dying in February 1588. Philip, faced with the urgency of finding someone quickly to replace him, passed over de Leiva and chose instead that reluctant orange-growing nobleman from San Lucar, Don Alonso Guzman el Bueno, Duke of Medina Sidonia and Captain-General of Andalusia.

There were compensations in store for de Leiva to erase the scars of having been bypassed for the leadership. Philip gave Medina Sidonia apparently secret instructions that in the event of his death de Leiva was to replace him, and he was also appointed, before the Armada sailed, as commander-in-chief of the land forces of the Armada should the Spaniards land in England. When the Armada sailed from Lisbon at the end of May, de Leiva commanded one of the ten vessels of the Levantine Squadron, the *Sancta Maria Rata Encoronada*, known more familiarly as the *Ratte* or *Rata*, an 820 ton converted merchantman with thirty-five guns. The *Rata* was not the Squadron's flagship: that honour was reserved for the *Regazzona*, a gigantic merchantman of 1249 tons, the largest vessel in the entire Armada, commanded by Don Martin de Bertendona. While Bertendona commanded the squadron at least nominally, at sea matters were different; during the Channel fighting, for instance, de Leiva had commanded an entire wing of the fleet and apparently gave orders to Bertendona – understandable given that Don Alonso was heir-apparent to the fleet command.

Bertendona, although overshadowed by de Leiva, has his own undeniable rights to a secure place in history. He was the sole principal squadron commander in the Armada to escape unscathed (of the others, one was captured by the English, one killed at Calais, one jailed in Spain, and two died shortly after reaching Spain) and survived the harrowing trip around Ireland to serve in three other Spanish Armadas against England. Throughout much of his career he kept up a running battle with Drake and the *Revenge*, tangling with him during the Armada, at Corunna in 1589, and finally gaining his revenge, if one will pardon the pun, at the fight in the Azores in 1592, when he was one of the Spanish vessels involved in the battle with the *Revenge* and Sir Richard Grenville, which resulted in the sinking of the English vessel and Sir Richard's death.

De Leiva's part in shaping the policy of the Armada during its campaign was vital; of that there is no doubt. He appears constantly in reports as being closely involved in important decisions, attending councils of war, proffering advice – and being listened to, for he was after all a King's favourite and a very possible future leader of the Armada. After the Duke himself, it could be argued that de Leiva played one of the most important roles in the Spanish chain of command. His vessel clearly reflected this; his military position, family background and glowing reputation had singled him out as one of the more glamorous figures of the Armada, and on board the *Rata* he quickly established a glittering social circle, entertaining lavishly with sparkling linen and gold and silver dishes – even the Duke came to dinner on the *Rata* in Lisbon.

De Leiva's glamour had attracted many noblemen adventurers aboard the *Rata* to take part in the campaign. They were common in those days – sons of titled families, wealthy and distinguished, short of an agreeable career, and anxious for the excitement and challenge which the Armada offered. Probably most ships in the fleet had some aboard, but to the *Rata* came the cream of the country's gentry and nobility, with their servants. They made a festive and glamorous list of passengers, these young scions of noble families: Don Ladron de Guevara, Don Rodrigo Manrique de Lara, Don Pedro de Guzman, Don Thomas de Granvela, Don Gaspar de Sandoval, Jeronimo Magno, Federico Vizconde, Don Manuel Paleologo, Captain Bartoleme Lopez de Silva, Don Luis Ponce de Leon, the Count of Paredes and many others – around sixty of the finest young and titled blood in the whole of Spain. The *Rata* was very crowded; an 800 ton ship such as she was would probably be about 90 to 100 feet long, and into that short length were crowded a listed 419 men – but this does not take into account the noblemen and their servants. She carried 335 soldiers alone, together with eighty-four seamen. Add the sixty or so noblemen-adventurers and their servants (de Leiva himself had no less than thirty-six servants, while some of the others were into double figures) and the overcrowding becomes clear. There can scarcely have been a spare inch of space on the *Rata*.

The Levantine vessel's high-born passengers received a rough baptism once the fleet entered the English Channel and battled its way along past Cornwall and Devon up to the Isle of Wight and beyond. As flagship of one wing of the crescent shaped fleet, the *Rata* was in the forefront of every fight, giving and taking punishment. By the time the fighting was over and the fleet had moved on into the North Sea and around Scotland, this punishment was showing its effects. When the fleet was to the northwest of Ireland, a series of gales caused her condition to worsen suddenly, and brought on an emergency meeting of her senior officers, at which it was decided to run for Ireland and take their chances there. The ship clearly would not make Spain. On September 10 the *Rata* turned and ran for the Irish coast on the wings of a furious gale. One week later, with his ship leaking and her crew in weakened condition, de Leiva sailed down the dreaded coast of Erris (he came in to the coast to the southward of Erris Head itself, thus missing being embayed above it to the north), and on the 17th brought his vessel into the mouth of Blacksod Bay in Co. Mayo.

They had sighted Ireland on the previous day and before coming into Blacksod had one melancholy duty to perform. Among several Irishmen aboard the *Rata* (and who undoubtedly helped in achieving the Levanter's precise landfall) was Maurice Fitzgerald. A well known figure among the Irish and a son of James Fitzmaurice, one of the leaders of the Desmond Rebellion some years back, he had long been exiled and had for years wandered the courts of Spain and Rome seeking aid for his country. His father was a cousin of Gerald, the Earl of Desmond, a vast fertile territory in Munster much coveted by Elizabethan settlers. In 1567 the earl had been incarcerated in the Tower of London and Fitzmaurice had taken over the running of his estates at a time when colonization was building to a peak in Ireland, with land-hungry Elizabethans flooding into the country from England in the hope of gaining rich and large tracts in the more fertile areas.

One of these colonists was Sir Peter Carew, who lodged a claim on lands belonging to the Earl of Desmond. Fitzmaurice and many other Irish noblemen and landowners saw Carew's outrageous claim as a clear threat not alone to the Desmond lands but to all land in Ireland, and Fitzmaurice rose in rebellion in 1569. His rebellion was doomed from the start and in the end he was forced to submit; fleeing Ireland, he petitioned Pope Gregory in Rome to raise an expeditionary force. He was successful to a point, since the Pope did eventually give him a small and inadequate force, led by Thomas Stukely, the fly-by-night adventurer of Europe's capitals. Fitzmaurice landed in Dingle in Co. Kerry in July 1579 but was killed in a skirmish on the Shannon. Thus ended his rebellion.

His son Maurice had evidently been allowed by Philip II to join the Armada force, possibly as a palliative to the many pleas which fell almost daily on Philip's head from the many exiles who then thronged Madrid and Lisbon, and possibly because his help might well be useful if the Armada should land in Ireland instead of England. Whatever the reason, Fitzgerald accompanied the fleet; and because he was a nobleman's son, he was given a berth on the *Rata*.

Fitzgerald was still a young man when he started on the long journey. What he hoped for can only be guessed at; his most wishful thoughts doubtless centred on a resounding defeat of Elizabeth by Philip's combined forces at sea and invading from the Low Countries under Parma, and after that a return to Ireland, a joyous reunion with the now landless members of his family, and a speedy regaining of all the lands which the English colonists had taken from them. But day by day, at first stoically enduring the long and irritating delays as the fleet tacked back and forth out of Lisbon, more often going backwards rather than forwards on its course and then resting to lick its wounds and recuperate in Corunna before setting off on the final leg to the shores of England, Fitzgerald must have lost hope. Throughout the running and mostly indecisive battles up the Channel he underwent a similar torment; and then came the night of the fireships at Calais, the panicky disruption and flight of most of the Armada, and on the next day the death blow to all of Philip's hopes – and Fitzgerald's – at Gravelines.

One of the more poignant stories in the Armada, the many hundreds of insignificant human tragedies, is this episode concerning an exiled Irishman who must have hoped for so much from the attempted invasion of England. As the fleet moved on northwards to round Scotland, swept by gales, Fitzgerald gradually weakened, a man with all hope lost. Somewhere at sea between Rockall and Ireland, he died. In early November a Patrick Eulane wrote to the Marshal of the Army, Sir Henry Bagenal, that 'James Fitzmaurice's son was in the ship that came to M'Sweeny ne Doe's country, and died forty leagues before they came to land' (it should be noted that Eulane mixed up the *Rata* and the *Duquesa Santa Ana*), but this was not the first intimation to the English authorities in Ireland that the Irish exile had died at sea; on October 10, probably close on a month after Fitzgerald had died, Edward Whyte, in his discourse on the Spanish wrecks, wrote that 'Maurice FitzGerald, son to archtraitor James Fitzmaurice FitzGerald, was cast into the sea in a fair cypress chest with great solemnity before Torane' (Tiraun on the Mullet peninsula, the western side of Blacksod Bay in Mayo). Fitzgerald had evidently died some 120 miles out to sea, about halfway between Rockall, the lonely speck of wave-washed rock some 250 miles northwest of Donegal, and the Irish mainland. His body had been kept aboard for three or four days, until the *Rata* sighted land, and then, within sight of his own soil, it was slipped with some ceremony into the Atlantic waters.

This last tribute paid to Fitzgerald, de Leiva sought anchorage along the Mayo coast. Fitzgerald's body was buried 'before Torane', today known as Tiraun, about halfway down the long peninsula of the Mullet, and on its western side. In the sixteenth century there was a castle at Torane, the remains of which were recorded as late as the middle of the eighteenth century; today there is just a raised mound, grass-grown and smoothed with the passage of years; the stones of the castle are commonly supposed to have gone to build the network of dry-stone walls which enclose the salt-whitened fields of this barren country. Looking across from Tiraun, as we will call it for the sake of modernity, to the islands of Inishkea, until quite recently (and incredibly) inhabited, the wild Atlantic dominates all, under a grey and lowering sky. It is a desolate scene.

Leaving the vicinity of Tiraun – he cannot have come too close in towards the land, since the outlying Inishkeas, the North and South Islands, and the Carrick rocks to the north of them form a threatening barrier to seaward – de Leiva moved southward down the coast. He evidently knew what he was about; there were Irishmen aboard, including some clerics, one of whom was the Bishop of Killaloe, and among these was a pilot. That he knew the area is certain, from the exact navigation of the *Rata* into what is described (in the Irish Cruising Club's *Sailing Directions for the South and West Coasts of Ireland*) as 'the best harbour of refuge along the whole west coast, accessible by day or night, with broad clear approach and entrance and splendid shelter and holding.'

This was Blacksod Bay, a deep and long indentation extending to the north from its wide mouth above Achill Island. To seaward of the bay is the

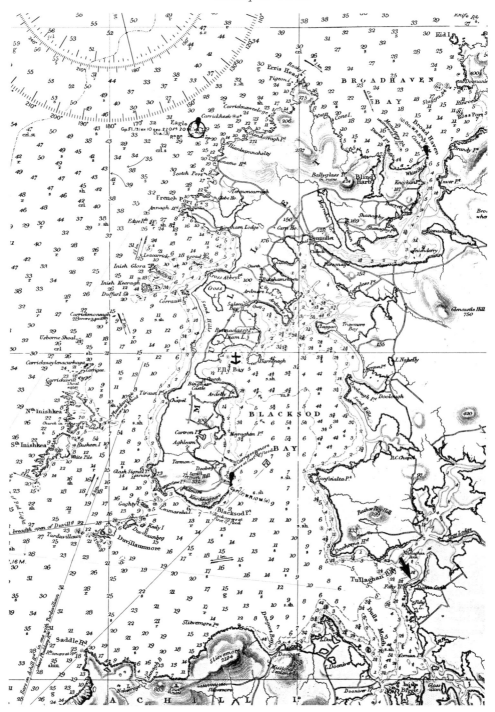

low Mullet peninsula, in reality an island separated from the mainland of Mayo by a short stone-lined canal linking Blacksod with Broadhaven Bay. The very top of the Mullet forms Erris Head and the land falls gradually from the precipitous cliffs of that barren headland to the low, windswept sand dunes of the Mullet.

Inland of Blacksod is utter desolation in the endless brown bogs of Mayo – the great Bogs of Erris, and the largest in Ireland by a long way. The Irish dramatist John Millington Synge, following one of his many visits to this bleak land in the early part of this century, wrote of the 'endless wastes of brown mountain and bog . . . the land is still utterly inefficient . . . the poorest in the whole of Ireland.' Synge's dominant impression, and one which encapsulates totally the pattern of life in this remotest area of even modern Ireland, was of the relentless rain that rarely ceases to fall on Erris; 'the rainfall of Belmullet [at the isthmus of the peninsula] is a heavy one and in wet weather this absence of stone gives one an almost intolerable feeling of dampness and discomfort . . . the people are now at work weeding potatoes in their few patches of tillage and their draggled, colourless clothes . . . added indescribably to the feeling of wretchedness one gets from the sight of these miserable cottages. . . .' Much of what Synge said seventy years ago is true even today. It is equally true that the people in general are better fed, housed, clothed and otherwise provided for; yet the low, rainswept, sodden landscape is as interminably dreary, half-misted in a drooping curtain of rain.

This landscape lay to the east of de Leiva, moving cautiously into the mouth of Blacksod Bay, picking his way among the scattered rocks and islands. His navigation had hitherto been admirable and almost faultless, but it was at this point, somewhere at the entrance to the bay, that he made the decision which was to spell the end for his vessel.

The best and safest anchorage within Blacksod Bay is Elly Bay, directly eastward of Tiraun and on the side of the Mullet facing inwards to the bay. It was then known as Pollilly, *poll* being the Gaelic for hole, a significant term since Elly Bay is basically a deepish hole with ample water even at low tide for quite large ships. Spotswood Green, who had sailed these waters in his capacity as Chief Inspector of Irish Fisheries, called it the best anchorage in the

Erris Head and Blacksod Bay in north Mayo, the centrepiece of several episodes involving the Armada. A small vessel may have been lost on Kid Island off Benwee Head, and at Inver on Broadhaven Bay evidence suggests that the urca Santiago *was wrecked. Further south, near Ballycroy, the* Rata Encoronada *went ashore on Fahy Strand in Tullaghan Bay with Alonso de Leiva on board. The men from the* Rata *fortified themselves at Doona (Fahy) Castle, and later marched round the eastern side of Blacksod Bay and down the Mullet Peninsula to join up with the* Duquesa Santa Ana *which had anchored in Elly Bay east of Torane (Tiraun). The* Duquesa *later left Blacksod, but was herself wrecked further north in Donegal while heading for a refuge in Scotland. (Produced from portion of BA chart 2419 with the sanction of the Controller, HM Stationery Office and of the Hydrographer of the Navy)*

A solitary stone marks the spot where Torane Castle formerly stood. On this bleak outpost of Tiraun on the Mullet Peninsula in Mayo, the men from two and possibly three Armada vessels gathered before sailing west out past the distant Inishkea Islands (left background) in the Duquesa Santa Ana. *(Denis Kendrick)*

A view southeast over Elly Bay, Mullet Peninsula, Co. Mayo. An excellent sheltering ground for ships, and where the Duquesa Santa Ana *anchored for some days, this broad bay is on Blacksod Bay on the inland side of Torane (now Tiraun), where the Spaniards fortified themselves. (Denis Kendrick)*

bay, a judgement underlined by the Irish Cruising Club's description of Elly as giving 'excellent shelter with good holding in the west or north parts of the bay according to wind.'

It is most probable that the *Rata* was not alone at this point and that somewhat in her vicinity was at least one other Armada vessel, the *Duquesa Santa Ana*, a 900 ton Andalusian ship with some 350 men aboard. The *Duquesa*, entering the bay, turned north and sailed up to Elly where she dropped anchor – a fine and accurate piece of pilotage. Once there, she was as safe as she would be in any anchorage along the coast. That de Leiva and those aboard the *Rata* had seen the *Duquesa* enter the bay and sail up deep into its safety is almost certain if one takes into account their subsequent action. But de Leiva did not follow the Andalusian's course, for what inexplicable reason is not known, and chose instead to move deeper and eastward into the other arm of the bay. Probably he sought shelter behind the towering bulk of Achill Island to the south, intending to sail between Ridge Point on its northernmost tip and Kinrovar, near Dohooma to the north. Inside of these two points was a considerable bay leading south down into Achill Sound; while there was shelter there, its navigation presented some difficulty.

By moving towards the eastern end of Blacksod de Leiva was entering an area of complex and difficult tides, the ebb stream reaching a speed of up to three knots. William Hamilton Maxwell's classic *Wild Sports of the West* describes the general area as 'deep and dangerous, for through them the waters which flow from Blacksod and Clew Bay, and fill this extensive channel and its surrounding estuaries, rush with amazing violence; and the rapidity with which the tides enter and recede is frightful.'

The *Rata* sailed into this tide-rip; by now, de Leiva may have been regretting his decision to run east, and somewhere there he anchored. Directly east was Doona, dominated by the high Fahy Castle, and to the northeast the Tullaghan Bay. To the south was Inishbiggle shoal and island and the treacherous channel of the Bull's Mouth. The Levantine ship was in a highly dangerous position. The wind was westerly or thereabout; the current and tides together were alarmingly strong, as the Spaniards could feel from the unease of the *Rata*. Afraid to move further south into the even more dangerous sound above the Bull's Mouth, obviously an area which he and his pilots did not know, de Leiva had no other choice than to anchor; but the tides were strong, and with only one large anchor (the other left on the bottom at Calais) the big vessel was clearly close to dragging it clear of the sandy bottom and drifting onto the shore.

It was probably well past midday: a decision had to be taken quickly. De Leiva decided that the wisest move would be to send a scouting party ashore to see if food and fresh water were obtainable and also to test the temperature of their welcome among the natives. He detached an Italian soldier, Giovanni Avancini, with fourteen soldiers to undertake this delicate operation. Considerable risk was involved, since they probably knew little of the area, its politics or the natives' possible behaviour towards strangers landing on its shores. Avancini and his men took the sole remaining small boat on the *Rata*, lowered it into the strong currents, and made off towards the shore to the east. They grounded gently on a sloping, sandy beach near the gaunt and deserted Fahy (Doona) Castle; there was no-one in sight. They pulled the boat up and after a short consultation moved off inland towards Ballycroy. Soon they were lost from the sight of those aboard the *Rata*.

Avancini and his men had landed in one of the wildest and most remote coasts in the entire island of Ireland, a part of Connacht that was perhaps least touched by English rule. Its natives were rebellious and unruly, the leading clan among them being branches of the Burkes of Mayo, a family which had for many years taunted Bingham from their strongholds in bog and mountain. The overlord, however, was not a Burke but a chieftain much further east, Sir Brian O'Rourke of Breffni, who controlled a great stretch of territory including parts of Sligo, Leitrim, Cavan and Mayo. O'Rourke was a despised and even feared figure as far as Bingham was concerned. Although formerly a loyalist at a time when that political alignment had probably suited his survival, he had later turned away from fealty to Elizabeth to such an extent that at one period he had made a 'wooden effigy on which was written the words "Queen Elizabeth", urged his retainers to hack it with axes, and tying it to his horse's tail, dragged it through the mire.' Such a tale is probably true; certainly it bears the characteristic stamp of this remarkable chieftain who for so long dominated much of the lower northwestern portion of the country, and in doing so eluded the vengeance of Bingham and Fitzwilliam. Later on, when defeat and capture seemed inevitable, he fled to the neutral James VI in Scotland who, however, turned him over to English hands. He died on the gallows at Tyburn, and was drawn and quartered.

O'Rourke's power extended as far west as the remote bogs of Erris and even to the area around Ballycroy, where Avancini and his men had now landed. The local chieftain was, however, a Burke – Richard Burke, known to all, including Bingham, as 'the Devil's Hook'. The Connacht Governor hated all Burkes and particularly Richard on whom he kept a close and watchful eye; as early as September 8 (18) we find him writing to Fitzwilliam from Athlone that 'This morning I had news brought to me that the Devil's Hook, a notable malefactor of the Burkes in Mayo, hath of late taken a dozen skiffs or small boats with certain kernes [Irish soldiers] into the islands there, by which should seem that they have knowledge of some foreign enemy to land thereabouts, for till now I have not heard of him a good while.'

It seems probable, indeed likely, that Richard Burke and his men had seen the *Rata* come to anchor outside Ballycroy. The coast was well populated and the entrance of such a huge ship would not go unnoticed. Word would have spread like wildfire; the natives may well have feared a change of tactic by Bingham, an attack by sea rather than by land in an attempt to bring them to heel. That they kept hidden, suspicious and watchful, is understandable.

Avancini's party was, it must seem, watched from cover. As soon as Burke judged they were out of sight of the *Rata*, he surrounded them and took them prisoner. Like many of the native Irish, once he understood that the landing party was Spanish and not English, Burke showed mercy in not killing his captives, although he did order them to be stripped of their clothes, and their valuables and weapons taken. This done, they were probably moved inland. They ended up in Bingham's hands and suffered the same fate as other Spanish prisoners in being executed in Galway.

Edward Whyte has a different version of what happened when the Spanish landing party came on shore, claiming that 'Giovanni Avanciny and fourteen Italians being ill-used desert'. This seems unlikely and is contradicted in other reports.

On board the *Rata* the hours passed slowly and anxiety gradually grew. Avancini had not reappeared on the shore, where the small boat lay unattended and alone. It was a valuable link to de Leiva and he could not afford to lose it; several of the best swimmers among the crew were detailed to go ashore on empty wine casks which were thrown overboard and on which they paddled and swam ashore. Once there they clambered aboard the small boat and rowed back out to the *Rata*. By now the evening was lowering and an early September dusk was beginning to fall. The wind was getting up, the tide was still strong, and de Leiva must by now have almost given up hope that the landing part would return. Even more worrying was the state of his ship and her anchorage, but with night coming on there was little he could do for the moment.

They spent an anxious and watchful night as the tide ebbed, and then began to flood again before dawn. The light brought with it a vista of a grey sea whitened by the freshening wind from the west, the worst possible quarter. It was clear that a safer anchorage must be found.

It may be that de Leiva chose this moment to up anchor and try to move further south, down towards what he hoped might be a better anchorage; it may equally be, and probably was, that under the strong flooding tide and the sweeping current the *Rata* at last dragged her anchor. Whatever the reason, she began to drift, unable to make any offing and gain some sea room. The shore loomed up – low, wind-swept sand dunes half hidden with breaking spray. And then the grating shock, the heave, the thunderous falling of loose tackle from aloft; the *Rata* struck sandy ground hard and rammed her great keel firmly into the bottom.

Matters could not have been worse: the Spaniards had paid the price of bad seamanship in taking risks on a coast they did not know. The big Levanter had gone aground on a rising tide and the chances of floating her off at highest water were therefore slim. The sandy bottom was yielding and the ship was settling into it quickly; even a single tide might well ensure such strong suction on the hull that it would be impossible to shift her. Moreover, there would be no chance of kedging her off, since they had just one small boat, far too small for that dangerous and complex task. Each successive tide would seal her fate with greater firmness.

This was a desperate blow for de Leiva. Undoubtedly he had hoped that he would have been able to find a safe and secure anchorage in friendly country and there patch up the *Rata*'s damaged and leaking hull, make other repairs and finally sail for either Spain or Scotland (the latter then being neutral). Now all this had come to nothing; the Armada ship had come to the end of her passage.

On the credit side, the *Rata* herself was not in immediate danger of breaking up, and her men were unharmed. There were few dangerous rocks where they lay; ahead to the east was the shelving strand of Fahy on which they had struck, with inland an almost limitless expanse of flat bog, backed by great mountains – Slieve Car, Knocklettercus, Corslieve, Nephin Beg, Glennamong and many other high peaks. Closer at hand and almost overhanging the low-lying land facing them was the sudden hump of Knockmoyleen (791 feet). Whatever awaited them lay somewhere in that region, for on the three remaining sides lay an unknown entanglement of land and sea, difficult terrain to the stranger.

The first task which faced the men on the *Rata* was getting ashore. She was not far off the land; tradition, which in this case can be relied upon as an accurate guide since the remains of the wreck were visible at low spring tides until about sixty years ago, places the site some 150 yards offshore and almost in the centre of the sickle-shaped hoop of strand northwest of Doona Castle.

Looking northwest from Fahy Strand in Blacksod Bay, Mayo, where the Rata *went aground at a point roughly midway between the centre of the picture and the tip of the distant spit of land. The wreck lies under shifting sands. (Denis Kendrick)*

Local people living there remember hearing their grandparents talk of the wreck and there are stories of intrepid children picking mussels from its weed-encrusted timbers. That this wreck was the *Rata* is without doubt, since tradition is still vibrantly alive in placing it as the Spanish ship. Spotswood Green, on a visit there at the turn of the century, secured 'one of her timbers of Italian oak, burnt at one end', a significantly revealing piece of evidence, since it indicates that, as was the custom with wrecked Spanish ships, the *Rata* was burnt to prevent enemy hands being usefully laid on her.

Getting ashore then, while difficult, was not overly so; many men, even hardened sailors, in those days had not learned to swim, but it would have been simple enough to construct a few makeshift rafts from hatch covers, loose timbers and so on, and float ashore on these and other contraptions. And there was the one boat – small, it is true, but probably capable of ferrying ashore perhaps thirty to forty men in a single journey. Many would have swum; others may have slid down once low tide came and half-swum, half-waded ashore. There is not great depth of water there today, but over four centuries the seabed can change. There is no mention anywhere of any of the men off the *Rata* being drowned, and probably this was the case. It may have taken a day or even longer to get them all ashore safely, but it was done, and possibly on the afternoon of the very day the *Rata* had drifted aground, all those who had been aboard stood on the the strand at Fahy.

How many were there? The official Lisbon muster of the Armada shows that when the ship left there at the end of May she had on board 335 soldiers, 84 seamen, and various officers, chaplains, hospital staff and so on: probably well over 450 men to begin with. On top of that there were something in the region of sixty or so noblemen; add to that the total of servants, and it is very possible that the *Rata* carried perhaps as many as 700 men. To get all these ashore without a soul being lost was a considerable feat. It was a formidable force: they were undoubtedly well armed, and around half of the total number were soldiers, probably well trained. That they could repulse any possible attack by natives goes without question, and from what we know of the strength – or the lack of it – of Bingham's forces, could contain any moves from that direction as well.

They now had to find shelter; the day was wild, with the westerly gale still blowing, the men were wet, unused to the climate, cold and hungry. Shelter and hot food were imperative. Close to the edge of the strand, and more or less marking its southern end, rose the tall form of Fahy or Doona Castle, apparently then deserted. It may not have been so – perhaps the inhabitants had fled when they saw the Spanish ship approaching – but at any event it was now empty and provided an ideal base. They began to fortify themselves into a strong, well-protected camp around the castle and its environs.

Fahy Castle in the late sixteenth century was not extensive, as its present remains reveal. Today there is not a great deal of it left. Maxwell, in *Wild Sports of the West*, suggests that it may once have been the home of the infamous Grace O'Malley whom we have already met in the previous chapter, but there is little corroboration of this. He writes, 'The castle of Doona was, till a few years since, in excellent preservation [Maxwell wrote this in 1830 or thereabouts] and its masonry was likely to have puzzled Father Time himself; but Irish ingenuity achieved in a few hours what as many centuries had hitherto failed in effecting.' He goes on to describe how the once-massively built castle came to be in its present state.

A rich hospitable farmer [John Conway], whose name will be long remembered in this remote spot, had erected a comfortable dwelling immediately adjoining the courtyard wall of the ancient fortress; and against the tower itself was piled in wealthy profusion a huge supply of winter turf. It was a night of high solemnity, for his first-born son was christened. No wonder then that all within the house were drunk as lords. Turf was wanted, and one of the boys was despatched for a cleaveful – but though Patt could clear a fair, and "bear as much beating as a bull", he was no man to venture into the old tower in the dark, "and it haunted". Accordingly, to have fair play "if the ghost gripped him", he provided himself with a brand of burning bog-deal. No goblin assailed him, and he filled his basket and returned unharmed to the company, but unfortunately forgot the light behind him. The result may be anticipated. The turf caught fire, and from the intense heat of such a mass of fuel, the castle walls were rent from top to bottom, and one side fell before morning with a crash like thunder. Nor was the calamity confined to fallen tower and lost fuel. Alas! several kegs and ankers of contraband spirits were buried beneath the walls, and the huge masses of masonry that came down, burst the concealed casks of Cognac and Schiedam.

Today, although one corner of the castle stands, along with what may have been at one time an oratory, there is little else left. The house where John Conway drank the health of his first-born son has been replaced by that of Jack Daly, who has, like Conway, put his own turf-rick against the grey stone walls.

Once de Leiva and his company had fortified themselves within the castle and the feeding of the large force had been organized, the question of what to do with the ship arose. It was against both custom and policy to leave her there intact as she was. No stranger would approach as long as the Spaniards were in the vicinity of the ship, but once they moved, as they must, it would be a different matter. If the English did not get to the wreck first, they would find it stripped within a day or so by the avaricious clansmen and not an item of value would remain.

At the next low tide, a group of men rowed out to the *Rata*, poured tar and pitch along her upperworks and rigging, set it alight, and as the flames grew scrambled overside and returned to shore. Before this had been done, anything of value which was easily transportable had been removed – 'all the goods they had in the ship of any value, as plate, apparel, money, jewels, weapons, and armour', although they had apparently left behind 'victual, ordnance, and much other stuff'. (Later Bingham was to learn that this 'other

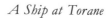

A corner of the remaining masonry of Doona Castle at Fahy Strand, Co. Mayo. (Denis Kendrick)

Doona Castle. Alonso de Leiva and the rest of the Spaniards from La Rata Encoronada *took shelter here after their ship went aground in the bay in front of the castle. (Denis Kendrick)*

The remains of Bingham's Castle built on the site of Elly Castle, looking to the northeast across Elly Bay. (Denis Kendrick)

stuff' consisted of 'great pieces [cannon] and other munition, wine and oil and many other things under water . . . treasure, cloth of gold, velvet . . .'.) The cannon, too heavy to carry, were left behind.

Word of the wreck of the *Rata* soon reached Bingham from the hurried messages of Gerald Comerford, his Sheriff, whose responsibility it was to keep a close eye on the area. The news that another ship was wrecked must have gladdened Bingham's heart, but that seven hundred Spaniards had taken over a castle on the shores of his province must have come as a great shock. Beleaguered as he was with the various wrecks lower down the coast towards Galway, he had his hands full; his forces were weak and despite constant appeal to Fitzwilliam were likely to remain so. (It is difficult to blame Fitzwilliam, since he was bombarding his superiors in England with constant and increasingly frantic calls for help, which were largely ignored.) All Bingham could do for the moment was entreat Comerford to keep a very close watch on de Leiva and his men, and to keep him informed of any developments. Ballycroy was more than seventy miles from Galway over difficult tracks and Bingham was fully occupied with the worsening situation closer to Galway, where reports of wrecks and shipwrecked Spaniards were reaching him almost daily.

It was lucky for Bingham that de Leiva's intentions far from being aggressive, were directed almost solely towards survival and escape. It was no easy matter to feed so many men for a lengthy period and food was difficult to come by from an elusive and almost hidden population. Some bartering may have been done, the Spaniards possibly exchanging arms or wine and oil for food, but we do not know. De Leiva's thoughts now turned to the *Duquesa Santa Ana*, which he knew was still somewhere in the bay to the north. His own position, while secure enough as long as food lasted and the anticipated English forces failed to arrive, was far from satisfactory; there was a big and well found ship from his own country somewhere in the bay and it seemed logical that they should try to join her and thus possibly get back to Spain.

Within a couple of days of their stranding at Ballycroy, the Spaniards were on the march. They may have got a local guide to show them the way around the bay to where the *Duquesa* lay; it would appear logical, since the path was by no means an easy one and even today is difficult to follow. Moving northwest from Doona, they would have crossed the Owenduff River somewhere where the present Shrahnamanagh Bridge stands today, and from there struck directly north towards Belmullet, crossing en route the Owenmore River somewhere in the vicinity of Goolamore, and then gradually following the rough contour of the eastern side of Blacksod Bay until they reached the isthmus at Belmullet. From there, the march south to Tiraun would have been the easiest part of the journey.

They joined another formidable company of their countrymen at Tiraun. Comerford records this episode briefly: '600 Spaniards who were at Bally-crauhie [Ballycroy] were conveyed to the Castle of Torane, a very strong place, and there joined with 800 more who came out of another great ship which lay at anchor in the road of Torane.' Edward Whyte, acting on an earlier report from Comerford, had already recorded in a letter to his brother Stephen that '400 Spaniards fortify at Ballycroohie'. Both were wrong in their figures, Comerford underestimating those from the *Rata* and at the same time, overestimating the company aboard the *Duquesa*. His combined figures of men now at Tiraun came to 1200, whereas in fact there cannot have been much more than 1000 men on the peninsula. Captain Don Pedro Mares of the *Duquesa* commanded a total force of 357 men according to the Lisbon muster, and this number had undoubtedly been reduced by the familiar twin spectres of war and disease until it was in all probability something in the region of 300. The *Duquesa*, incidentally, is commonly supposed to have been named in honour of the wife of the Duke of Medina Sidonia who was an Andalusian.

While all this was going on, Comerford was flitting about anxiously. When he heard that de Leiva and the seven hundred strong party had left Doona he immediately sent an armed guard to watch over the charred remains of the *Rata* and to take anything of value left aboard. But he was too late; the locals had already descended on the bones of the ship and picked her clean like a pack of famished wolves. On September 23 Comerford dolefully informed Bingham that 'James Blake, Ferriegh M'tyrrell, Richard Iccoggy, Moilmory M'Ranyll, Marcus Roe M'Tyriell and Thomas Burke M'inabbe took out of the wreck a boat full of treasure, cloth of gold, velvet &c.'

At Tiraun, de Leiva took overall command. The formidably large force had now fortified itself in two castles, one overlooking Elly Bay from its southern shore, the other half a mile away on the other side of the Mullet peninsula at Tiraun. From a high mound beside the castle at Elly the castle at Tiraun was clearly visible and so signal communication between the two was possible. Today the crumbled remains of Bingham's Castle, the ancestral home of the Mayo branch of the Binghams, marks the site where Elly Castle stood; the high mound on the eastern side of the castle is unchanged. Nothing is left of Tiraun but a raised mound. They were in an impregnable position: Tiraun commanded an extensive and comprehensive view over all the seaward approaches to the peninsula while Elly overlooked the land approaches and any possible routes of attack from the eastern side by sea. They had chosen well, with the soldier's eye for terrain and defensive positioning, and with a force of a thousand men were clearly well beyond Bingham's or Fitzwilliam's capacity to capture.

Here was a fresh nightmare for Bingham. A thousand well armed Spaniards on his territory, with a large ship; probably two, as there is some evidence to suggest that another Armada vessel, the *Nuestra Senora de Begona*, was somewhere close by. The *Nuestra Senora* was a 750 ton Castilian merchantman with twenty-four guns and 297 men aboard; she later reached Spain and one of her crew deposed there that they had met up with and talked to the *Duquesa* and her crew, apparently while the Andalusian was anchored in Ireland.

The Governor of Connacht or for that matter the Lord Deputy need not have been so concerned. There is not a single shred of evidence to suggest that de Leiva had any intention of either remaining in Ireland or of making any attacking moves. His sole thought, and presumably that of all his men and senior officers, was to get away as quickly as possible and home to Spain. Bingham, of course, did not know this, just as de Leiva knew little of Bingham's own fears. If each man had guessed the other's mind, particularly de Leiva that of Bingham, how different matters might have been!

Wherever the Spaniards now sailed, it would be tight squeeze for them all. The *Nuestra Senora de Begona*, if she was indeed in the vicinity, had by now left and the sole ship remaining was the *Duquesa*. There may have been one or two smaller ships, such as *pataches* or *zabras*, but this is doubtful. Thus about a thousand men had somewhat to be fitted into one ship; if the *Rata* had been crowded, then the *Duquesa*, a slightly bigger vessel, would be doubly so. A conference of senior officers, led by de Leiva and Pedro de Mares, decided that the ship would find it difficult to reach Spain. She was damaged (how badly is not known) and although she had been repaired by the ship's carpenters while lying at anchor, they were makeshift repairs. Fears were freely voiced that the Andalusian would not survive the strong gales they must expect out in the Atlantic; these, coupled with strong headwinds, would make any proposed voyage to Spain a hazardous one.

The alternative was Scotland. Under James VI it was both independent of England and neutral in the war between Elizabeth and Philip II – and supposed also, if we are to judge by what Armada survivors believed, to have been sympathetic to Spain. This was at least partly true: James did harbour many shipwrecked Spaniards who reached Scotland from Ireland and helped them back to Spain.

Scotland it was, then. By this time what repairs were possible had been completed and the ship was stocked with fresh water and as much fresh food as they could obtain. The men filed on, packed like sardines in the confined spaces above and below decks; not an inch of room was left. The *Duquesa*, weighing anchor, took sail in a strongish wind and left Elly Bay.

Her going was joyfully reported by Comerford: 'the ship that was at Pollilly, by Torane, has sailed, taking the company that was wrecked', a report which Bingham passed on to the Lord Deputy in a note of Sunday morning, September 25, from Castle M'Garratt in Mayo, adding that 'the Spaniards, about 1400, who were at Torane, are gone to sea.' The laconic comment no doubt concealed a great deal of relief. But in a day or so Comerford was frantically signalling that the *Duquesa* has been driven back into Blacksod by 'a contrary wind'. However, she 'afterwards put to sea again.'

It had been a false start; the Andalusian had met a strong gale once she had cleared the mouth of the bay, and after fighting it for a time, gave up and returned. Shortly afterwards, she sailed once more for Scotland.

V

Disaster in Donegal

FOR much of Elizabeth's reign over Ireland, the most remote section of the country, and that least affected by English rule, was the furthest north-west corner known as Tirconnell (*Tir Conaill*, Land of Conal), a modern approximation of which would include Donegal and parts of Derry, in Northern Ireland. Tirconnell had achieved a near autonomy which it held perilously and with a weakening grip for the latter part of the sixteenth century, a state which it owed to a variety of factors. It was one of the last strongholds of the great Gaelic chieftains, with their clan systems of land ownership and self-government, fortified by the settlement in the area of a number of Scottish mercenary families who took over land from smaller local septs and established themselves, in time becoming as Irish as the Gaelic clans themselves.

Elizabeth struggled, with varying success, to make Tirconnell secure under English rule. It was a difficult task; the land was poor for much of its area, the climate even wetter than in most other parts of Ireland, the clans were elusive and evasive, and above all, Tirconnell was so far removed from the centre of government and from the consequent ease of garrisoning which would spring from such closeness that to put much-needed soldiery into its mountain fastnesses was, for most of Elizabeth's reign, beyond her power.

There was no mistaking the strength of the clans who peopled this distant corner of Ireland. Apart from the warlike mercenary or gallowglass families, there were the native clans, above all the O'Donnells, themselves intermarried with a Scottish clan, and whose sway in the farthest tip of the northwest was absolute and virtually unchallenged. And the geography of Tirconnell, protected from west and north by the Atlantic, and by the deep landward thrust of Lough Swilly to the east, made it almost impregnable to any but the largest and most determined forces.

From the very first attempts by English rulers to exercise full authority over west Ulster, there had been trouble. King Henry VIII, acting through Lord Leonard Grey, had spent many years in trying to persuade the Gaelic chieftains and lords to acknowledge him as their king and was eventually successful (under Grey's successor St Leger) in persuading the O'Donnells to accept an agreement which allowed O'Donnell (at this time Manus O'Donnell) to retain his lands under a stringent set of conditions. These, which were to ensure a relative peace of mind for Henry, effectively tied O'Donnell's hands; he was forced to renounce the Pope, to not consort with rebels, to retain his lands with a new title from the king, and (a final and insulting blow) to send a son to England to be educated there. Henry was relieved at O'Donnell's agreement in 1541; earlier he had written to St Leger on the difficulties of ousting O'Donnell by force that 'we think [they] lie so far from our strength there, as, without a greater force, it would be difficult to expel them out of their country.'

When Elizabeth came to power she continued the English interest in gradually weaning the full loyalty of the other west Ulster natives. In 1566 Henry Sidney, the new Lord Deputy, took the castle of Donegal from Hugh Dubh O'Donnell without a blow being struck and at the same time ensured that the eastern part of Tirconnell, around Derry, was loyal. Calvagh O'Donnell took over the castles of Donegal and Ballyshannon to the south; the great Shane O'Neill, whose power had gradually been eroding that of O'Donnell, was repulsed and the influence of the now loyalist O'Donnells restored.

Even at this, however, the English authorities could not rest. The loyalty of the northwestern clans was almost always questionable, and this was to be underlined in the ensuing years by Hugh Manus O'Donnell who, however, after some dilatory wavering, reaffirmed his allegiance to the Crown in 1574. When the Spanish ships came down upon the coast of Ireland some fourteen years later almost to the day, that situation was unchanged. But the years in between had not been uneventful; the O'Neills and the O'Donnells, the two greatest clans in the whole of Ulster, had begun to heal the bitter differences which had divided them for so many years, and O'Neill, the Earl of Tyrone (*Tir Eoghain*, Owen's Land, in east Ulster), had actually married O'Donnell's daughter to cement a growing relationship. It was this gathering alliance which most worried England.

Perrott was Lord Deputy during this difficult period and he had made several attempts to protect his queen's interests in Tirconnell, including a proposal to send a sheriff there, which to Perrott's surprise and annoyance was flatly and firmly turned down by O'Donnell. The clan had agreed to be subject to England, but O'Donnell drew the line at the close watch which would inevitably ensue from the presence of an English sheriff at his front door. But Perrott was equal to the situation; he sent an English ship to Lough Swilly, on the east of Tirconnell, where O'Donnell's son, Red Hugh, and one of the MacSweenys were staying at a Carmelite monastery. O'Donnell was inveigled on board on a pretext of wine being sold to him; he drank too much and he and MacSweeny were taken prisoner; the ship sailed back to Dublin, and within a week Red Hugh O'Donnell was a prisoner in Dublin Castle.

With O'Donnell's most treasured son under English guard in Dublin,

Perrott knew that the older O'Donnell would not raise a finger against English rule; by the kidnapping of Red Hugh he had therefore ensured that Tirconnell at least would be quiet. And so, when the Spanish ships arrived along its coast in 1588, it was.

Perrott's move against O'Donnell was to have far-reaching effects which have never been fully appreciated in the historical and political context of the Armada. Perrott did not foresee that Armada survivors would land on Tirconnell's shores in huge numbers, but inadvertently he had ensured that the two most powerful clans in that area, the O'Donnells and the MacSweenys, could give them little serious help, with a son from each family locked up as ransom insurance by the English. Had any warlike alliance with the shipwrecked Spaniards in Tirconnell developed, English rule over the whole of Ulster and perhaps ultimately over all Ireland would have been severely threatened.

When Alonso de Leiva and the surviving men from the *Rata* and the *Duquesa Santa Ana* left Blacksod Bay and turned north towards Scotland they can have had no intention of landing again on Irish soil, except in emergency: Scotland was their goal. Clearly they neither expected nor hoped for anything from Ireland. Mayo had given them a cold welcome, a welcome coloured by the intimidating Bingham and the treachery of the Burkes. If they had thought of making a further landing in Ireland, they cannot have expected a different reception from the one they had been given on the rough shores of Mayo.

Out at sea they were only slightly better off. They faced a voyage of great danger through some of the roughest seas in the world, at a time of the year when strong gales were almost constant. Even at the height of summer and in fine weather, the Irish coast from Erris Head northwards to Malin presents a maze of strong currents, winds, islands, outlying rocks and reefs, and includes a prominent example of almost every navigational hazard, including dense fogs and sea mists which fall like a sudden curtain. Few sailors even today brave this stretch of coast during the onset of winter; in a leaking, overcrowded vessel with pilots who probably knew little of what they were facing, the *Duquesa*'s voyage was doubly dangerous.

From the start, when they were forced back by westerly gales into Blacksod Bay, the Spaniards were beset with difficulties. Overcoming the initial setback of being blown back to where they had originally started, they set off again, skirting the maze of rocks and islands called the Duvillauns (Black Islands) at the southern end of the Mullet, beating westward past the Black Rocks, and then and only then bearing northwards to slip by the outlying Inishkeas. Once past, they were directly to seaward of Erris Head and eastward of that again, the towering Benwee Head, with its great cliffs tumbling sheer into the sea.

This was one of the most dangerous parts of the voyage. To clear Erris required plenty of sea room and it is likely that the *Duquesa* beat westward from Blacksod for perhaps ten or even twenty miles before her officers could feel confident of having enough offing to clear the head. Once past Erris a simple enough passage lay ahead across the fifty mile mouth of Donegal Bay, where there was open water and plenty of room.

Donegal Bay, a deep, wide indentation separating Mayo from Donegal, presents few navigational hazards in its outer approaches, but there were other more hidden dangers at work. Its northern and southern seaward entrances are flanked by mountain ranges, from the high cliffs which are a feature of the Mayo coastline from Erris to Killala and on the northern side of the bay in Donegal, the massive bulk of Slieve League, almost 2000 feet high. On a clear day it is possible to see from one side of the bay to the other at the seaward entrance; but the weather there, especially on a wild and wintry October's day, is rarely that clear.

Precise information is needed to navigate here with any safety. At first the sailor is faced with a battle to keep to seaward of the Mullet and Erris; he is then suddenly in the clear into the approaches to Donegal Bay. And when he has negotiated the wide mouth of the bay, he is once more faced with the dangers of the coast on the opposite side.

It can be assumed that the *Duquesa*'s pilots were aware of this danger and that all the time the Andalusian sought more sea room, which was of paramount

The towering cliff-faced Slieve League in Donegal. Alonso de Leiva in the Duquesa Santa Ana *narrowly escaped being wrecked here after leaving Killybegs, to the south, but the ship drove ashore further north in Loughros More Bay. (Noel Habgood/J. A. Cash)*

77

importance. The best course was as near to north as could be sailed; a course with any easting whatsoever would bring them nearer the coast north of Donegal Bay, and if they approached it closely they were in great peril. Donegal's Atlantic flank is as hazardous as any in Ireland and more hazardous than most, and an ample clearance in such a clumsy and unweatherly sailor as the *Duquesa* was essential.

The Spaniards failed in navigating this passage. There can be several reasons for this failure to keep clear of the land, which spelled the end for their ship, just as they had feared: the wind was westerly and blowing a gale – we have an eye-witness account from an Irish sailor aboard the *Duquesa* that she was caught by a 'contrary wind' at the northern side of the bay. And the ship found it almost impossible to make any offing to windward, heavily laden and possibly leaking as she was. Above all, taking into account the winds and the geography of the coastline, they had failed miserably to keep enough sea room to ride out a gale under bare poles and still not drift ashore. The blame for what happened next lies with whoever took the decision, made somewhere west of Erris Head, that they were far enough off the coast for safety and could make northeast.

The *Duquesa* did, however, clear Rossan Point, with the outlying Rathlin O'Birne Island which marks the northern tip of Donegal Bay, and thus escaped destruction inside the bay. Inland to the east now were the massed peaks of the Slieve League peninsula – Leahan (1418 feet), Croaghacullion (1230 feet), Slieve Tooey (1458 feet), Crockuna (1268 feet) and several others, some even higher and more inland. To the north were clear waters beyond Gweebarra Bay. It seems probable that at the time the *Duquesa* was being blown hard by the west wind towards the shore, and those aboard must have been fully occupied with trying to keep her from being wrecked on this terrifying coast next to Tormore Island, a jagged pinnacle of rock rising sheer out of the surf at the western foot of Port Hill and a signal warning to all who sail these waters.

At some point the Spaniards decided that the only way to save their ship from being wrecked by what clearly was a strong wind freshening up into a gale was to seek what shelter they could find and anchor. They were at the mouth of Loughros More Bay, between Slieve Tooey on the southern side and Dawros Head and the low-lying Dawros peninsula on the northern. Somewhere in this bay they dropped anchor and came to a halt, rolling heavily in the growing seas. They were anchored in some seventy feet of water, on a sandy and rock bottom, possibly between Dawros Bay and Loughros Point, the peninsular finger of land which separates Loughros More Bay from the more southerly and smaller Loughros Beg Bay (*More* and *Beg*, big and small).

This was a very unsafe anchorage. The *Sailing Directions* says quite bluntly of Loughros More Bay that there are no secure anchorages easy of access; the bottom was sand over rock, in other words a shallowish skim of sand lying on a rocky underbed – the poorest holding for any anchor. Above all, they were

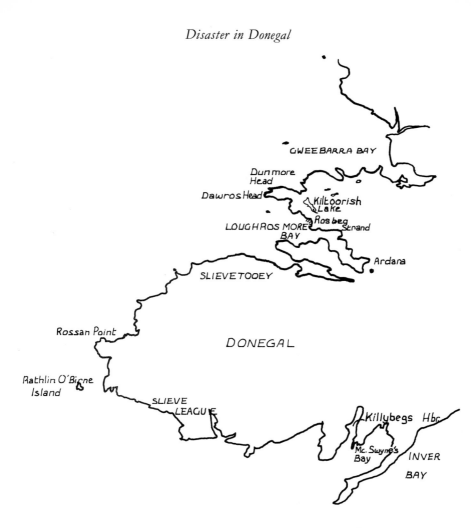

Loughros More Bay in Donegal, where the Duquesa Santa Ana *was wrecked. The survivors, including Alonso de Leiva, came ashore on the beach southeast of Rosbeg and then fortified themselves on O'Boyle Island in Kiltoorish Lake nearby. From there they marched south through Ardara to Killybegs, where they embarked in the* Girona. *The galleass was sheltering there while her crew made repairs, in part with planks and timbers from the two other small Armada vessels which had been wrecked in Killybegs, one inside and the other outside the harbour.*

trapped inside a bay and on a lee shore, with no hope of escape unless the wind either dropped or swung to the south quarter. With the gale growing and the seas rising visibly, there seemed little chance of either possibility.

It may be – we have no way of knowing – that the Spaniards thought there was deeper water in Loughros and that the bottom there would be rocky and good holding ground even under a gale; perhaps the bold profile of the coast

79

they had just sailed along led them to believe that. But north of Slieve Tooey, the coast assumes a much lower outline, with little sandy bays and shallow, winding inlets; the waters here shallow considerably. Another three or four hundred yards deeper into the bay where the *Duquesa* now lay, she would go aground at low water. But the Spaniards probably failed to realize this.

The account of the subsequent events is short on detail. It can be taken as accurate, however, and it does help somewhat in enabling the chain of events which led to the wrecking of the *Duquesa* to be pieced together. An Irish sailor, variously called James Machary or McHarg (more probably either McGarry or McCarthy), who came from Holycross, in Co. Tipperary, survived the wrecking in Loughros and was later interrogated by the English authorities. Here is that section of Machary's short account which touches on the *Duquesa*'s wrecking: 'by a contrary wind they were driven back upon M'Sweeney ne Doe's country to a place called Lough Erris, where falling to anchor, there fell a great storm which brake in sunder all their cables and struck them upon ground'.

The 'Lough Erris' which Machary spoke of is of course Loughros More; that they anchored he confirms. Evidently the gale worsened ('there fell a great storm') and broke the anchor cable (in all probability it shifted the anchor as well: the *Duquesa*, like many other Armada ships, had left most of her big anchors in the mud at Calais), and thus helpless before wind and sea, drifted deeper into the bay towards the mainland. She struck the sandy bottom of Loughros More beside a rocky spur southeast of the present-day village of Rosbeg, to the seaward of a fine-sand beach facing westward into the bay. It is one of the most approachable of all Armada wreck sites (driving from Ardara, take the left turn where the signs show 'Strand' just before Rosbeg, walk down onto the beach and then westward onto the shoulder of rocky headland that juts out a sharp finger into the bay).

Additional light on how the ship was wrecked has been shed through the somewhat confused testimony of two other shipwrecked survivors of the Armada, Juan de Nova and Francisco de Borja, who were told in turn by survivors of the *Duquesa* whom they met in Antrim while awaiting transport to escape to Spain. While Machary's account is first hand (he did, of course, speak English and what he said was instantly intelligible to those who interrogated him), we are on shaky ground in dealing with the story of the other two.

Both de Borja and de Nova were in the home of one of the McDonnells in Antrim after the wreck near there of the *Girona*; they had come off one, and possibly two, other Armada wrecks and had been sheltered by the McDonnells. They were joined there by survivors from the *Girona* (who were also survivors of the *Duquesa*'s wreck in Loughros More) and it was from them that de Nova and de Borja learned the details of the *Duquesa*'s loss. Later they were able to make Scotland and there were again aided in their attempts to reach Spain. They got at least as far as Calais, where they met and gave their

Loughros More Bay, Co. Donegal, seen towards the southwest across low-lying reefs and islets.
(Denis Kendrick)

Waves break on the strand at Rosbeg in Loughros More Bay. To the west is the open Atlantic; at
the left the cliffs of Slieve League. And in the right foreground, the reef on which the Duquesa
Santa Ana *was wrecked. (Denis Kendrick)*

account to Captain Marolin de Juan, the Armada's chief navigator, who had been left behind in the French port by the dispersal of the fleet by the English fireships, at a time when he was ashore on some mission. There he had remained throughout the campaign, and he was there still when the two survivors reached him some months after they had been wrecked. Marolin de Juan took down a lengthy and involved story from these two men, an abbreviated version of which he sent on to Philip early in 1589 as proof positive of the wreck of the *Girona*. Together with his own longer and more detailed account, and Machary's own short account, that is all the survivors' evidence we have of the wreck of the *Duquesa*.

Unfortunately, while Machary's information has the benefit of being first hand, Marolin de Juan's has not: it is the report of a man taking down an account from two people, who in turn heard it from others, or rather one other, since Marolin de Juan does say that both de Nova and de Borja got their information from one of the *Girona* survivors, who had also apparently been on the *Duquesa*. This constant transferrance may have affected the accuracy of the original report told in Antrim to de Nova and de Borja: we do not know that, but there are puzzling and apparently inexplicable statements scattered throughout Marolin de Juan's report whose mystifying contents can only be ascribed to either the navigator's having taken them down wrongly or through de Nova and de Borja taking them up wrongly.

Still, it is all evidence and must be taken into account. In fact it differs from Machary's account only in one essential aspect: both de Nova and de Borja appear to state that when the cable broke and the *Duquesa* began to drift towards the shore, the Spaniards tried to attach a mooring line to a spur of rock upwind and running out from the north shore to hold the ship. This manoeuvre if it did occur (and we must suppose that it did) failed and the vessel drove onto the sand near Rosbeg.

At Rosbeg, de Leiva and the rest of those aboard the grounded Andalusian vessel faced a series of dangers. The most immediate was the threat to their lives; the seas were running heavily, washing over the *Duquesa*, but she was holding her own and not yet beginning to break up. It was in all probability high tide or very close on it and the flooding tide may well have helped carry her up onto the sand. With the ebb would come lower water and a lessening of the battering she was now taking. Most of all, it would enable men to get ashore without drowning.

When low tide came, the men began to go overside, dropping down the bellied sides of the big merchantman into the cold and still turbulent Atlantic waters. The *Duquesa* had some small boats – cock-boats as they were known – and in these the senior officers were ferried ashore. Among them was Don Alonso; and he was carried ashore.

Machary says of this, 'Don Alonso before he came to land was hurt in the leg by the capstan of the ship in such sort as he was neither able to go, nor ride, neither during the nine days of his encamping, nor upon his remove, but was carried. . . .' This is curious, to say the least. Machary uses the word *capestele* (in the Spanish State Papers, cited by Duro) which undoubtedly means capstan. The mystery lies in deciding how de Leiva was struck by this normal piece of ship's equipment, since on a typical merchantman such as the *Duquesa*, the capstan was normally below deck just aft of midships and was used to hoist the main yard on the mainmast. Above it and a deck higher was the half-deck, and aft of that again the poop deck which is where one would expect to find de Leiva. But Machary was on the spot and his word must be taken.

There is another and possibly more plausible theory. The anchors were worked by a windlass well forward just under the main deck, at the forward end of the gun deck. It would normally take perhaps half a dozen men or more to raise an anchor by using the long handles of the windlass to turn it. These handles were thrust into holes in the centre of the windlass and removed alternately to other notches as the anchor cable was hauled in. If indeed, as de Nova and de Borja appear to suggest, the Spaniards had tried to stop the ship's drift by throwing a rope onto a projecting reef as they floated past, there must have been a small anchor on the end of that line; had this anchor taken hold and the rope snapped under the pulling strain of the big ship, rolling like a great barrel in heavy seas, then it is conceivable, as was known to happen aboard vessels of a later period with a similar system, that the anchor windlass could have flailed about with terrible violence, scattering men in every direction. The long handles may have been flung from their sockets by the force, and anyone who got in their way could have been seriously injured. All this is pure supposition; yet de Leiva was injured by a piece of nautical equipment which was normally far removed from where a senior officer on board would be. Can he have been forward and overseeing the handling of this crucial operation, which if successful might have staved off disaster, and thus was injured when the cable snapped?

With de Leiva hurt and in some pain, the company began to gather on the rocks and sand as the men gradually struggled ashore, some swimming to the rocks and scrambling to dry land, others being washed in towards the shelving beach by the waves, some coming ashore by boat, many on improvised rafts, barrels, hatches and baulks of timber.

The landscape which they saw remains much the same today, a low, hummocky land of little lakes and rocky outcrops, flanked by sandy beaches and rugged headlands. Rising to the north was the hump of Dunmore Head, some 430 feet high, and between that and the shore the land sloped down gradually to a long, irregularly shaped lake with an island at its southeast corner. This was Kiltoorish Lake and the Island of O'Boyle, with a ruined castle halfway along the crest of the island on its eastern bank, commanding an extensive view over the surrounding country. Between Kiltoorish and the strand at Rosbeg was a line of high sand dunes, thick with marram grass. To the east and inland stretched an expanse of low land, with a backdrop of mountains, brown with heather and dotted with stands of native timber.

O'Boyle Island in Kiltoorish Lake, seen from the south. (Denis Kendrick)

Kiltoorish Castle on O'Boyle Island at Rosbeg, where the survivors from the Duquesa Santa Ana *encamped before moving south to Killybegs. The* Duquesa *was wrecked about half a mile away. (Denis Kendrick)*

Today it is a homely, friendly landscape, built on in an almost miniature scale and with an indefinable but very tangible charm of its own; on that late September day in 1588, with the gale whipping up the grey seas under a lowering sky, it must have appeared very different to the Spaniards.

None of the surviving accounts state whether the natives had by this time approached. This was McSweeney country: originally a Scottish mercenary family who had come to Tirconnell to serve under O'Donnell, they afterwards spread out and gradually assimilated themselves into the Irish way of life. In Tirconnell they split into three distinct groupings, McSweeney na dTuath, Fanad, and Baghuine. McSweeney na dTuath (otherwise known as ne Doe) had his castle further north, up the coast from where the Spaniards had landed, and to the south, controlling the northern side of Donegal Bay, was McSweeney Baghuine (otherwise Bannagh). The remaining sept controlled the area around Fanad, in the north of Donegal; all were underlords to the Earl of Tirconnell, Sir Hugh O'Donnell.

These McSweeneys were gallowglasses (*Galloglaigh* or *Gall Oglach*: foreign young fighting men). The term describes their warlike character perfectly; they were fierce and independent and at no time could even O'Donnell feel secure of their peace and friendship. Although the gallowglass McSweeneys occasionally fought among themselves, they created their own powerful clan structure, proving stronger than the native clans on numerous occasions, as was to be expected from professional fighting men. In time the gallowglass McSweeneys became utterly absorbed into the Irish clans; today their descendants have taken the name of Sweeney or Sweeny.

The area around Dawros was by no means depopulated in the later sixteenth century and it is certain that many eyes had seen the *Duquesa* being wrecked and afterwards all her men coming to the shore. It is more probable than not that shortly after reaching shore contact was established with the clan by the Spaniards. Within a short while the Spanish party had crossed the sand dunes to the north and had begun to wade out to the island in Kiltoorish Lake. At the very southeast corner of the island where it almost meets the mainland, it is possible today to wade in some two feet of water (winter level) out to the island; the water doubtless was deeper then, since modern methods of drainage have lowered the level since that time.

The Spaniards now began to fortify themselves around the ruined castle on the island. Today little is left except the remains of a staircase entrance and a pile of flat stones; cattle graze on the bare fields. They had brought a cannon from the ship and mounted it just south of the castle on the flank of the island facing southeast; food and other provisions were brought from the ship, as were supplies of clothing, weapons, ammunition and other necessities. Gradually the camp assumed a soldierly appearance; guards were placed on strategic points around the island, and similarly on the beached *Duquesa* half a mile away.

Over the next couple of days the Spaniards appear to have concentrated on continuing to dig themselves in on the island. Relations with the McSweeneys were begun: the local sept was that of McSweeney ne Doe. De Leiva sent off an Irish cleric who had been aboard the *Rata*, Father James ne Dowrough, to see McSweeney ne Doe further up the coast, where it seems he was well treated and assured that the Spaniards would receive as much help as he could give. The Donegal people had given a significantly warmer welcome than had those in Mayo; but they were under less pressure, freer from English control and probably better accustomed to the divided loyalties of war.

Fitzwilliam's first intimation of what was going on in Donegal probably came by way of unmentioned spies; however, the first confirmation in detail of events in McSweeney ne Doe's country came in a letter from one Patrick Foxe, one of Walsingham's officials in Ireland, who wrote from Dublin on October 6:

My bounden duty most humbly remembered unto your Honour. It may please you to be advertised that lately after my Lord Deputy hath sent away the packet upon news had of the sinking of certain ships, and the killing of a great number of Spaniards in divers parts of Ireland, Captain William Mostyn came up from the north, and hath here reported how that certain other of the Spanish ships came to a haven in M'Sweeny ne Doe's country called 'Loughesullemore' and how that the said M'Sweeny joined with them and received them into the country, where (as it is thought), he meaneth to guard and guide them. This course is dangerous and most likely, as I think, to grow much to the annoyance of that part of the realm, for of himself the said M'Sweeny is a man of great power and no doubt if he continue in that action O'Rourke [of Breffni] and other the neighbours of like disloyal minds by his procurement will join with them also, which if it shall so fall out, as it is much to be suspected, great hurt will grow thereby. But I hope my Lord Deputy and Council will take that course as their purpose shall be quickly prevented. It is reported that a great number of the Spaniards that were stript naked by the soldiers that serve under the heading of both the Hovedens are now come to the other Spaniards that landed in M'Sweeny's country, and thither brought by the Bishop of Derry, a most seditious papist, and a man very like to procure great aid to the Spaniards if he can; O'Donnell is lately come up with a company of Spaniards that were taken prisoners, to the number of thirty, and is a suitor for the liberty of his son now pledge in the Castle of Dublin, in consideration that he lately hath served against the Spaniards.

Foxe had put his finger on Fitzwilliam's great fear. Tirconnell was a sensitive area, the part of Ireland least controlled by English force, beset with rebellious clansmen who although professedly loyal, continually defaced that loyalty with seditious behaviour. There was a great underlying strength of Gaelic clanship, both native and immigrant (such as the Scot McSweeneys), and all that was needed, as Fitzwilliam well knew, was a strong and well armed force of Spaniards to land and join the clans already there in an uprising against the English. The barrel of gunpowder that was Tirconnell was primed to explode: the Spaniards now being harboured under McSweeney ne Doe's wing were the match to set it alight.

84

Alarm now began to spread among the English authorities. The reports from their spies were coming in daily confirming the strength of the Spanish force and also that they were being given help by McSweeney. The English spies were finding it difficult to get their reports through to Fitzwilliam, wrote Sir Geoffrey Fenton and Sheriff George Bingham from Sligo, the McClancys of Leitrim and Sligo being largely responsible; Gerald Comerford had a report to hand of the Spaniards in 'M'Sweeny Ne Doffe's country' which he sent on to Sir Richard Bingham; the great Earl of Tyrone, O'Neill, wrote to Fitzwilliam advising him that there were '1500 Spaniards in M'Sweeny ne Doe's country' and asked for 'munition and a commission of martial law'; he would, he wrote, provide a 'month's victuals for his company to go against the Spaniards.'

This was exactly what Fitzwilliam had most feared, and his fear was daily increased as the alarmed and often exaggerated reports came flooding in. Fenton wrote urgently saying that O'Neill [highly unlikely] 'has relieved the Spaniards in Tirconnell with 500 beeves' and also that 'O'Rourke, M'Glannogh (McClancy), Maguire (of Fermanagh to the east), and the Burkes of Mayo are combined with the Spaniard. O'Rourke hath already sent all his galloglasses to Hugh Maguire, and hath let slip his son whom he had in hand, and meant himself to go out.'

Around this time, a band of native kerne burned the castle of George Bingham, the Sligo Sheriff, at Ballymote, not far from Sligo, an event of which Fenton alleged that the kerne said they were 'making way for King Philip', although Sir Richard Bingham afterwards corrected this by telling Fitzwilliam that the burning was in fact in revenge for the earlier recovery of Sligo town. It was, however, enough to further alarm Fitzwilliam, still snowed under by reports of the Spaniards in Donegal. Henry Duke wrote from 'Castle Jurden' (Castlejordan) that O'Rourke 'hath written to the Spaniards in the north to join with them.' He also told Fitzwilliam that 'it is most true that M'Mahon [of Monaghan to the east] and Maguire's eldest son, Hugh Maguire, will assist O'Rourke.' Bingham himself told the Lord Deputy that reports that Tirlach Lynagh O'Neill 'hath entertained the Spaniards to make war on the Earl of Tyrone, to be suspected'. He warned Fitzwilliam to stand on his guard, 'for between O'Neill, the Earl, and the Spaniards you may too deeply engage yourself.'

Fenton and George Bingham next wrote to Sir Richard in a panic, saying that the Spaniards had come within twenty miles 'of this side of M'Sweeny ne Doe's country' and that 'if the Castle of Sligo had not been taken as it was, the Spaniards would have had it by now.' That was on October 16 when, unknown to them, de Leiva was sailing from the coast of Donegal for Scotland. Three days later, they were despairingly telling Bingham of their 'expectation of a general revolt'; a day later, William Taaffe was writing to Fenton that '2000 Spaniards are camping at Forreside-more, within six miles of Strabane' and that he had heard a report stating that 'the Spaniards are going to aid Turlough Lynagh O'Neill to make war on the Earl of Tyrone.' And on the same day came another frenzied appeal from George Bingham to his brother, saying that the 'Spaniards will be in Sligo in five days.'

It is easy to understand the panic which swept among the English authorities as the reports came in of Spaniards and Irish massing together and marching south. This was the underbelly of English power in Ireland, and bad luck would have it that the largest force of Spaniards ever to land in Ireland had done so at the most vulnerable point as far as England was concerned. That they had done so inadvertently was beside the point; they were there, and the indications that their very presence would unite the Irish in the north-west and bring about a concerted attack on English forces were very clear.

Back in Donegal, however, the real situation was very different. De Leiva, injured, clearly had not the slightest intention of creating trouble or of joining with the Irish. His thoughts were preoccupied with getting out of Ireland as fast as he could and sailing home to Spain somehow; there is absolutely no positive indication that he thought at any time of an alliance which had every chance of seizing all Sligo and Donegal from English hands, and perhaps precipitating a general revolt throughout Ireland which would result in the entire country being regained into Irish hands. In furthest Tirconnell, Sir Hugh O'Donnell held his cards close to his chest and made no move of consequence; his son, Red Hugh, was still firmly locked in Dublin Castle and Perrott's long-held trump card was now being played. McSweeney ne Doe, his own attitude possibly coloured by O'Donnell's reluctance to act with the Spaniards, did little except provide food for them lower down the country. All the key figures who had they combined would undoubtedly have created the most serious threat to Elizabeth's rule in Ireland before the Battle of Kinsale in 1601, failed to take any action. Hesitancy and not decisiveness was the order of the day.

De Leiva stayed at Kiltoorish for nine days. Daily trips by the Spaniards to the wreck of the *Duquesa* stripped her of anything of value except the bigger guns, and probably McSweeney got those. All the valuables, plate, silver, gold, weapons, money, jewellery and so on were removed and taken back to the camp on the island. And then a message came from the south that three Spanish ships lay at anchor in the harbour of Killybegs, on the northern side of Donegal Bay and less than twenty miles south across the mountains from the Spanish encampment.

It had taken a long time indeed for this news to reach Kiltoorish Lake, and it may seem strange that the report that there were three ships waiting in Killybegs had not reached de Leiva sooner. What makes it stranger still is that those ships were in all probability the very first ships from the Armada to reach Ireland – they were certainly the first reported, George Bingham having written to his brother on September 15 from his castle in Ballymote that 'three Spanish ships bore down towards the harbour of Calebeg'; it is certain that if Bingham reported this on the 15th, the ships had been seen at least several

What remains of Kiltoorish Castle. Though in ruins at the time it sheltered the Spaniards, its position provided some protection and a view over the surrounding country. (Denis Kendrick)

Killybegs approaches: two small ships were wrecked here, one inside and one outside the harbour. From Killybegs the Girona *sailed for Scotland on October 26, to be wrecked two days later in Co. Antrim. (Denis Kendrick)*

days earlier, which would probably make them the first to reach harbour in Ireland.

Later reports clarified what had happened to these three ships. As late, in fact, as November 5, when Henry Duke reported that he had sent a spy into the north to obtain information about the Spaniards:

Three of the Spanish ships coming into the harbour of the Killibeggs in M'Sweeny's country, one of them was cast away a little without the harbour, another running aground on the shore brake to pieces. The third being a gally, and sore bruised with the seas, was repaired in the said harbour with some of the planks of the second ship, and the planks of a pinnace which they had of M'Sweeny.

Two of the ships therefore had been lost, one each inside and outside the harbour, while another was repaired. The third vessel was the Neapolitan galleass *Girona*, and she was still there when the report reached de Leiva: the other two ships had, of course, been wrecked some weeks before this, a fact which had apparently not been reported to de Leiva.

The long delay before the Spaniards further to the north heard of the ships in Killybegs was accounted for by the fact that Killybegs was in the territory of McSweeney Bannagh, an entirely different person to his sept-cousin who controlled the area around Kiltoorish. He was probably much poorer and had not sufficient food to feed an army of hungry Spaniards; he was also closer to Sligo and therefore to English influence and may have feared retribution for anything he did to help the Spaniards. Furthermore, relations between the two clan chieftains were strained, and a high mountain range separated their territories, making communication difficult, though certainly not impossible.

McSweeney Bannagh had not, however, been unhelpful to the men from the ships wrecked at Killybegs. He had given them food and shelter (reports later indicated that he was well paid for his trouble), and even a pinnace from which they had removed planks to repair the damaged galleass. Henry Duke's spy claimed that the Spaniards would have given the local clansmen a caliver (a musket some 4½ feet long) for a mutton, and said that many had dispersed into various castles scattered throughout Bannagh's territory. There is no doubt that McSweeney did harbour the Spaniards, but he was recompensed to the full for everything he provided. Mutton was plentiful but calivers were not.

Once de Leiva heard that Armada ships lay at anchor a day's hard marching from where he lay on an improvised litter, he decided at once to leave the fortified camp on Kiltoorish Lake and head south for Killybegs. He was placed on a litter carried by four men, and the Spaniards left the island and started towards Killybegs, leaving behind on the island the gun which they had taken off the *Duquesa* to guard the entry to the island from the mainland. There the gun remained, rusting away quietly and undisturbed down the centuries until Robert Stenuit found it in 1968; shortly afterwards, it was sold and removed from the island by an unnamed person – shabby and unforgiveable treatment of a priceless and hitherto unique relic of the Armada.

What McSweeney ne Doe thought of their going is not known, but he must have felt relief. His clanspeople had been finding it a great strain to find sufficient food for the camp, and he may well have become increasingly embarrassed by their continued presence. He had treated them well and with sympathy, however, which was not the way of all the Irish; and for that if nothing more the Spaniards had much to thank him for.

The thousand-strong party headed southeast along the coast from Rosbeg to Ardara, then probably no more than a scattered collection of huts. From there they turned directly south and began to climb from the low country around Ardara to the steep hill of Mulmosog (1157 feet) along a winding path that linked the territories of the two McSweeney septs. From the top of the pass near Mulmosog the path began to drop, following the course of the Stragar River, gradually descending to Killybegs.

Killybegs harbour lies at the northern end of a deep winding creek leading out into the open Atlantic in Donegal Bay. For centuries it had provided a base for fishing, affording excellent shelter from winds from every point of the compass – the ideal harbour in fact, advantages which today confirm it as one of the busiest ports anywhere in Ireland. Then, it was in all probability quite large for the area; it does appear to have harboured many of the more prestigious members of the McSweeneys, and the State Papers allude here and there to numerous castles in the vicinity.

But an unpleasant surprise now awaited: the report was of three Spanish ships, but only one, the *Girona*, remained afloat. This was a severe blow; doubtless every Spaniard who finished the arduous march over the mountains from Ardara had had the expectation of finding room on a ship at the end of it all, a ship which would bear him home. But one ship could not carry an extra thousand men together with its own complement and those from the two smaller ships wrecked around the harbour.

The *Girona* was one of four Neapolitan galleasses in the Armada; essentially fair weather vessels, they were a bastard cross between a galley and a galleon and combined the disadvantages of both without the advantages. The *Girona*'s displacement (weight) is not given in any of the Armada lists, but she was probably between 700 and 800 tons and in length some 150 feet; she carried thirty-six oars, eighteen on each side, pulled by 244 rowers who lived a wet and demanding existence, most of it spent in the open. The galleass's high freeboard combined with the mobility given by her oars gave her a high degree of manoeuvrability but made her vulnerable to gunshot and, above all, to bad weather. The galleass also carried three long masts and had high stern and bow castles. These 'striking beautiful' ships were highly regarded in a social sense; the officers aboard lived in a manner foreign to most of the other vessels of war, and the *Girona* was no exception.

The complements of no less than five ships – the *Rata*, the *Duquesa*, the *Girona*, and the two smaller vessels – were gathered in Killybegs. There is a very slight possibility that they had been joined by men from a Spanish ship

An anchor, possibly an Armada relic from one of the Killybegs wrecks, lies mouldering in the grass on an old quay in the harbour. (Denis Kendrick)

supposedly anchored in Donegal harbour with her mast gone, but this is doubtful. The *Girona* alone carried 102 sailors, 196 soldiers, and 244 rowers of which almost exactly half were impressed convicts (the remainder of the rowers, surprisingly enough, included 68 volunteers; one can only hope that they had not been disappointed in their expectations). On top of that there were undoubtedly servants, hospital staff, clerics and so on; the overall total was therefore around 550 men.

Thus there were, in the first week of October, the largest force of Spaniards ever assembled on Irish soil (it is as well to point out at this juncture that the term 'Spaniard' indicates only those who served with the Armada; they were of course not all Spanish and included Portuguese, Italians, Yugoslavs (Ragusans) and men from many other nations). It has been said before that there were over 2000, but how this figure was arrived at is a mystery. In addition to the 550 men from the *Girona*, together with a further 100 or so from the two small vessels (and even this is a generous estimate), there were around 270 men from the *Duquesa*, and perhaps 600 or 650 from the *Rata*, making a very approximate total of around 1700. This is a generous figure and does not take into account the inevitable toll exacted by war, disease, and other hazards. A figure in the region of 1600 is acceptable, taking every factor into account: certainly not 2000.

But even 1600 men constituted an enormous threat to English rule. As Major Martin Hume says,

> Here, then, was the crucial point. A swift despatch boat was sent to Spain, begging and praying Philip to send aid at once [this is doubtful]. News went through France to Spain that at last the Spaniards had conquered Ireland, and if de Leiva had been more determined, Philip more prompt, and McSweeny ne Doe had been more confident, then certainly the O'Donnells would have joined the O'Rourkes, Sligo and Donegal made common cause, and all the west of Ireland would have been up, and Ireland would probably have been lost to England.

Undoubtedly the chances were there for the taking, and were not taken. De Leiva was injured, McSweeney ne Doe had in the end been relieved to see the back of the Spaniards, and McSweeney Bannagh was at his wits' end trying to find food for an extra 1600 mouths, even though he was well paid to do it. O'Donnell remained obdurately aloof in his Tirconnell fastness.

If O'Donnell was obdurate, his wife Ineen Dubh (the 'dark daughter' of James MacDonald and of Lady Agnes who later married Tirlach O'Neill) was equally so but in an entirely opposite manner. She was Scottish and warlike, like so many members of her clan, and although her son was locked up in Dublin Castle, this did not deter her from threatening Fitzwilliam in an indirect way, as is evident from a report to the Lord Deputy from Henry Dowgan and Salomon Faranan on October 23 that

> The Spaniards in M'Sweeny ne Doe's country have repaired one ship. O'Donnell's wife, James McDonnell's daughter, Ineen Duv, saith openly that she will hire the

Spaniards to stir up wars except she can get her son, that is in the castle, on the return of her husband.

A day later came a report from Patrick Eulane to Sir Henry Bagenal, Marshal of the Army, warning that

the Spaniards from the two ships wrecked off M'Sweeney Banagh's country have joined those in M'Sweeny ne Doe's. M'Swiney's fear to hunger his country. The Spaniards are buying garrons and mares for food. The best of the Spaniards in M'Sweeny's country are going away and will leave the rest to shift for themseves [this was the first intimation to Fitzwilliam that the Spaniards might pose less of a threat than he had feared] because the ship cannot receive them all. If those who are left can get any guide, they will go to O'Rourke's country, or else if they can get any passage they will go into Scotland.'

In the meantime, the Spaniards concentrated on getting the *Girona* seaworthy once more. They repaired and slung her rudder, which had been damaged by the September gales off the northwest coast; they replaced planks which had shot holes; they repaired rigging, took on fresh food and water, rearranged what scant accommodation there was, sewed every seam in every sail to withstand the October weather, and made final preparations for the voyage which would bring them back to Spain. Because of the strong prevailing westerlies, it is likely, but not known for certain, that they would have chosen to go north and eventually reach the neutral ground of Scotland.

First, however, there was the problem of choosing who should go and who should stay. The ship could not carry them all. Eventually around 1300 men packed into the galleass, leaving some 200 behind. Some of those who stayed were Irishmen, glad to be home after months at sea and unwilling to take their chance on a ship again (among them was James Machary); others were wounded and dying; undoubtedly there were Spaniards who felt that they might have a more pleasant and profitable life in this strange land than Spain would provide and stayed of their own choice. But this did not account for all the 200 men left on the quay at Killybegs; some had to be picked out from the crowd as dispensable – a harsh but necessary decision. What their feelings were as they watched their colleagues climb aboard can only be imagined.

On October 26, 1588, repaired and ready for sea, the *Girona* slipped out of Killybegs on the full of an ebb tide, sometime shortly before dawn. Henry Duke's spy reported

The 16th [26th] of this instant October the said gally departed from the said harbour with as many of the Spaniards as she could carry. . . . As it is judged they have left in one Brian M'Manus's house at the Killibegg's vicar of that place, one of the chief of their company, being very sore sick of the flux. They have likewise left with M'Sweeny an Irish Friar called James ne Dowrough, who first went into Spain with James Fitzmaurice . . . the Spaniards gave M'Sweeny, at their departure, twelve butts of sack wine, and to one Murrough Oge M'Murrough I Vayell, four butts. The M'Sweenys and their followers have gotten great store of the Spanish calivers and muskets. . . .

VI

⟨✦⟩

A Fair Wind for Spain

HE voyage which now faced the men on the *Girona* was by any
standards difficult and dangerous, with hazards heightened by the
emergency repairs to the galleass. They had to cover about 200 miles of ocean,
through seas that were cold, rough and exposed, at the onset of winter and in
an overcrowded vessel. But the passage was short enough; four days with the
wind in their favour would enable them to cut corners and thus save distance
and reach the outlying isles of Scotland.

The course which the galleass took from Killybegs is unknown to the
extent that there is no evidence to reveal how close inshore she kept; but it is
safe to suggest that she stood well out to sea, possibly at times out of sight of
the coast and up to twenty miles or more out into the Atlantic. There were no
eye-witness reports of her sighting, which adds a little extra weight to
suggestions that she sailed well away from land. It meant a longer voyage,
but gave sea room to drift before a wind without fear of piling up on the coast.

Clearing Drumanoo Head to the north and St John's Point to the south, the
galleass began a long seaward sweep out of Donegal Bay. To the north lay the
massifs of Slieve League; to the south, mostly unseen, the great cliffs of Mayo.
Muckros and Carrigan Heads were passed; the wind was southwesterly, the
weather cold. Soon they had weathered Rathlin O'Birne, the island sentinel at
Slieve League marking the northern tip of Donegal Bay. At this time they
were probably on a heading west into the Atlantic.

A few miles out at sea – probably at least ten or twelve and very possibly
more – the galleass's bow was turned north. Now the wind was almost
directly astern; they crowded on as much sail as they dared, but this cannot
have been much. The rudder was weak despite the repair, and the replacement
planking had to be treated with caution. Too much sail would strain the
damaged hull.

As the day wore on, the *Girona* gradually began the long slant northwards.
To the east now were the tips of the Slieve League mountains which de Leiva
and many of those aboard had already passed in the *Duquesa*. She passed
Loughros More where the *Duquesa*'s bones were being picked by McSweeney
ne Doe's men; they were too far out to sea to catch a glimpse of the wreck.

Then past the long stretch of sands at Naran and Portnoo and across the mouth of Gweebarra Bay.

By the afternoon they may have been able to make out the dimpled peaks of Aranmor Island – Frenchman's Hill, Cluidaniller and Cronagarn, all close to 700 feet high. Aranmor is the seaward bastion of the low-lying Rosses on the mainland, a wide tract of rocky ground dotted with bogs and little lakes, and the largest of a scattered group of islands in which, unknown to the Spaniards now weathering it far out to sea, lay the remains of at least two more Armada ships (Chapter XI on the Rosses). To the northeast of Aranmor are Owey and Gola, two islands of roughly similar size and distance off the coast; and northeast of those again the imposing thousand-foot-high brow of Bloody Foreland, the extreme northwest corner of Donegal.

This was all dangerous coast, full of outlying rocks and reefs, threaded by swift and powerful currents and tides, an intricate maze of islands and water navigation without the most expert pilotage and local knowledge was impossible. The *Girona* did not attempt to near it but stayed well out to sea. The course was probably still almost due north. It is probable that the pilots knew of the existence of Tory Island some miles north of Bloody Foreland and that a course was set which would bring the galleass wide of Tory to the seaward; the passage between the island and the mainland, although easily navigable, was in all probability ignored. Once again, there are no eye-witness reports to suggest otherwise. Now and only now did the *Girona* begin to bear east a little, on a course which would clear Tory well to seaward but which would enable her to start to swing around the corner of Ireland.

By now it was nightfall, and if they saw Tory at all it would have been the vaguest of glimpses away to the east. During the night the galleass bore northeast with the wind still favourable; they had cleared the west coast at last, had made good some sixty or seventy miles of ocean, and with the wind still damped down had gone a good deal of the way towards Scotland. Another two or three days' sailing and the Isles would be reached. By then, they were probably reaping whatever benefits their extra pilots had brought; they would have been helped in navigation by information picked up in Killybegs from the natives as well as their knowledge of the coast.

Daylight on the 27th brought with it further anxiety: the *Girona*'s hull had begun to complain under the press of a freshening wind; the song of accompaniment that every sailor knows had changed from the slow creaking of long glides over the water to the rattling and banging of gear and the protests of straining timbers. The sea in that grey northern latitude had begun to change with the wind to a dirty leaden colour, flecked here and there with the white of broken water.

Bad weather was what the Spaniards feared most. They had avoided any navigational problems by simply keeping clear of all the possible trouble, but they could not escape a storm. The *Girona*, overburdened, leaking and with a suspect rudder, was capable of weathering a normal blow but anything beyond that would be of great danger. Every wave was now watched with growing anxiety; the after decks on the high stern castles were far above the water and the officers could assess clearly the effect of the following waves as they combed up behind the galleass and broke in flooding sprays against her stern. They cannot have liked what they saw. This sort of weather was anathema to a galleass, and hardest on the banks of rowers; forward of the stern castles, on which the officers stood high and dry, the waters surged inboard and drenched the rowers, slopping onto the main deck. Sail was shortened, a matter of regret since the wind was a following one; but the ship, now labouring heavily, could carry only limited canvas even in a following blow. To pile on more in the hope of making Scotland was at this stage out of the question, as she would simply have ploughed her bows under.

The course was east, the wind westerly. All that day it freshened. To the south showed fleeting glimpses of great mountains and deep bays; Fanad Head was passed and then Dunaff, split by the deep inland thrust of Lough Swilly. To the starboard quarter now began to show Malin Head and the Garvan Islands; they had plenty of sea room and probably altered course whenever land showed. To keep well out to sea was still vital, but was simple enough with a following wind, except in severe conditions.

A typical mixture of cliff and reef on the Donegal coast. At least eight Armada ships were wrecked along this coastline, but sheer cliffs and deep bays on a lee shore may well have claimed others. (Robert Dawson/Barnaby)

Towards the afternoon the wind began to change, not in strength but in direction, and to the worst possible quarter – the north. A northerly wind made the coast a lee shore, and pushed the galleass inshore towards the rocks and reefs. Malin Head loomed closer to the south. The situation was not yet critical. The galleass could sail reasonably well: they had, after all, covered well over a hundred miles in a day and a half. Another day and possibly less would undoubtedly be sufficient for the ship to reach Scotland and safety. If they could keep moving east and at the same time keep far enough from the coast, they should be safe. The biggest danger now lay not in the possibility of foundering but of being blown onto the shore of Donegal, Derry or Antrim.

It is not clear whether the *Girona* sailed inside or outside Inishtrahull, the remote island in latitude 55°26′N longitude, 7°15′W near Malin Head. From her later course and taking into account the fact that the wind changed at around this time, it seems more likely that she had weathered the island sometime during the late evening of the 27th; the passage through the sound between the island and the mainland of Donegal is simple enough but the question of whether or not the Spaniards knew exactly where they were is very pertinent. According to what a survivor later said, those aboard the *Girona* had only a very hazy idea as to their whereabouts.

It was also during the 27th that a curious incident occurred, one whose significance has never been satisfactorily examined. Francisco de Borja and Juan de Nova testified in France that a survivor from the *Girona* had related to them a conversation between de Leiva and his pilot aboard the *Girona* somewhere off this coast, as to whether they should alter course for Spain; on the face of it this appears highly unlikely, but as one of the scarce details relating to the *Girona* it must be taken seriously. De Borja's and de Nova's statement contains the following references:

They could, [de Leiva] thought, manage to get to Scotland, where they would obtain succour. They therefore went around Cape Clear and when they arrived between the Spanish Sea and the island of Scotland, they had a fair wind to carry them to Spain. The pilot therefore represented to Don Alonso that if he would allow him to set sail he would arrive in Spain in five days. Don Alonso replied that if he was sure the weather was favourable, he could do so. But he was deceived in thinking that the weather was settled, for it now changed. . . .

This extract from a lengthy deposition is riddled with navigational error. 'Spanish Sea' was the sixteenth century term for the waters at the mouth of the English Channel ('the Sleeve') at its southwest extremity. 'Cape Clear' could mean anything – it was applied by mystified Spaniards to literally dozens of headlands on the Irish coast from Antrim to Kerry. 'Spanish Sea', misleading though it appears, was nevertheless a widely accepted description of the Channel approaches and appears on maps of the period. If the account is taken literally, it would seem as though de Leiva and the pilot believed themselves off the *south* coast of Ireland rather than the *north*, which is nonsense. Evidently

The Girona's *last voyage, from Killybegs on the north side of Donegal Bay.*

the survivor, in addition to the two Spaniards who had listened to his tale, got the details hopelessly confused.

The 'fair wind for Spain' is just as confusing. A fair wind could only be a northish wind; they had indeed a north wind at some stage during the 27th, but by then must have been in some trouble with the ship. At this point the pilot suggested that they make for Spain, which he claimed they could reach in five days. This is again nonsense: even in good repair and in excellent sailing conditions the *Girona* would probably take at least ten days to reach Spain from the northeast tip of Ireland. And would de Leiva have risked the English Channel?

In any event, the 'fair wind' was scotched by the weather, which 'now changed'. Changed to where? It could only have been to north or east for it to drive the ship onto the shore, and that would have been a favourable wind for Spain if they had had sufficient sea room to take advantage of it.

Clearly, the pilot was either wrong or he has been totally misrepresented in the depositions in the Spanish State Papers. The latter is highly probable; the survivor from the *Girona* was from all evidence a common seaman who would therefore hardly be privy to conversations between de Leiva and the pilot in the officers' quarters or perhaps on the poop deck. He was in all probability relating 'tween-deck gossip, twisted and distorted by uninformed repetition. That there were Irish pilots on the *Girona* is confirmed by James Machary, who was at Killybegs and testified that when de Leiva left for Scotland in the *Girona*, the vessel carried 'for his pilots three Irishmen and a Scot'.

Regrettably this entire story must be disregarded; it simply makes no coherent sense, at one stage appearing to suggest that the *Girona* was sailing *west* instead of *east*. At some stage between the galleass's loss and the depositions at Calais, confusion set in and stained the possible truth beyond reconstruction.

As night came down there were immediate problems to be faced. The following seas had helped the galleass on her way, but the rudder had taken the full brunt of two days' sailing in fairly heavy weather and during that afternoon had been struck repeatedly by heavy seas. There was nothing that could be done to prevent this; all the men could do was to watch as comber after comber reared a great fist and banged hard on the loosely-swinging rudder. Probably it had begun to work loose in its fastenings, thumping and grating against the stern timbers, an ominous sound that would have gone through the vessel and found an echo in every listening ear.

That night must have been the most anxious which de Leiva had spent in the entire campaign, his anxiety sharpened by the fact that for the first time he was close to relative safety: fifty miles from Scotland. He had been shipwrecked and escaped with his life twice, and it must have appeared most unlikely that he would be as lucky if disaster should strike for a third time. All that was needed was for the wind to shift back to a point in the west and for the seas to go down. But the wind held north, pushing the *Girona* inshore, and the rudder continued to work against the timbers.

Dawn came on the 28th, with the galleass significantly closer to land, wallowing and plunging in the heavy seas. The rudder was in a worse state; the ship was leaking and the pumps hard pressed to cope with an increasing inrush of water. But they were still floating, closer to Scotland, and hopes were still high. Had de Leiva known where he was with any exactitude he would have been in little doubt that his ship was in serious straits. It was no longer a question of sea room: that they were getting perilously near the coast was obvious to all. The rudder was close to breaking loose and the wind was relentlessly in the north; both factors were fatal. It was now a question, given a continuation of these circumstances, whether she could weather the northeast tip of Ireland (Antrim), and if so possibly escape destruction on the rocks by running before the northerly down the Irish Sea between Ireland and Britain. If she failed to weather the corner, she was doomed.

Sometime around mid-morning, the rudder answered every question. By then they were off the mouth of Lough Foyle, close to where the wreck of another Armada vessel lay, the *Trinidad Valencera*. Lough Foyle divides Donegal to the west from Derry to the east; further east of Derry is Antrim. Another thirty miles and they would be clear of Ireland and have saved the ship. It was at that point, however, that the rudder finally broke.

The *Girona*'s steering equipment, like that of most ships of her period, was complicated and difficult to use. The helmsman probably stood just forward of the break of the poop deck, underneath the half-deck (if there was one on the *Girona*, which is highly debatable). Under the deck on which he stood ran a long tiller which met the rudder connections right aft at the sternpost. The end of the tiller close to the helmsman was attached to a long vertical pole which projected upwards through a hole in the deck and was grasped by the steerer. By manipulating this, he manoeuvred the rudder, but because he was some distance away from the rudder itself and could neither see the seas or where he was going, there must have been an inevitable time-lag before the ship answered. Though a cumbersome system, it worked; in heavy weather such as the galleass was now experiencing it usually required at least two or three men to control the vertical pole or whip-staff. The rudder was hung on the sternpost by means of great iron brackets; probably these had now worked loose, repeating a similar previous failure. Whatever the details, the rudder now went, finally and irrevocably.

A sailing vessel is not altogether lost without her rudder; a good sailor will keep some degree of control through judicious trimming and balancing of his sails, spilling and filling them alternately to tack from port to starboard. But it is a poor substitute, and the *Girona* had not even this slight benefit. She fell away off the wind, unable to keep her head up to the seas; the wind caught the sides of the high bow and stern castles and held her broadside-on where she lay wallowing in the troughs of the rollers, her rigging and gear thrashing and flogging. Probably the rowers tried desperately to give some measure of control, and may even have succeeded to a slight extent, but a great galleass, offering so much rigging and superstructure to a searching wind, must have been unmanageable in such a situation. The exhausted rowers, at one moment catching fresh air, at the next burying their sweeps immovably in the ocean as the *Girona* rolled wildly from side to side, must have been helpless.

It was getting dark, but the coast was now hideously clear, even in the failing light. The wind kept strong, the seas roared as before. The last glimpse the company had of land was an angry coastline, dim in the almost opaque dusk, marked by flashes of dirty white where waves broke on the rocks of Antrim.

The *Girona* drifted on through the night, steadily nearing the coast. Unknown to those aboard, she drifted down close to Portrush and the Skerries rocks which lie northward of that. East was Benbane Head. Between the two is a terrifying coast of sheer cliffs and reefs hidden underwater. Probably the lookouts heard the confused roar of broken water before they saw its pale line in the darkness. The crew may have tried to drop anchor. There would have been time to shout a warning, but little more. Just before midnight, with the night as black as pitch, the *Girona* came staggering through the darkness and struck a long reef running seawards from the land.

She struck hard and sideways-on to the reef, ripping open her bottom and breaking her back almost at once as the great force of wind and water together pushed her over the reef and down the other side. She probably turned turtle at this point, spilling a rush of men, cannon, casks, shot and all the multitude of odds and ends that a ship carries into the water. Rigging and loose tackle rained down from aloft; timbers cracked and split and were thrown aside like flimsy matchwood by the waves as the *Girona* heeled over, laid her high castles flat with the surface and buried her head deep into the ocean. Around her in the welter of breaking spray men sank or floated and tried to swim; hundreds were trapped inside the hull, caught without chance or hope of escape and entombed in the sinking galleass. More were struck by falling gear, some battered by flailing spars; encumbered by clothes and money-belts, many sank quickly in the cold waters.

Once the ship struck, she was demolished with diabolic swiftness. She broke in two, fore and aft, and not a section of the hull came ashore in a sizeable piece but instead as great baulks of timber, casks, hatches, spars, lengths of mast, splinters of wood, richly-carved doors, chests, deck beams, etc. The havoc caused by huge timbers thrashing around in the din and darkness was incalculable.

To add to all this, the night was dark, as black as a tomb. To the swimmer trying to keep above water in a confusion of screaming and clutching men, drowning and dying, with timbers thrown everywhere in the breaking seas and a tangle of rigging, any attempt to find the shore and safety was next to impossible. A tidal stream was sweeping out to sea and as the men began to drown, their bodies were pulled eastwards – ironically, towards Scotland. Within half an hour the pathetic few who came alive out of this terrible episode had scrambled ashore. Out of the 1300 men who had left Killybegs in the *Girona* less than three days before, just nine lived.

The most plausible reconstruction of the actual wrecking of the *Girona* is that by Robert Stenuit, the Belgian underwater archaeologist, who discovered the ship's remains in the late 1960s and who dived for three seasons in and around the scattered remnants.

I watched the waves breaking off Lacada Point, fifty yards to the northwest. They catch on a reef there, a submerged mound, rising up in some forty feet of water. At low tide, the top of it is only about twelve feet below the surface . . . the *Girona* struck the top of the reef, or maybe she just rolled over it, caught athwartships by a breaker. As soon as the Spanish realized that they were about to go on the rocks they dropped anchor . . . the vessel had begun to turn round on herself, but the next moment she was being broken apart on Lacada Point . . . the after castle broke away from the shattered hull and drifted eastwards . . . Another part of the *Girona* was carried along the west side of Lacada Point . . . from there the swirling currents drove it onto a reef to the west of Spaniard Cave . . . this was almost certainly part of the prow, containing the crew's quarters. . . .

A look at a map of the immediate coastline shows the clarity of this argument. Lacada Point, which the *Girona* hit following her initial collision with the outlying reef off the point; Spanish Rock; Spanish Cave; and Port na Spaniagh, all of which have a direct relationship with the wrecking and the subsequent finding of remains and artefacts, lie just to the west of Benbane Head, on the extreme northern coast of Antrim.

From what Stenuit and his divers found on the ocean bed, it seems clear that the galleass split up around the reef. The captain's cabin had ripped away from the hull, drifted with the current, and finally came to rest against a rock east of the point, splitting up there. What Stenuit thought to be the fore part of the ship containing the fo'c'sle was carried along the other side of the point and ended up southwest of Lacada, this apparent anomaly being explained by the currents being diverted when they met the bulk of the point and switching direction.

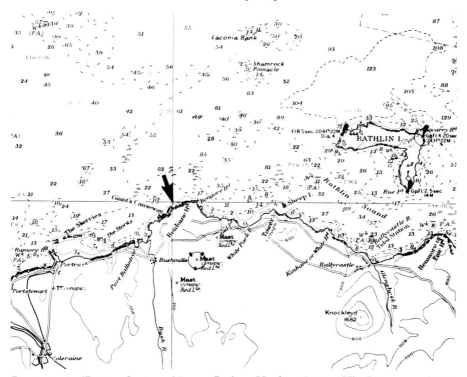

Portnaspania (Port na Spainneach), near Benbane Head in Antrim. The Girona was lost at Lacada Point on the night of October 28 while en route from Killybegs to Scotland. (Produced from portion of BA chart 2723 with the sanction of the Controller, HM Stationery Office and of the Hydrographer of the Navy)

It left behind a 'trail of perrier balls' on its path from the point to Spanish Cave where the divers found 'cannon balls, ballast and debris'. There were some small coins, but little of great value. Lead plates were picked up at the base of the point, part of the *Girona*'s ballast which had been nailed to the top of the frame timbers and which proved that it was here that the main part of the hull sank.

The ship's anchor was discovered at the foot of the reef. It may have spilled out when the *Girona* hit, but it is equally likely that it was left there when the cable broke as the crew tried to hold her off the reef. Cannon and lead ingots were found at the base of the point, proving that the ship did hit there and split open at the same time (the heavier objects would sink immediately and would not be swept around by the current). A load of coins and jewellery was found on the sea bed at the rock east of the point, and must have come from the captain's cabin, after the stern part had split off Lacada and drifted onto the rock, where it sank to the bottom and there opened, releasing its contents.

The most striking aspect of the wrecking was the speed with which wind, sea and rock broke up the galleass. Probably within ten minutes or so it was all over; a great ship of possibly around 700 tons was in a thousand pieces of scattered wreckage and some 1300 men were dead, drowned or battered to death against the rocks or by floating and falling wreckage.

Only nine men survived; they included sailors, soldiers and one artilleryman but no officers of any rank. All the senior officers, captains, noblemen, adventurers, clerics and those of any other distinction were drowned or killed. Apart from de Leiva, the noblemen who died included Don Thomas de Granvelle, a nephew of the one-time Prime-Minister of Spain, Cardinal de Granvelle; the Count of Paredes; Don Rodrigo Manrique de Lara (although his death has been questioned); Don Gaspar de Sandoval, Jeronimo Magno, Federico Vizconde, Capitan Bartolomé Lopez de Silva and Don Luis Ponce de Leon.

An even heavier and more complete toll was taken of the various officers, military and naval, who were on board. Three ships' captains died: Fabricio Spinola, the nobleman-captain of the *Girona*; Francisco Vidal, captain of the *Rata Encoronada*; and Don Pedro Mares, captain of the *Duquesa*. Among the high-ranking soldiers were Don Diego de Leiva (perhaps a brother of Don Alonso), Don Hieronimo de Herrera, Don Juan de Baraona, Gonzalo Beltran, Don Rodrigo Tello and Antonio de Silva, most of whom had commanded large companies of soldiers.

Among the many clerics who had accompanied the *Rata, Duquesa* and *Girona* had been the exiled Irish Bishop of Killaloe. He may have officiated at the sea burial of Maurice FitzGerald off the *Rata* at Blacksod Bay: it is known that the Bishop was aboard the *Rata* and that later on he was on the *Girona*'s final voyage. A gold reliquary, an exquisite piece of miniature craftsmanship discovered by Stenuit's divers, may well have contained the Bishop's *Agnus Dei* tablets.

Much of the detail of what happened to the ship when she struck must remain speculation, as is the case with almost all of the Armada wrecks around Ireland. Stenuit's reconstruction is probably as close as anyone will get to the truth. What can be more fully explained, however, is the apparent mystery of the length of the *Girona*'s last passage from Killybegs to Lacada Point. Stenuit, who has achieved so much with his careful study of the whole episode that he could with justification claim that he knows more about the galleass than any other man, states:

From the time he [de Leiva] set out, say before dawn on the 26th to the time of the shipwreck at midnight, 100 nautical miles further on, twenty hours had passed. With a good following wind the *Girona* could do five knots, and twenty hours would be about right to cover 100 nautical miles but it wouldn't be anything like long enough to get all the way to the [Scottish] isles, bearing in mind that the wind dropped, then changed, and then that they doubtless waited until the new wind seemed properly established, before working back to the west.

This estimate is based on the evidence of both the Irish and Spanish State

Papers, containing the evidence of de Nova and de Borja, and also the reports of Fitzwilliam to Burghley (Nov. 6), Henry Duke (Oct. 26), Bingham (Dec. 13), and two other reports by Patrick Foxe and Captain Nicholas Merryman. From a close study of these the real truth can be elicited. I cannot find any other significant reports dealing with the wreck which bear on the date on which she struck Lacada Point. Neither de Nova nor de Borja (who were not even aboard the vessel) are clear on when she sailed and when she was wrecked; their evidence is simply confusing. Bingham and Burghley's reports are equally unhelpful. Henry Duke reported on October 26:

The 16th of this instant October the said gally departed from the said harbour with as many of the Spaniards as she could carry, and sailing along the coast towards the Out Isles of Scotland, whither they were then bound, struck against the rock of Bunboyes, where both ship and men perished, save only five who hardly got to shore; three of which five men came the next day, being the 17th, in company with Sorley Boy M'Donnell, unto O'Neill's house at Strabane where they certified of their late shipwreck.

The clear statement here is that the galleass was wrecked on the day that she departed. Patrick Foxe says merely that 'the Spanish ships . . . are lately departed from M'Sweeny's country in the night-time . . .', but his report is dated Oct. 2 (12th) at which time the *Girona* was still in Killybegs harbour.

Another report, perhaps the most vital in the tenuous chain, from Captain Nicholas Merryman, who was commanding a patrol vessel off Antrim at the time of the *Girona*'s wreck, reads: 'The Spanish ship which arrived in Tirconnell with the M'Sweeny was on Friday the 18th [28th] of this present month descried over against Dunluce and by rough weather was perished, so that there were driven to the land, being drowned the number of 260 persons, with certain butts of wine which Sorley Boy [McDonnell] hath taken up for his use.'

Let us now examine the physical aspects. The distance sailed from Killybegs to Lacada Point depends on the course taken out at sea. It was highly unlikely that the *Girona* would take the most direct course, that closest in and through the various sounds and so on, since while she had three pilots aboard, later evidence appears to suggest that they knew little of the coast; moreover, since de Leiva was now in command, and a veteran of two shipwrecks already on this coast, he would be more than wary of the danger of a course that lay close to land. It is therefore reasonable to assume that the *Girona* sailed very wide of the coast, possibly ten to twenty miles out and just keeping the land in sight as a navigational check. Such a course, far from being the 100 nautical miles or so which Stenuit suggests, would be (from Killybegs to Lacada) some 175 (land) miles or 155 nautical miles; to Scotland the passage would be 200 miles, and that only to the Outer Isles.

Under ideal sailing conditions it is possible that the galleass could make five knots (one nautical mile per hour or knot = 1.15 statute miles) as Stenuit suggests. But this was a vessel overloaded to the danger point, probably leaking, certainly patched up and with a frail rudder. Her rate of progress would have been good had she managed to make even 2.5 knots. Assuming that she left Killybegs at dawn or before on the 26th (dawn in Killybegs in October is around eight o'clock) and was wrecked at midnight on the same day, having covered the course here outlined, she would have had to cover 155 nautical miles in 16 hours at an average speed of 9.75 knots an hour – twice her swiftest pace in *normal* sailing.

Even this, however, is not taking into account the evidence of Captain Merryman which states that she was 'descried' near Dunluce on the day she was wrecked; this implies that she was near Dunluce during the hours of daylight sometime before seven o'clock in the evening and some five or six hours before she was wrecked at midnight. Henry Duke's report that she both departed and was wrecked on the same day (16th/26th) must be doubted; he had sent a spy into Killybegs and got back a report on November 5, ten days after the *Girona* had sailed – speedy enough news from remote Antrim. His report that the ship left on the 16th (26th) can be taken as literal – after all, the sources in Killybegs would at least have been right about that. But is it safe to assume that news which had percolated from an unnamed source on the other side of Ireland back to Killybegs was correct? I doubt it.

One further element which must place in the strongest possible doubt the theory that the *Girona* sailed from Killybegs to Lacada/Dunluce in a day is the fact that if she left at, say, eight o'clock in the morning and had arrived at Dunluce by, say, six o'clock, she would have covered some 150 nautical miles in 10 hours, for an average speed of 15 knots (nautical miles per hour); in statute miles per hour, the figure is 17 mph. This is clearly impossible. Taking Merryman's account as the most reliable, supplemented by the various reports that the galleass left Killybegs on the 26th, we can estimate that from eight o'clock in the morning of the 26th to around six o'clock on the evening of the 28th, she had covered 150-odd nautical miles in 58 hours, for an average speed of 2.6 knots.

If this seems an inordinately slow speed, it was not so by Armada sailing standards. After leaving Lisbon, the fleet's best run up to the first week in June was on June 2nd when it had covered 30 nautical miles in 24 hours for an average speed of 1.25 knots, while in sailing from Lisbon to Finisterre the dismal figure of half a knot was achieved! It is fair, however, to point out that this was not always the case. From August 12 to September 22 Medina Sidonia's *San Martin* and accompanying vessels covered 2000-odd miles of ocean for an average daily run of 39.4 knots (45.4 statute miles), an average pace of 1.6 knots. Admittedly they were beating against rough seas and headwinds for a great part of the way, but even allowing for that the evidence is clear that the Armada ships were distinctly slow, even in fair winds.

That nine men survived (Henry Duke's report, third-hand at least, suggests only five) is evident from the statement made by a survivor to de Borja and de Nova while the shipwrecked Spaniards were sheltering in Antrim. Here again

Duke's report must be doubted, since eye-witness reports, while still open to question, are almost always more reliable than information which has filtered through several hands at least.

Although the survivors were few, they were lucky in that they had landed on the shores of a part of Ireland which, like Tirconnell, was remote from English rule, although not to the same extent. This was McDonnell territory. The McDonnells were a Scottish clan, originally Norse, who had repeatedly raided into Antrim across the narrow strip of water separating the two countries, and who had gradually taken over large tracts of land in Ulster, primarily in Antrim. Once settled, like other originally Scottish clans such as the McSweeneys, their influence spread quickly and they became absorbed into the Irish way of life, their clan name of MacDonald being also altered. Their most illustrious member was Sorley Boy McDonnell, who himself married one of the O'Neills: another member of the clan was the famous Ineen Dubh, who was married to Sir Hugh O'Donnell: she was a daughter of James MacDonald of the Isles and Lady Agnes MacDonald, herself a daughter of the Campbell Earl of Argyll.

By the time of the Armada Sorley Boy was an old man (he lived to be well over eighty, a unique age in those days). During his long years in northeast Ulster he had run the wide gamut of diplomatic manoeuvre from fickle loyalty to downright rebellion against the English; at one time he had been forced to swear loyalty to Elizabeth, then for two years he was a prisoner of Shane O'Neill, and was later beaten by the Lord Lieutenant Essex during the latter's campaign in Ulster in which he burned down one of Sorley Boy's castles on Rathlin Island and massacred his wife and youngest sons together with some 600 people. By 1585 McDonnell could muster some 2000 Scots to protect his Ulster interests, a force large enough to give Elizabeth pause. In the following year he again acknowledged Elizabeth as his Queen and agreed to split his territory with another Scottish clan, the MacQuillans, thus finally legalizing his ownership of lands taken by force when he had first come to Ireland.

Sorley Boy owed his strange name to his yellow hair (Somhairle Buidhe, yellow haired Charles). He lived at Dunanyme Castle, near Ballycastle, some twelve miles or so to the east of where the *Girona* was wrecked; his son James occupied Dunluce Castle, just west of Port na Spaniagh. Dunluce is a castle out of Grimm's fairy tales, perched on an isolated rock high above the water, connected by a swaying causeway to the mainland: an impregnable fortress. The McDonnells, like the McSweeneys, gave considerable help to the Spaniards. Both Sorley Boy and James sheltered them in their castles and shipped many of them back to Spain, at the same time shielding them from Fitzwilliam's wrath. Sorley Boy was particularly kind to many of the survivors from the *Trinidad Valencera*, who had come to him for help following the massacre of many of their countrymen by a force of soldiery under the Hovenden brothers near Derry. These survivors had been sent begging him to provide them with a boat, as they were Catholics as he was; this gentleman possessing vessels as he lives on an arm of the sea. He received them with much kindness and kept them for twenty days, Mass being said for them. There were at the time no boats there but he sent for some three miles off. Two boats were sent and eighty soldiers embarked in them, to be taken to an island off Scotland, which is only ten miles off, the rest remaining in the castle until the boats should return.

Fitzwilliam's network of spies was sufficient to bring this information to the ears of the Lord Deputy, who immediately demanded that the McDonnells give up their hostages, threatening Sorley Boy with death and the confiscation of his lands if he failed to obey. In reply, Sorley Boy

dedicated his sword to the defence of the Catholic Faith and those who held it, and in spite of the Governor, the Queen and all England, he would aid and embark the rest of the Spaniards who came to him; and he came back to them with tears in his eyes, and told them the Governor's demand and his reply thereto. So when the boats came back, he shipped the rest.

The *Girona*'s survivors certainly reached Scotland, as Sorley Boy shipped them there, and some of them at least reached Spain. It is entirely possible that among the nine who survived the wreck were men who had also been aboard the *Rata* and the *Duquesa*: three shipwrecks in six weeks. It was a reprieve well deserved.

It was a long time before the news of the *Girona* filtered through to Philip II in his retreat in the Escorial in the Guadaramma mountains outside Madrid. From Paris, the Spanish Ambassador to France, Don Bernardino de Mendoza, had been sending to the King a stream of optimistic reports compiled, it would seem, largely from the bottomless well of his own imagination, and in one of these he had claimed that de Leiva had landed 2000 men in 'Mac Win land' (this report was received by Philip in January 1589). He was accurate as far as that went, having written the despatch just before Christmas. But Philip was shortly afterwards to learn the full and shattering facts from Captain Marolin de Juan, who wrote to the King from Calais enclosing his summary of the depositions of de Borja and de Nova which contained their version of the final moments of the *Girona*.

Don Alonso de Leiva with his ship's crew and that of the *Santa Ana* set to sea in the galleass *Girona* [wrote Marolin de Juan in words which must have pierced Philip to his very depths], which previously had sought shelter in an unknown port. Scarcely had she sailed towards Spain when she was struck by a terrible storm which broke her rudder and flung her at midnight upon the rocks. . . .

It was the final blow. For months Spain had been counting the growing toll of ships and men; some two-thirds of the fleet had limped home in small groups or one by one, struggling silently into northern ports with men dying by the score each day from sickness, wounds and even hunger. But as long as de Leiva lived, Philip felt that the final disaster had been somehow staved off. Now that news of his death and that of sixty sons of the noblest houses in

Spain had reached the King, the significance of the whole campaign was clarified. Philip had lost, and with it dozens of ships, thousands of men and a fortune in money; worst of all he had lost his favourite, a man whom he regarded as fondly as any son.

The story of the *Girona* has a striking poignancy and sadness which far outweighs any similar emotional response to the many other Armada wrecks around the Irish coast. Some of this – perhaps all of it – is undoubtedly due to de Leiva and the aura of dashing and chivalrous invincibility which he bore like a brilliant banner wherever he went, lending a vivid colour and excitement to everything he did. James Machary's description helps to bring home, after four centuries, the magnetism which attracted so many followers of fortune to de Leiva. 'D. Alonso for his stature was tall and slender, of a whitely complexion, of a flaxen and smooth hair, of behaviour mild and temperate, of speech good and deliberate, greatly reverenced, not only by his own men, but generally of all the whole company.'

About the deaths of this chevalier-like figure and of his young and noble company of Spanish grandees, with their glittering clothes, their gold and jewels, their retinues of servants, hovers a mantle of immortality. De Leiva, unlike most figures on the Spanish side during the Armada, has secured a niche in the hall of great Elizabethans alongside the names of Drake and Grenville, Raleigh and Hawkins, Santa Cruz and Recalde.

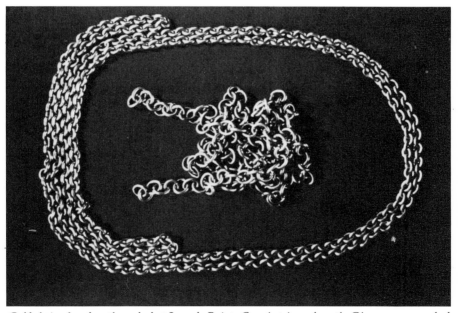

Gold chains found on the seabed at Lacada Point, Co. Antrim, where the Girona *was wrecked. In perfect condition after almost four centuries on the seabed, the outside chain is about 2.5 metres long and weighs over four pounds.*

VII

The Escape of Captain Cuellar

WHEN the Armada left Lisbon at the end of May, there sailed with it many captains who had no ships. In most navies this has been a fairly common occurrence, and that of Spain was no different. There were many *entretenidos* in the fleet, men who had commanded ships in the past but been passed over for promotion; some served throughout the campaign as senior officers, while others were lucky enough to gain commands during the reorganization of the fleet at Corunna. One of these was Don Francisco de Cuellar.

De Cuellar's career is shadowy in the extreme, but it seems probable that he came from Cuellar, a smallish town in Segovia. Some forty miles from Cuellar is a shrine of Our Lady of Hontanares, with which it is known de Cuellar was familiar. His birthplace therefore can be tentatively said to be somewhere in the region. Of his early naval career nothing is known. He joined the Armada at Lisbon, where his name was entered, with many others, on the list of captains waiting for a command. They were paid as captains even though they had no ships; de Cuellar received twenty-five escudos a month and had a servant. When the Armada sailed he went with it, still without a command.

After the Armada had made its painfully slow way from Lisbon to Corunna, battered by gales and several times being blown backwards, the Duke of Medina Sidonia ordered that the fleet should stay in the Groyne until it had refurbished its ships, taken on fresh stores, raised its level of efficiency, cured some of the many sick men and in general regained its composure, already badly dented by a dismal performance in Atlantic waters. At Corunna a reshuffle of ships' personnel took place and de Cuellar was given command of a galleon, the *San Pedro*.

The *San Pedro* was a member of the Castilian squadron under the overall command of General Diego Flores de Valdes. Of 530 tons displacement, she carried 24 guns and 272 men on leaving Lisbon, figures which remained substantially similar after Corunna. In addition to her crew of 131 men, she carried 141 soldiers and probably another twenty or thirty others, bringing her likely complement to around 300. She had been commanded by Don Pedro de Mendoza, who transferred to the *Gran Grin*, the Biscayan *almiranta* which was later wrecked in Clew Bay. There was nothing unusual in this; transferrence to the *Gran Grin* under Recalde's overall command could be looked on as a form of promotion for Mendoza, and many officers switched ships at Corunna. De Cuellar was one of the lucky ones.

Of the role which the *San Pedro* played during the subsequent fighting in the Channel little is known. The galleon is simply not mentioned; in general, the Castilian ships do not appear to have been as prominent in the several battles as, say, the Portuguese galleons or the converted merchantmen of the Levant. It is safe to assume that the *San Pedro* saw some action at least: she was most certainly damaged, and it was this damage which led to her assuming a sudden significance. Following the battle of Gravelines, when the Spanish ships had been dispersed and comprehensively defeated by Lord Howard's fleet, the Armada sailed north towards the tip of Scotland. It was a time for recrimination and a general licking of wounds. De Cuellar, exhausted by the strain of battle ('for ten days I had not slept nor ceased to assist at whatever was necessary for me') went below to rest, leaving command of the galleon to 'a pilot, a bad man whom I had'.

Previously, an order had gone through the fleet warning that strict formation must be kept among all the vessels – no easy matter with some of the ships leaking badly and limping along, losing distance all the time, and others being slow sailers even in good conditions. Ship station was an indispensable part of the Armada's discipline; when the fleet had managed to keep its crescent formation, it had defeated with comparative ease every English attempt to destroy it, and only when the formation had been broken, as at Gravelines, did the Spanish ships become vulnerable.

Because of the stress laid on keeping formation, to transgress was a serious crime. De Cuellar had kept station, despite the 'many heavy cannon balls which the enemy lodged in her in various parts' which must have slowed the *San Pedro*. While he slept, the second in command put on more sail and gradually forged ahead of the fleet, drawing away from the formation. When the galleon had gained about two miles on the leading ship, sail was lowered and the *San Pedro* came to a near halt on the water. The purpose of this manoeuvre was simple. By gaining two miles on the rest of the fleet, the galleon's temporary commander had given himself perhaps an hour's leeway to examine the shot-damaged hull while the ship was stationary and without delaying the remainder of the fleet. Normally it would have been a smart, seamanlike act, but in the light of the fleet order it could only have appeared as direct disobedience.

The *San Pedro* had barely begun to stow her sail when a fast tender from the Duke came alongside and a messenger sprang onto the galleon's deck with a curt message to de Cuellar to go at once to the fleet flagship. Retribution was clearly in the air, not only for de Cuellar but also for another captain, Don Cristobal de Avila, whose storeship lay ahead of the *San Pedro*, having taken a similar course of action. The two captains came together on the deck of the

San Martin and were taken before the *Maestro de Campo General* (Camp-Master General). He sentenced both to death.

If this abrupt treatment seems unnecessarily harsh, it must be remembered that this was just a day after Gravelines and that the fleet's senior officers had much more to concern themselves with than the behaviour of a couple of junior captains who had flouted orders and thereby weakened the chain of command's influence. The Camp-Master General, Don Francisco de Bobadilla, was noted for his harsh authority: 'alone was he who ordered and countermanded in the Armada.' Neither de Avila nor de Cuellar could expect mercy. Medina Sidonia played no part. He was in his cabin in a state of despair over the sinking on the previous day of the two great Portuguese galleons *San Mateo* and *San Felipe*; 'in retirement and very morose', the Duke was 'unwilling that any one should speak with him.'

De Cuellar was taken to the ship of the Judge Advocate, Don Martin de Aranda. It was a Levantine ship, and although there is no firm proof it was in all probability the *Lavia*, vice-flagship of the squadron. Like her squadron sisters, she was a converted merchantman, displacing 728 tons and carrying 274 men at Lisbon, increased to 302 at the Corunna muster. As a vice-flagship or *almiranta*, she was a ship of some importance and it is this fact more than any other which has led to general agreement that she was the vessel which harboured de Cuellar. A personage as important as the Judge Advocate, in effect the principal legal figure in the fleet, would more likely than not be in a ship of equal importance, such as a flagship. De Aranda was not in the Levantine flagship, the *Regazzona*, which reached Spain safely; that he was in the squadron is confirmed by de Cuellar, and if not in the flagship it seems most likely that he was in the ship of next importance, which was the *Lavia*.

While de Cuellar was aboard the *Lavia*, his colleague in error, de Avila, was hanged and his body, strung from the yardarm of a pinnace, paraded through the ships of the fleet as a grim warning to further transgressors.

De Cuellar had been sent to de Aranda to have the death sentence carried out, but he evidently argued his case strongly and eloquently enough to persuade de Aranda to shelve the execution temporarily while seeking further information from the *San Martin*. In a brief note, the Judge Advocate told Medina Sidonia that unless he received a personal note from the Duke authorizing the execution of de Cuellar, he would not carry out de Bobadilla's order 'because he saw that I was not in fault, nor was there cause for it.' De Cuellar also wrote to the Duke in 'such a nature that it made him consider the affair carefully'. Both letters had the desired effect: Medina Sidonia sent back a note from the flagship informing the Judge Advocate that de Cuellar was not to be executed. (No such mercy was shown to de Avila.)

After this incident the fleet sailed on as before. De Cuellar was not allowed to return to the *San Pedro* and resume command but remained aboard the *Lavia*, a virtual prisoner even though the 'Judge Advocate was always very courteous to me'. He stayed on the Levantine vice-flagship as the fleet sailed on past the shores of England and rounded the tip of Scotland between the Orkneys and the Shetlands, and bore westwards towards the open Atlantic.

If the *San Pedro* had been in poor condition after Gravelines, the *Lavia* was scarcely any better. 'We were in imminent danger of death because she opened up so much with a storm that sprang up that she continually filled with water, and we could not dry her out with the pumps,' wrote de Cuellar. But the vessel survived as far as the northwest of Ireland, where they were separated from the rest of the fleet by the great storm which began in the first week of September and scarcely let up for the next three weeks. The *Lavia* and two other large ships (which de Cuellar does not name) were probably detached from the main bulk of the fleet by the first tremendous gale of September 2; another gale followed just over a week later, by which time they were off the Irish coast.

Erris Head once more enters the picture. De Cuellar does not name it – it was unknown to the Spaniards – but says simply that 'being not able to round Cape Clear in Ireland, on account of the severe storm which arose upon the bow, he was forced to make for the land . . .' Once again Spanish ignorance of the coast was underlined: 'Cape Clear', to judge by later events, could have been no other headland but Erris. Clearly, the three big ships had sighted land, probably west Donegal, sometime during the week preceding the second series of gales which began on September 20. They had worked their way along the coast into Donegal Bay and there found themselves trapped by the seaward bulk of Erris, unable to round it in the strong headwinds of the gale of the 20th. It not only prevented the ships from weathering Erris Head but forced them back under bare poles deep into Donegal Bay. Drifting along the coast, the ships passed the inlet leading into Sligo, then held fearfully by Sheriff George Bingham, and anchored in a final attempt to avoid drifting further and being wrecked on the shore.

They were to the south of Inishmurray Island and about one and a half miles from the mainland some twelve miles due northwest of Sligo town. The shore here is low, with high sand dunes breaking its profile; behind it and much further inland are the peaks of Ben Bulben (1730 feet) and King's Mountain (1527 feet) and several other mountains, the range dominated by the great Truskmore at 2120 feet. Immediately inland of the ships was the headland terminating in Roskeeragh Point, and to the northwest above that the long curving strand at Streedagh, directly northwest of the present-day village of Grange. It was a dangerously exposed anchorage, open to almost every wind except an easterly (a rare wind on the west of Ireland in late September). There would have been slight protection from a southwesterly, but none if the wind went into the west.

The ships held at anchor for four days. On the fifth, however, the weather grew worse. 'There sprang up so great a storm on our beam, with a sea up to the heavens, so that the cables could not hold nor the sails serve us' wrote de Cuellar. 'On our beam' could only mean a westerly wind, the very worst

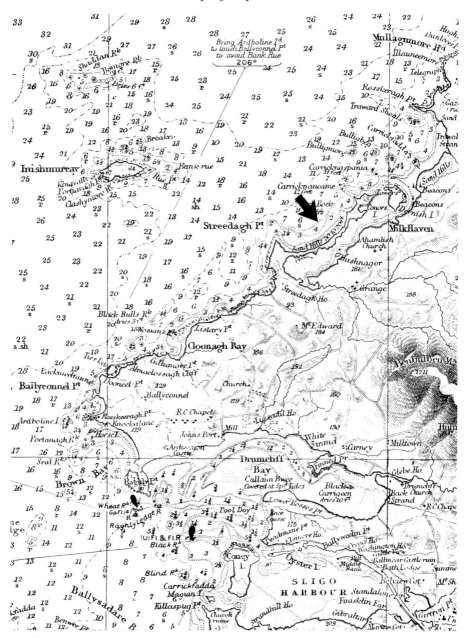

At Streedagh Strand, near Grange, north of Sligo, three ships were wrecked: the San Juan *of* Castile, *the* Lavia *and the* Santa Maria de Vison. *Captain Francisco de Cuellar of the* Lavia *survived and eventually escaped to Scotland, and later Antwerp, travelling northeast through Sligo, Leitrim, Fermanagh, Antrim and then back to Derry. (Produced from portion of B.A chart 2440 with the sanction of the Controller, HM Stationery Office and of the Hydrographer of the Navy)*

direction from which it could blow. The anchor cables parted, and once that had happened there could be only one result.

We were driven ashore [wrote de Cuellar], with all three ships upon a beach covered with very fine sand, shut in on one side and the other by great rocks. Such a thing was never seen; for within the space of an hour all three ships were broken to pieces, so that there did not escape three hundred men, and more than one thousand were drowned, among them many persons of importance – captains, gentlemen and other officials.

Of all the many Irish shipwrecks of Armada ships, this one at Streedagh is easily the most horrifying (apart perhaps from the *Girona*). Evidently all three ships broke their cables more or less simultaneously, or within an hour or so of each other, which testifies to the sudden rising of the storm. They drove aground in similar fashion, all together as it were, and within an hour were broken up by the strength of wind and wave. They went ashore on Streedagh Strand, between Streedagh Point to the south and Black Rock to the north. The strand runs in a quarter circle between those two landmarks, curving inland and about two miles long. Directly to the north of Black Rock is a low rock half-hidden in spray which at the turn of the seventeenth century was named on contemporary maps Spaniards' Rock; today it is known similarly as Carricknaspania – the 'Rock of the Spaniards'. But it is doubtful if this played any part in the wrecks, being well north of where de Cuellar very clearly states the ships were wrecked. And he himself does not mention any rock. Although tradition has named the rock after the wrecks, local tradition insists that the ships were driven ashore on the strand itself and this de Cuellar's own evidence appears to confirm.

In a gale, the seas running onto the strand are tremendous. The beach shelves very gradually and the ships struck bottom some distance out. A ship very quickly breaks up on sand, where there is no holding surface; on rock, the hull is frequently impaled and so transfixed and able to withstand quite heavy seas for some time before beginning to break. But on sand even large vessels thump and grind their keels on the unyielding smooth surface, and nothing breaks up a wooden hull more swiftly. This explains why the three ships were destroyed within an hour.

De Cuellar here gives the first and only clue as to the identity of one of the two accompanying vessels. Hitherto he had described them merely as being 'very large'; and that in one of them sailed Don Diego Enriquez, the 'hunchback', and it was at Streedagh that Enriquez 'died there one of the saddest deaths that has ever been seen in the world.'

With Enriquez we are set back abruptly into the tortuous channels of sixteenth century Spanish nomenclature. There were at least two men named Don Diego Enriquez among the Armada personnel, one being a camp-master, the other given the appellation 'Tellez'. Tellez has since been proven the commander of another Levantine ship, the *San Juan de Sicilia* which was blown up by an English agent in Tobermory Bay in the Hebrides. It has sometimes been asserted that Tellez and the *San Juan* perished together at Streedagh, an error no doubt due to the similarity of names: this is clearly untrue.

The second Don Diego Enriquez was a person of considerable importance in the Armada; de Cuellar clearly infers that he was the leader of the little group of three ships once they had parted company with the main body of the fleet. He was a camp-master, a prestigious and influential position in the hierarchy of the fleet's senior officers. Nowhere other than in de Cuellar's account, however, is he referred to as the 'hunchback'. Enriquez commanded a Castilian galleon, the *San Juan*, an exact sister apparently of de Cuellar's *San Pedro*. Being in the same squadron, de Cuellar must have known Enriquez, which may account for the 'hunchback' appellation. The *San Juan* was 530 tons (like the *San Pedro*) and carried a similar number of guns (twenty-four) and complement of men. This was the ship which in company with the *Lavia* and a third unnamed vessel, was wrecked at Streedagh on September 25.

If the identification of the *Lavia* has hitherto appeared vague, there are further shreds of evidence to strengthen the theory that it was on the Levantine vice-flagship that de Cuellar and Martin de Aranda were wrecked at Streedagh. The master of the *Lavia* was Manuel Orlando and in one of the many lists of Spanish prisoners taken by the English along the west coast the same name appears. But is it the same man? There is no other Manuel Orlando

The Sligo coast at Mullaghmore, north of Streedagh, with Classiebawm Castle in the centre. Three ships were wrecked south of here, with the loss of at least a thousand men. (Noel Habgood/J. A. Cash)

listed with the Armada, the inference being that the Orlando taken by the English forces was indeed the Orlando of the *Lavia*. Another pointer in the same direction is the appearance of survivors of the *Lavia* in O'Donnell's castle in Tirconnell in 1596, by which time they had apparently helped in the training of Irish soldiers with O'Neill, and possibly O'Donnell himself.

This of course goes to prove only that the *Lavia* was wrecked somewhere along the northwest coast, between Sligo and Donegal. The Levanter could therefore be one of several unidentified ships wrecked on the same coast. Yet the presence of the Judge Advocate aboard the ship at Streedagh does suggest strongly that it was a ship of some importance; that it was of the Levant squadron we know from de Cuellar. It may never be proven satisfactorily, but most of the scanty evidence does point strongly to the *Lavia*.

De Cuellar's graphic description of the drowning of Don Diego Enriquez from the deck of the *San Juan* is certainly the most detailed account of any similar incident to survive through Armada records on either side.

In consequence of fearing the very heavy sea that was washing over the highest part of the wrecks, he took his ship's boat that was decked, and he and the son of the Count of Villa Franca and two other Portuguese gentlemen, with more than sixteen thousand ducats in jewels and crown pieces, placed themselves under the deck of the said boat, and gave the order to close and caulk the hatchway by which they had entered.

Thereupon more than seventy men who had remained alive jumped from the ship to the boat, and while she was making for the land so great a wave washed over her that she sank, and all on deck were swept away.

Then she drifted along, rolling over in different directions with the waves until she went ashore, where she settled wrong side up, and by these mischances the gentlemen who had placed themselves under the deck died within. More than a day and a half after she had grounded, some savages arrived who turned her up for the purpose of extracting nails or pieces of iron; and breaking through the deck, they drew out the dead men. Don Diego Enriquez expired in their hands and they stripped him and took away the jewels and money which they [the dead men] had, casting the bodies aside without burying them.

The force of the waves at Streedagh is emphasized. The water is not deep and the rollers are consequently short and turbulent; in a strong gale, to make the shore in such a sea was a distant hope. Diego Enriquez and the others entombed within the ship's boat would have had a better chance of survival had they clung to a piece of timber and allowed themselves to be carried by wind and wave to the shore. De Cuellar was saved thus, although he was a non-swimmer.

I placed myself on top of the poop of my ship and from thence I gazed at the terrible sight. Many were drowning within the ships; others, casting themselves into the water, sank to the bottom without returning to the surface; others on rafts and barrels, and gentlemen on pieces of timber; others cried aloud in the ships, calling upon God; captains threw their chains and crown pieces into the sea; the waves swept others away, washing them out of the ships.

While I was looking on at this scene, I did not know what to do, nor what means to adopt, as I did not know how to swim, and the waves and the storm were very great; and on the other hand, the land and the shore were full of enemies, who went about jumping and dancing with delight at our misfortunes; and when any one of our people reached the beach, two hundred savages and other enemies fell upon him and stripped him of what he had on until he was left in his naked skin.

De Cuellar found a piece of wreckage floating in the water beside the ship and clambered down onto this, followed by Martin de Aranda; the wreckage was held fast to the ship by iron chains, and unable to break it loose, they had to leave it.

I managed to find another resource, which was to take the cover of a hatchway, about as large as a good-sized table [wrote de Cuellar]. When I tried to place myself on it, it sank with me to a depth of six times my height below the surface, and I swallowed so much water that I was nearly drowned. When I came up again, I called to the Judge Advocate and I managed to get him upon the hatchway cover with myself . . . there came a huge wave breaking over us in such a manner that the Judge Advocate was unable to resist it and the wave bore him away, and drowned him, crying out and calling upon God while drowning.

I could not aid him as the hatchway cover, being without weight at one end, began to turn over with me, and at that moment a piece of timber crushed my legs. With great exertion, I righted myself upon my supporting timber; and supplicating Our Lady of Ontanar [an evident reference to the shrine near his home town] there came four waves one after the other and without knowing how, or how to swim, they cast me upon the shore where I emerged unable to stand, all covered with blood and very much injured.

He had had a remarkable escape from death; the irony was that de Aranda, the man who had earlier in the campaign intervened to have the death sentence on de Cuellar commuted, should himself drown. The Judge Advocate had stitched some crown pieces into his waistcoat and trousers; loaded with the heavy weight of coin, he must have gone almost straight to the bottom.

De Cuellar came on shore at Streedagh to a savage and appalling scene, doubly so for him in that he was a stranger on these shores. Everywhere were dead and dying men, and running among the bodies hundreds of native Irish – de Cuellar called them 'savages' although the sixteenth century usage of this term referred more to the word 'native' than to a blanket description of the Irish as savages. The natives were not killing the Spaniards: they were stripping them of their arms, jewellery, coins and valuables and even their clothes. If force was necessary for this purpose then force was used. But it is clear that there was no large-scale attempt to massacre the survivors of the wrecks. De Cuellar was not touched or molested in any way when he staggered ashore out of the surf, and he explains this apparent anomaly by suggesting that the natives left him alone because 'my legs and hands and my linen trousers [were] covered in blood.' He did not stay long on the beach but moved inland seeking shelter, passing many naked and shivering Spaniards.

Streedagh Strand is a long peninsula separated from the mainland, to which it runs almost parallel; it is connected only at the southern end, just east of Streedagh Point itself. In all probability it was similar in 1588, and if so it would have been necessary for de Cuellar to go south before he could get off the strand. Probably he climbed the high dunes which today form a backdrop to the wide sweep of fine sand; if so, he would have seen a narrow stretch of mud and water separating him from the mainland.

Sligo was in English hands, the town itself being under Bingham's brother George as Sheriff. The local clan was the O'Conor, and it was probably a branch or branches of this family which descended on Streedagh after the ships were wrecked. Their prompt appearance in so isolated a landscape is explained by the fact that the ships had been in the vicinity for five days, ample time for the clan to gather and await developments. Now the chance had come for plunder and salvage, and in the manner of the native they were taking full advantage of this rare opportunity.

It is difficult to blame them for this action which at a distance appears cold and heartless. But it was customary then in the west of Ireland (as indeed also in other localities in the British Isles) to claim any wreckage or similar trove which came ashore as the finder's property; this native custom was widely accepted and regarded as normal behaviour, especially after shipwrecks. In this light, the action of the natives in taking everything the survivors owned seems less despicable. Some Spaniards were harmed, but nowhere does de

Looking northwest along the curving sands of Streedagh Strand, Co. Sligo, the graveyard of three great ships and over 1,200 men. The three vessels were driven ashore in the centre of the Strand. (Denis Kendrick)

Cuellar suggest that the Irish intended to murder the survivors: all they wanted was any article of any use or value.

De Cuellar made his painful way from the beach towards the mainland until he reached 'a deserted place' where he lay down, in great suffering from his damaged leg. He was joined by another Spaniard, so dazed that he could not speak; presently two natives arrived and instead of seizing the two survivors and stripping them of whatever valuables they possessed, they cut rushes and covered the two men.

During the night de Cuellar was disturbed by about two hundred soldiers riding past him towards the beach; this party was evidently part of the garrison at Sligo, along with some reinforcements. His companion had died, and at dawn de Cuellar began to move inland again, seeking a 'monastery of monks' which he had evidently heard of. Sometime that morning he reached it – the Abbey of Staad, almost two miles southeast of Streedagh; but there were now no monks but a dozen of his countrymen hanging by ropes from the window grills, executed by the 'Lutheran English'. The monks had fled to the woods.

De Cuellar left the abbey as quickly as he could by a road that led through a large wood. There he met an old woman who, recognizing him as Spanish, warned him not to go near her house 'as there were numerous enemies in it, and they had cut off the heads of many Spaniards'. Uncertain as to what to do, de Cuellar went back to the beach at Streedagh, where he met some of his countrymen. Although there were large parties of natives still hunting through the hundreds of dead bodies lying on the sand and carting away whatever spoils they could lay their hands on, de Cuellar and his companions were able to find the body of Don Diego Enriquez and bury him in a hastily dug grave in the sand beside the water's edge.

When this had been done, a native who may have been a chieftain ('for they respected him') showed them another road away from the beach. It may or may not have been some sort of trap, since after he had gone a considerable distance along the route de Cuellar was waylaid by three men and a girl of twenty. One of the men, whom de Cuellar describes as English, attacked the Spaniard with a knife but the others intervened and saved him from further injury. The trio then stripped him, taking a gold chain worth more than 'a thousand reals', together with forty-five crown pieces which he had sewn into his jacket. They went away then, but the girl sent back a boy with food and medicines for the Spaniard. The boy then showed de Cuellar another route, which he said led part some mountains to another area where a chieftain was known to help Spaniards.

It took de Cuellar many days to reach the desired land. On the way he met with every sort of misfortune, being stripped again and beaten, narrowly missing being taken by a force of English horse troops, starving, and still in great pain from the wound in his leg. Along the way he met other Spaniards and together they travelled on deep into Leitrim, living on blackberries and watercress and whatever else they could find to eat. At almost every turn the party was assisted by the natives, who guided them and in some cases gave shelter.

De Cuellar does not say how many days it took him to reach the safety of the territory of the 'important savage'; probably the time amounted to a week at least. The chieftain to whose safety the Spaniard had fled has been mentioned already: Sir Brian O'Rourke of Breffni. His territory covered a vast area of the more inland regions of the northwest, centring around Leitrim; next to O'Neill and O'Donnell, he was perhaps the strongest native chief in the area and a bitter opponent of Elizabeth. O'Rourke had helped many Spaniards and some of them appear to have stayed with him for a considerable time, even to the extent of training his own soldiers. He was not there, however, when de Cuellar reached his home, being away defending 'a territory which the English were coming to take'.

O'Rourke's main settlement at this time was near Newtown, on the Sligo-Leitrim border at the eastern end of Loch Gill, but it is accepted that when de Cuellar arrived on his doorstep along with the other fugitive Spaniards, the chieftain had moved his entire entourage to Loch Glenade, near Glencar. Glencar, one of the most beautiful small lakes in Ireland, possesses several crannogs, the lake dwellings of stone to which O'Rourke's clan could flee to during siege.

It was at Glencar that a curious incident occurred, curious in that de Cuellar's description of it gives tantalizing glimpses of another mysterious Armada vessel in the vicinity. When the Spaniards had been with O'Rourke's clansmen for some days, word reached them that a 'very large' Spanish ship was 'at the coast . . . and came for those Spaniards who had escaped.' Without delay, de Cuellar and nineteen others left Glencar and returned to the coast, a journey which probably took them far less time than had the original. For some unspecified reason (perhaps his injury), de Cuellar could not keep pace with the rest of the party and was left behind. The others reached the vessel and 'they embarked on board her, as she belonged to the Armada and had arrived there in a great gale with her mainmast and rigging much injured.'

We know little more than that of this intriguing ship. What happened to her afterwards is indicative of the repeated good fortune which enabled de Cuellar to survive.

Fearing that the enemy might burn her or do her some other injury, for which energetic preparations were being made, they set sail from thence in two days with the crew that came in her and those they had picked up, returning, to run aground and get wrecked on the same coast. More than 200 persons were drowned, and those who reached the shore by swimming were taken by the English and put to death.

What was this ship? It has been suggested, with apparent real foundation, that she was either the *Rata* or the *Duquesa Santa Ana*, or a combination of both. This appears unlikely at best: the *Rata* was wrecked much further to the southwest of Sligo/Leitrim to enter into the calculation; the *Duquesa* simply does not fit de Cuellar's description of the wreck of this mysterious ship. Hardly a man was lost during the wreck of the *Duquesa*, and the English failed to take even one prisoner, from most accounts. There is a possibility, explored in a later chapter, that she was the Armada ship towed into Donegal harbour by a turf-boat and with her mainmast gone, and which may have been wrecked later on further down the coast. And there for the time being we must leave it.

De Cuellar never reached this ship; instead he resumed his wanderings, keeping to the hidden forest paths and little frequented byways to avoid the English soldiery. Aided by a clergyman's directions he set off to find another chieftain, a 'very brave soldier and an enemy of the Queen of England', but while on the way was taken virtual prisoner by a blacksmith, for whom he had to work in the forge for more than a week. Eventually the same clergyman who had helped him previously came by once more and had him released, and de Cuellar finally reached his second objective with the aid of a guide party which the clergyman had arranged should be sent to him from the chieftain's castle.

If all this appears complicated in the extreme, it must be remembered that de Cuellar could not speak English and that he was loose in a country of which he knew absolutely nothing. He was therefore dependent on the natives for any help, hoping in a vague way to make his route always to the northeast corner of the country, from whence it would be possible to escape to Scotland. He covered remarkably little ground during the course of his various wanderings, at least initially. Much of his effort had been taken up with finding places to sleep, getting something to eat, keeping warm (it was October), travelling warily along little-used paths, constantly afraid of being captured by the English.

In reaching the castle of the 'very brave soldier', however, de Cuellar had again been in luck. Like O'Rourke, the man whom de Cuellar had now stumbled upon was a bitter and implacable enemy of England and its Queen. Dartry was the chief of the MacClancy clan, who governed a sizeable area of the northwest close to O'Rourke's territory. His castle was at Rossclogher, an island fortress to the west of the island of Inisheer, near the southern shore of Loch Melvin which divides Co. Sligo from Fermanagh in Northern Ireland. Rossclogher stands today, but only barely; its walls have largely crumbled away into the deep waters of the lake and those few stones which are left are held together by tendrils of ivy. Bushes have sprouted everywhere and an arm of green reeds stretches from the shore almost to within feet of the little island. Hugh Allingham, perhaps the very first local historian to trace de Cuellar's route, wrote of Rossclogher:

The Castle of Rossclogher is built on a foundation of heavy stones laid in the bed of the lake and filled in with smaller stones and earth to above water level. The substructure was circular in form, and the entire was encompassed by a thick wall, probably never more than five feet in height. The walls of the castle are very thick, and composed of freestone, obtained from an adjacent quarry on the mainland. They are cemented together with the usual grouting of lime and coarse gravel, so generally used by the builders of old; the outside walls were coated with thick roughcast, a feature not generally seen in old structures in the locality. Facing the south shore, which is about one hundred yards distant, are the remains of a bastion pierced for musketry. The water between the castle and the shore is deep, and goes down sheer to the foundation.

On the shore, close to the castle, are the remains of military earthworks, evidently constructed by some enemy seeking possession of the castle. On the summit of a hill immediately over this is a circular enclosure about 220 feet in circumference; it is composed of earth, faced with stonework. Here the MacClancy clan folded their flocks and herds, and from this ancient 'cattle-booley' a bridle path led to the mountains above. Portions of this pathway have recently been discovered [Allingham was writing in 1897]; it was only two feet in width, and regularly paved with stones enclosed by a kerb.

On the mainland, close to the southern shore, and within speaking distance of the castle, stand the ruins of the old church which was built by MacClancy, and which is of about the same date as the castle to which it was an appendage. In the immediate neighbourhood of the shore, guarded on one side by the lofty mountain range of Dartraigh, on the other by the waters of Lough Melvin, was MacClancy's 'town', an assemblage of primitive huts, probably circular in shape, and of the simplest construction, where dwelt the followers and dependents of the chief, ready, by night or by day, to obey the calls to arms. . . .

Almost every word of Allingham's detailed description of Rossclogher is of interest in the light of events during de Cuellar's stay.

MacClancy was a chieftain of considerable importance by any standards; his determined resistance to, and implacable hatred of, the English allied to the difficulties which subjecting his territory posed to any attacker made him an elusive and dangerous opponent. His lands, although small by comparison to those of the O'Neills, O'Donnells, O'Rourke and several other northern chieftains, were just as difficult to traverse, consisting of great stretches of low-lying bog, some quite sizeable lakes, including Melvin, and even mountains (the Dartry range).

MacClancy's territory was in Bingham's province of Connacht, and from no other nominal subject except the Burkes of Mayo did the Governor receive such trouble. As early as September 15, when the Armada scare was just beginning to make itself felt in the circle of English authority in Ireland, Bingham was reading a letter from his brother George in which he wrote, 'M'Glanathie [MacClancy] hath made proclamation that all the woodkerne [native Irish soldiers] shall resort unto him, and they shall have entertainment.' As Sheriff of Sligo, George Bingham's powers extended to MacClancy's territory; but like his brother, he seems to have been unable to make that power felt to any appreciable extent. Both Binghams waged a war of attrition on MacClancy, repeatedly sending minor expeditionary forces deep into his territory, hoping to catch him by surprise. They failed every time; probably he was able to retreat in times of extreme stress to a crannog dwelling which he had on an island, Iniskeen, not far from Rossclogher.

MacClancy was a major figure in that he helped many shipwrecked Spaniards to escape from the English forces. When the fugitives reached the safety of his territory they were given food and shelter, and when strong enough passed on through a chain of sympathetic aid to the northeast. There were many links in this chain, most both unknown and forgotten, but among them were several prominent names such as the Bishop of Derry, Raymond (or Redmond) Gallagher, the McDonnells of Antrim and the O'Cahans of Derry. Both of the Binghams, and more sporadically, Fitzwilliam, tried everything to stem this steady flow of refugees but to no avail.

Part of the difficulty in attempting to seal off this escape route was the slender hold which the English had on that part of the country. George Bingham lived in constant fear of Sligo falling into native hands, since he was almost surrounded by Irish sympathetic to MacClancy, O'Rourke and, further north, to the MacSweeneys and O'Donnells. On October 18 both he and Secretary Fenton were writing to Sir Richard from Sligo that they were finding it difficult to communicate with Ballyshannon, north of Sligo and a stronghold of O'Donnell, 'as M'Glannoghs [MacClancys] hinder our espials' (Ballyshannon is quite close to the western end of Loch Melvin). A day later Fenton at least was in receipt of more definite news, telling the Connacht Governor from Ballymote, fifteen miles south of Sligo, that 'O'Rourke, M'Glannogh, Maguire [the Fermanagh chieftain] and the Burkes in Mayo are combined with the Spaniards.' Early the next month, William Taaffe was complaining to Bingham that 'the nephews of Hugh Oge M'Hugh Duff have come to M'Glanchie's country to aid the rebels, and threaten to burn Taffe's [*sic*] land.'

MacClancy lived in a state of almost perpetual siege or fear of siege: the habitual lifestyle of a local Irish chieftain who had retained his independence of, and defiance to, the Crown. He had sheltered other Spaniards from Fitzwilliam's forces, and now he took de Cuellar into his castle and his household, apparently without question, and there the Spaniard remained for three months 'acting as a real savage like themselves'.

De Cuellar's observations on this period, during which he lived more or less as one of MacClancy's family, are of enormous interest; this is one of the few instances where any Armada survivor was able to leave a wealth of detail and comment on what he saw and underwent, but particularly so in view of the light cast on the varied aspects of native Irish life in the later sixteenth century. De Cuellar's position was unique: he was educated, observant, with a sense of humour, adaptable and persevering; endowed with these qualities, he was able to compile a remarkable and virtually unique picture which retains its graphic interest even to this day.

Besides the qualities mentioned above, de Cuellar apparently possessed a very definite attraction for the women in MacClancy's household. 'The wife of my master was very beautiful in the extreme and showed me much kindness,' he wrote.

One day we were sitting in the sun with some of her female friends and relatives, and they asked me about Spanish matters and of other parts, and in the end it came to be suggested that I should examine their hands and tell them their fortunes . . . I began to look at the hands of each and to say to them a hundred thousand absurdities, which pleased them so much that there was no other Spaniard better than I or that was in greater favour with them. By night and by day men and women persecuted me to tell them their fortunes, so that I saw myself [continually] in such a large crowd that I was forced to beg permission of my master to go from his castle. He did not wish to give it to me; however, he gave orders that no-one should annoy me or give me trouble.

It is significant that MacClancy was reluctant to let de Cuellar leave; later on a similar refusal was again made, but in a very different context.

During his three months or so with MacClancy, de Cuellar had time to observe the habits and customs of the clan, and was not overly impressed with what he saw.

The custom of these savages is to live as the brute beasts among the mountains, which are very rugged in that part of Ireland. . . . They live in huts made of straw. The men are all large bodied, and of handsome features and limbs, and as active as the roe-deer. They do not eat oftener than once a day, and this is at night; and that which they usually eat is butter with oaten bread. They drink sour milk, for they have no other drink; they do not drink water, although it is the best in the world. On feast days they eat some flesh half-cooked, without bread or salt, which is their custom. They clothe themselves, according to their habit, with tight trousers and short loose coats of very coarse goat's hair. They cover themselves with blankets and wear their hair down to their eyes.

De Cuellar's eye for the fair sex enlivens his narrative. 'The most of the women are very beautiful but badly dressed. They do not wear more than a chemise and a blanket with which they cover themselves, and a linen cloth, much doubled, over the head and tied in front. They are great workers and housekeepers after their fashion.'

This simple style of living allowed MacClancy's men ample time for warfare, of which there was plenty.

They carry on perpetual war with the English who keep garrison here for the Queen, [noted de Cuellar] and do not let them enter their territory which is subject to inundation and marshy. . . . The chief inclination of these people is to be robbers and to plunder each other so that no day passes without a call to arms among them. For the people in one village becoming aware that in another there are cattle or other effects they 'go Santiago' [a Spanish slang term for 'attack'] and kill one another.

And here he adds his own wry comment that 'the English from the garrisons, getting to know who had taken and robbed most cattle, then come down upon them and carry away the plunder.'

MacClancy possessed an unusual yet effective reply to any English attacks. His system of outlying spies was evidently effective enough to ensure early warning, and the entire clan withdrew to the mountains, probably leaving a skeleton garrison behind to defend the castle, which was unassailable without boats. With the clan went their cattle, their one source of wealth and most valuable possession.

During his three months in Rossclogher, de Cuellar and his companions had time to regain strength. They were safe, but for how long was another question. The brief idyll on Loch Melvin was coming to an end; sometime early in December word reached MacClancy that a great force of English soldiers, about 1700 men, had marched from Dublin to Sligo to counter possible moves by shipwrecked Spaniards, and having executed every survivor they could lay hands on had turned towards MacClancy's territory in pursuit of the remainder.

That the English force did execute as many Spaniards as they could find, with the exception of a handful of hostages, is undeniable. Neither Bingham nor Fitzwilliam, for instance, make any bones about it – on the contrary, they make it plain that they felt they had done a good job. The State Papers are peppered with reports of massacres, minor or otherwise: '140 who came on land executed'; '300 Spaniards that came to land put to the sword'; '1100 [Spaniards] who escaped to land executed' (this signed by Bingham himself); and Bingham again, writing to Fitzwilliam in late September, 'there hath perished at the least a 6000 or 7000 men, of which there hath been put to the sword first and last by my brother George, and in Mayo, Thomond and Galway, and executed one way and another about 700 or 800 upwards . . .'. Bingham reporting to Elizabeth from Athlone on December 3: 'the men of these ships all perished, save 1100 or more which were put to the sword . . .'. These are but few reports. De Cuellar for instance, shows that on the day following the Streedagh wrecks the English garrison from Sligo arrived there presumably to take care of any straying Spaniards – he himself saw at least a dozen hanged in Staad Abbey. De Cuellar said that the natives did not intend to kill the Spaniards but only to rob them, and the inescapable inference is that whatever Spaniards were left alive around Streedagh were executed by the English.

There was a great deal of truth in the report which reached MacClancy, though Fitzwilliam did not have anything like 1700 men to spare to send halfway across Ireland. He had asked London for 2000 soldiers (this also was beyond immediate capabilities), feeling that with such an army he could suppress any possible trouble in the northwest.

It is hardly necessary to find further excuse for the treatment which Fitzwilliam's soldiers meted out to Spanish prisoners and fugitives, but the necessity for this apparently thoughtless butchery is made even clearer by a full realization of the situation in which the Lord Deputy now found himself. Clearly he could not begin a war with O'Donnell on the basis of mere suspicion, a war which he might very well lose in the short run whatever the long-term possibilities, but the Spaniards were a different kettle of fish, something tangible into which Fitzwilliam's teeth might bite with impunity.

The best – indeed the only – way that he could eliminate any possible alliance was to kill every Spaniard as quickly as possible. It was as simple as that: only through a comprehensive and ruthless programme of slaughter could the Lord Deputy ensure that all danger of a rebellion was erased. And this programme he now embarked on.

Fitzwilliam started such an expedition into Connacht and northwest Ulster on November 14 from Dublin and finished it in the same city seven weeks and one day later, on January 2, 1589 – a formidable achievement. He had broken all the rules, marching through wet and boggy Ireland during the wettest months of the year, and at an age (sixty-three) when most men of his standing would undoubtedly have sent a capable younger deputy. Fitzwilliam's dedication and determination are legendary, but of all the many instances of his devotion to his position as Lord Deputy, none is more revealingly impressive than this winter forced march. In a letter to the Privy Council written a week after his return, Fitzwilliam underlines his achievement thus: 'returning without loss of any one of Her Majesty's army, neither brought I home, as the captains informed me, scarce twenty sick persons or thereabouts, neither found I the waters nor other great impediments, which were objected before my going out to have been most dangerous, otherwise than very reasonable to pass.'

On this journey he visited Streedagh Strand and saw the remains of the three Armada ships, including the *Lavia*.

As I passed from Sligo, having then gone 120 miles, I held on towards Bundrowes and so to Ballyshannon, the uttermost part of Connacht that way, as some say, but denied so to be by O'Donnell and his followers, and riding still along the sea coast, I went to see the bay [Streedagh] where some of those ships wrecked, and where, as I heard, lay not long before 1200 or 1300 of the dead bodies. I rode along that strand near two miles (but left behind me a long mile and more), and then turned off from that shore, leaving before me 'a mile and better's riding', in both which places they said that had seen it, there lay as great a store of the timber of wrecked ships as there was in that place which myself had viewed, being in mine opinion (having small skill or judgement therein) more than would have built five of the greatest ships that ever I saw, besides mighty great boats, cables, and other cordage answerable thereunto, and some such masts for bigness and length, as in mine own judgement I never saw any two could make the like.

It must have been at this time that the reports reached the ears of MacClancy in Rossclogher that Fitzwilliam was on his way to capture de Cuellar and the other Spaniards. Here was the biggest danger he had yet faced: English attack on his castle was not an unusual occurrence, but never had he met such apparent numbers. His reaction was dismaying to de Cuellar. 'This savage, taking into consideration the great force that was coming against him, and that he could not resist it, decided to fly to the mountains, which was his only remedy . . . we decided to say to the savage that we wished to hold the castle and defend it to the death; that he should . . . lay in provisions for six months and some arms.' The Spaniards' decision to remain at the castle while MacClancy, clan and cattle retreated into the mountains was a calculated one; de Cuellar was an experienced strategist and recognized the basic impregnability of the castle itself, which was 'very strong and very difficult to take . . . founded in a lake of very deep water . . . the castle could not be taken by water nor by the shore of the land that is nearest to it.'

MacClancy left Rossclogher in the Spaniards' hands, having extracted a promise that they would not desert it; de Cuellar and his companions made their preparations to withstand the siege. Within a short time the English force ('about eighteen hundred men' wrote de Cuellar) reached the shore about a mile and a half away from the castle. From there, sundry threats and even promises were delivered 'by trumpeter' but to no avail. The Spaniards simply waited; they saw two of their captured countrymen hung in their full view by the English. Seventeen days later, there came 'severe storms and great falls of snow'. The English were not prepared to stick it out any longer, and left.

MacClancy was overjoyed: he had every reason to be. 'He very earnestly confirmed us as most loyal friends; offering whatever was his for our service, and the chief persons of the land [did the same] neither more nor less.' This was not all: he offered de Cuellar his sister in marriage. Through many trials, having been sentenced to death, reprieved, shipwrecked, ill treated, wounded, besieged, he had borne all with a stoic fortitude that we can only admire. But here his composure broke and panic set in; where the seas and the English had failed, the humble sister of an Irish chieftain now succeeded brilliantly. There is no record of how young or pretty she was or whether MacClancy placed real value on her attraction. 'I thanked him much for this' wrote de Cuellar, tough man of arms, 'but contented myself with [asking for] a guide to direct me to a place where I could meet with embarkation for Scotland.'

MacClancy refused, evidently with a sense of injured reproof; later, de Cuellar was told by MacClancy's son that the chieftain had decided to keep the Spaniards in Rossclogher, even if he had to imprison them to achieve this. It was worrying news, and sometime around the 15th of January de Cuellar and four of his fellow Spaniards slipped forth from the castle in the dead of night and fled Rossclogher.

For the next twenty days they travelled 'by the mountains and desolate places, enduring much hardship' and at the end of that 'got to the place where Alonzo de Leyva, and the Count of Paredes and Don Tomas de Granvela, were lost, with many other gentlemen'. This was undoubtedly Dunluce Castle in Antrim, which had sheltered survivors from the *Trinidad Valencera* and the *Girona*. De Cuellar had come to this haven of shipwrecked Spaniards from Melvin to Strabane, possibly to Derry (although this might be doubtful) and thence northeast again through Antrim to Dunluce. Here he sheltered, possibly 'in the huts of some savages' until, seeking for a boat to bring him to Scotland, he heard that vessels were shortly leaving Ireland for Scotland from the territory 'of a savage whom they called Prince Ocan'.

Ocan was actually O'Cahan, the principal native sept in the area west of where de Cuellar now found himself. They were kin of the O'Neills, O'Cahan himself being a cousin and one of the principal chieftains in Ulster, bitterly opposed to the English. Dungiven, south of Limavady, was the main stronghold of the clan but there were others at Dunseverick (not far to the east of the Giant's Causeway); near Limavady southwest of Coleraine, and Castleroe, near Coleraine. In view of the fact that only Castleroe Castle stood near a port (Coleraine), we must presume that it was to this last of O'Cahan's four main habitations that de Cuellar now went in an attempt to reach Scotland.

Luck deserted him; he reached Coleraine only to find that the ship had left two days before; worse than that, however, he now found himself in a part of Ireland heavily populated with English soldiery. Moreover, his old leg wound, which had healed at Rossclogher, had begun to open under the strains of the journey. Some native women 'pitied me and took me away to their little huts on the mountain'; there he stayed for six weeks while the wound healed. As soon as he was well again he made his way back to Castleroe and O'Cahan.

Here again he met disappointment. O'Cahan would not see him, having apparently given his word to the English 'not to keep any Spaniard in his territory nor permit one to go about in it'. The chieftain had been under severe pressure from the English to take such action; Derry and its environs were already in danger of full occupation by English forces and evidently O'Cahan had agreed to cold-shoulder any Spanish refugees as a measure to protect his own interests for a while longer.

De Cuellar, by this stage, had tired of running, for which he cannot be blamed. He stayed in O'Cahan's village at Castleroe, in full view of the English, and inevitably they came to know of him. He was apprehended in a hut where he had gone to visit some girls; but the Spaniard, creating a diversion, leapt through the doorway and ran across the countryside, leaping banks and ditches until he hid in some brambles. Later on, two local boys helped him to find the castle where the English kept the Bishop of Derry, Redmond Gallagher (or Raymond Gallagher), whom the State Papers called 'a most seditious Papist'. The Bishop had previously helped Spaniards to escape and now found time to help de Cuellar as well. There were twelve Spaniards already there, and he had arranged for a boat to take them all to Scotland. At last it appeared as though de Cuellar's luck was in.

Within a week, they were at sea 'in a wretched boat . . . and the wind being contrary the same day, we were forced to run before it, at the mercy of God, for Shetland, where we reached the land at daybreak, the boat being nearly swamped, and the mainsail carried away.' Shetland was not Scotland, but it was near enough for de Cuellar 'to give thanks to God for the mercies he had bestowed upon us in bringing us here alive.' In two more days he was in Scotland. He does not say a great deal of his six months there save that he went around 'as naked as when we arrived' and that he 'suffered the greatest privations'. Probably he expected too much from a king who had need of diplomatic caution.

De Cuellar was supported by Catholic sympathizers until such time as a Scottish merchant in Flanders agreed to come to Scotland and ship all the Spaniards in four vessels to Flanders, which was comparatively safe in the control of the Duke of Parma. Parma himself was evidently involved in this transaction, and the Scottish merchant was to receive five ducats for every Spaniard who reached the Netherlands.

Once more they found themselves at sea and bound for friendly territory. But 'all was treacherous', says de Cuellar, 'for an arrangement had been made with the ships of Holland and Zealand that they should put to sea and await us at the same bar of Dunkirk, and there they should put us all to death, without sparing one, which the Dutch did as they commanded.' At this final hurdle it seemed that at last de Cuellar must fall, but 'God willed that of the four vessels in which we came, two escaped and grounded, where they went to pieces . . . so that we were forced to cast ourselves afloat and we thought to end it there . . . the sea and wind were very high . . . I reached the shore in my shirt. . . .'

As at Streedagh, he had had a miraculous escape. He entered Dunkirk stripped naked and half-drowned but indomitably alive. 'God has brought me to the State of Flanders,' he wrote 'where I arrived twelve days ago with the Spaniards who escaped from the ships that were lost . . . this I have wished to write to you, from the City of Antwerp, October 4, 1589, Sgd. Francisco de Cuellar.'

A sketch, made c.1890 by J. W. Carey, of a figurehead commonly supposed to have come from one of three Armada ships wrecked at Streedagh Strand, Co. Sligo. It was last traced to the house of a Justice of the Peace in Sligo around the turn of the century, but its present whereabouts are unknown. The armorial bearings are those of King Philip II of Spain and include the Arms of Castile, Leon, Aragon and Sicily. It is probable that the figurehead came from the galleon San Juan *of Castile, one of the former Indian Guard of galleons which Philip commissioned especially to guard his Plate Fleet carrying silver back from Spanish possessions in the west.*

VIII

❧

The Brothers Hovenden

A week or so after the Armada had shot the narrow passage between the Orkneys and the Shetlands, the ships had all begun to feel the strain. The crescent formation was not kept: in any case, its usefulness was confined to actual warfare. But the Duke of Medina Sidonia had been specific in his fleet orders: to survive, the vessels must stay together. Those who fell behind did so at their own peril.

At the beginning of the fourth week in August four ships lost contact with the rest of the fleet. There were two hulks or storeships in this group, the *Castillo Negro*, a 750 tonner carrying 27 guns and some 273 men, and the *Barca de Amburg*, a 600 tonner with 23 guns and 264 men. The others were much more noteworthy; the *capitana* (flagship) of the *urcas*, *El Gran Grifon*, a 650 ton vessel with 38 guns and 286 men, under the overall command of Juan Gomez de Medina, and the Levantine vessel *La Trinidad Valencera*. Of this little group, all were to founder, three of them probably within sight of Ireland.

The *Valencera* was one of the biggest ships in the entire fleet, her 1100 tons making her also the second largest ship in her own Levant squadron after the flagship *La Regazzona*. She carried 42 guns, a significant armament, and some 360 men, 281 of whom were soldiers. The soldiers were in three companies under the overall command of Don Alonso de Luzon, a Maestre de Campo, and one of the most senior officers in the entire Armada. De Luzon commanded the crack Regiment of Naples of almost 3000 men; all three companies, the other two commanded by Captain Don Garcia Manrique and Captain Hieronimo de Aybar, were of the Neapolitan *tercio*.

The captain of the *Valencera* was Horatio Donai. Like the ship herself, he was Venetian. The *Valencera*, like the rest of her squadron, was originally a merchant ship, now converted for war. A year before the Armada sailed she had been commandeered to bring Sicilian troops to Lisbon to assemble for the voyage to England. She had then been forced to stay; it was in the Portuguese capital that she was converted into a warship and her complement of guns brought up to the necessary standard. She was not the only Venetian merchantman to suffer this fate; in the same port, under largely similar circumstances, the *Regazzona* and the *Lavia* were held despite the strong protests of the Venetian authorities. Philip II needed every ship on which he could lay his hands, and could afford to brook no arguments.

The *Valencera* was doubtless involved fairly heavily in the Channel fighting, although her name is not at all prominent. She may have been damaged, and probably was although to what extent is unknown. While this may have caused her to lag behind the remainder of the fleet and in the company of the three *urcas*, it is more likely that her Mediterranean build and lightness of construction, coupled with poor sailing ability, caused her laggardly progress. By the end of the third week of August she was finding progress difficult. Her companions were slow and clumsy sailers in any weather, great pot-bellied, tubby vessels designed merely to hold as much cargo as possible without sinking. Their speed was a matter of derision among Armada sailors, but at the same time they could withstand bad weather far better than the lightly built Mediterranean ships, as most of them came from the Baltic.

By September 1 the little group of four was breaking even its own pathetic formation. The *Barca de Amburg*, battered by seas and almost constant headwinds which made progress nearly impossible, could take no more. For days she had been shipping and leaking water and now her pumps jammed. She signalled for help and the *Valencera* and *El Gran Grifon* came alongside and took off her complement, around 260 men. They were just in time; shortly afterwards, the hulk slowly slid under the surface.

The remaining vessels struggled on, but three days later, in darkness and heavy seas, they were finally separated. The *Castillo Negro* must have sunk somewhere off the northwest coast; she was never heard of again. *El Gran Grifon*, unable to make headway and with her bows still damaged by English shot, was driven back before the wind and eventually wrecked on Fair Isle, between the Orkneys and the Shetlands.

The *Valencera* was left, and by now her condition must have been a cause of great concern. On September 12 she was hit by yet another storm from the southwest; her bows, like those of *El Gran Grifon*, could take no more and she began to leak heavily, beyond the capacity of her pumps. With increasing and unwanted extra weight forward, she was in great danger of sinking. Reluctantly, the officers decided that the only course was to let her run before the wind in the hope of reaching land before she went under.

Evidently the *Valencera*'s navigators had not the slightest idea of their exact position. Running on before the wind, they sighted land which the pilots thought was the group of islands known as the Blaskets, which are actually at the other end of Ireland, off Kerry. Their navigation was about 300 nautical miles out; the land they sighted was Malin Head and the island Inishtrahull, to the north of Malin; the fact that Inishtrahull is a single island with some outlying rocks is not significant, as closer inshore were the Garvan Islands, which undoubtedly led the Spaniards into thinking they were off Kerry instead of Donegal, mistaking the Garvans for the Blaskets.

In one respect at least the *Valencera* was lucky; the wind, probably from the southwest, eased behind Malin Head and she was able to hug the shore quite closely before entering Glenagivney (now Kinnagoe) Bay, east of Malin Head and at the tip of the remote peninsula called Inishowen, which forms the western boundary of the entrance to Lough Foyle, itself dividing Donegal and Derry.

The *Valencera* sought shelter in Glenagivney on September 14. It is not a sheltered bay except in a south or southwest wind, but it probably represented haven to hard-pressed sailors. For two days and nights they had been constantly at the pumps in an effort to keep the ship afloat. Now they were within swimming distance of the shore. Some two hundred yards off the mainland the ship stopped and dropped anchor. As it happened, she was almost on a reef which lies underwater at that point. Perhaps she struck it, ran a little way up and then stopped (if this was so, the depositions of the survivors fail to make it clear).

The *Valencera* was obviously now in such poor condition that her officers had to decide whether to abandon or not. She was perilously close to sinking, and the first task had to be to get her complement ashore as soon as possible before they too went to the bottom. This was easier decided than performed; there was just one boat aboard the Venetian and even that apparently was damaged.

Help came from an unexpected quarter. On shore small groups of men had already appeared. The O'Doherty clan, although under English control, inhabited this remote and almost inaccessible peninsula. Sir John O'Doherty, the sept chieftain, had his headquarters in a castle at Alliagh, some three miles north of Derry, then increasingly under the thumb of English forces seeking a stronger foothold in the north of the country to drive a wedge between the O'Neills and O'Donnells.

Sir John had been loyal to the English for some time, but like all the northern chieftains, his loyalty had a questionable ring – it was for survival's sake rather than of the heart. His territory and lands were vulnerable and he knew it; at the same time he was prepared in secret to help the Spaniards if he could, although any aid he could give was limited and must not reach the ears of the English.

O'Doherty had probably had the *Valencera* under close scrutiny once she had passed Malin Head, because by the time she anchored in Glenagivney something of a reception committee was waiting on shore. The Spaniards would have been unable to determine whether the natives were friendly or not, and so a reconnaissance party embarked in the single small boat and rowed ashore. 'They landed with rapiers in their hands,' says a contemporary report, 'whereupon they found four or five savages who bade them welcome and used them well until twenty more wild men came unto them, after which time they took away a bag of money.' Another report, this time to Fitzwilliam, says merely that 'part of O'Dogherty's men have been familiar amongst the Spaniards'. Probably the Spaniards stepped ashore prepared for anything, to be met by a few natives, later augmented by a much larger number. Bargaining took place, and 'O'Dogherty's men went unto them with boats and did bring them to the shore.'

Agreement had been reached quickly: the natives were paid for their services and gave them. Bringing the entire complement of the sinking *Valencera* to the mainland was begun immediately with small boats, some of them belonging to O'Doherty and augmented by the ship's damaged cock-boat. By then the wind and seas had probably gone down, helping the ferrying operation, yet it was a huge task for such small craft and took two days, working day and night. Even then it was not fully accomplished when, on the 16th, the *Valencera* sank suddenly in the bay. About forty men were drowned, the remainder of those aboard swimming ashore or being saved by the boats. About 350 men survived on the mainland.

By now de Luzon and the senior officers would have known their precise whereabouts and have been disillusioned of their earlier belief that they had doubled 'Cape Clear, in Ireland' and were 'towards Blasket'. They were well armed and under the command of one of the most experienced soldiers in the Armada, de Luzon. But against that they were probably short of food and dependant on the natives and the barren countryside for survival. The extent of the aid which they needed to survive was doubtful too: while O'Doherty may have been willing, his hands were tied by his own equally desperate need for survival.

The only possible solution was to march towards the extreme northeast corner of Ireland, deep into Antrim, where they might get a ship to take them to Scotland. That part of Antrim was, as we have seen, controlled by the Scottish McDonnells and almost free of English interference at the time. Certainly it represented the best chance of both keeping freedom and reaching Spain.

There was, however, one crucial barrier. Between Inishowen peninsula and the haven that was Antrim stretched the deep waters of Lough Foyle, to the east of where the survivors of the *Valencera* were assembling on the shores of Glenagivney Bay. To reach the opposite shore, it was necessary to march along the western shores of Foyle until Derry was reached and the Foyle River could be crossed. And Derry was rapidly becoming an English stronghold, the chieftains around it (including O'Doherty) subservient to the Queen, including even the great O'Cahan. To find a vessel big enough to cross the mouth of Foyle and so to the opposite shore, within a few short miles of Antrim (which itself starts close to Portrush, a few miles east of Lough Foyle) was beyond the natives. The only solution was to march to Derry, under the guidance of the clansmen for much of the way. Once near Derry and in the area of English influence, however, the Spaniards would be on their own; they could expect no help from O'Doherty once within his immediate area.

De Luzon had undoubtedly weighed up the many factors before making his decision. The most pressing reason for prompt action was the supply

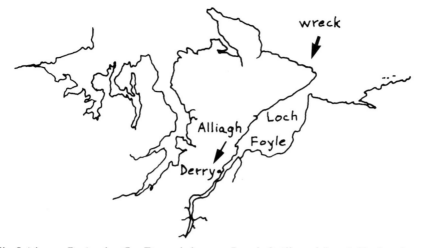

The Inishowen Peninsula, Co. Donegal, between Lough Swilly and Lough Foyle, where the Trinidad Valencera *was wrecked in Glenagivney (now Kinnagoe) Bay. The survivors hoped to reach Antrim and sail to Scotland, and marched along the shore of Lough Foyle towards Derry. At Alliagh (Illagh) they were massacred by a force of Irish soldiery under English command. Some Spaniards escaped; others were marched to Drogheda. The wreck of the* Trinidad *was discovered in 1971.*

situation; feeding 350 men was not an easy task in a strange country surrounded by enemies on one side and water on the other. They must start at once and march towards Derry, hoping by their strength of arms and numbers to intimidate possible attackers. The appearance of such a small army would, however, have been illusory; they had been trained and well equipped soldiers it is true, but there the resemblance to a formidable force would have ended. These men had been at sea on and off since the end of May, subsisting on food which had grown almost inedible; they had been through several sea battles and repeated storms, both of which had sapped strength and morale. Like all ships' crews of the period, following a voyage of any length many would have been sick and weak. Certainly, however well led, they were in no fit condition for a long march in cold weather with perhaps a strenuous battle or two. Only limited stores, arms and ammunition would have been brought ashore in the short time before their ship sank.

Good soldier that he was, de Luzon would have known this, but there was nothing else he could do. The columns formed up into something resembling a military formation and the straggling army set off south for Derry. Army discipline nevertheless prevailed. De Luzon made his men march in order, with drums beating and banners flying. Undoubtedly their appearance would have been impressive; de Luzon must have hoped so.

Slowly the Spaniards made their way down along the western shore of Lough Foyle towards Derry. It is by far the most direct route, then as now,

A bronze and wrought-iron swivel gun raised from the Trinidad Valencera *at Kinnagoe Bay, Co. Donegal. The piece was found loaded and ready to fire. (Colin Martin)*

but it may well have been that de Luzon hoped to commandeer enough boats to bring his men across the rapidly widening waters of Lough Foyle. If so, he was disappointed. It was a march of perhaps thirty miles, mostly along the loch shore, and in all that distance de Luzon found no boats in sufficient numbers to take the party across Foyle. It was a slow march also; assuming that they had left Glenagivney on either the 16th or 17th of September, it was certainly at least three to four days, and possibly longer, before they came within three miles or so of Derry. The march, with dying and wounded men as well as those who were ill and weak, cannot have been an easy one.

They had reached Sir John O'Doherty's castle at Allagh (or Alliagh, now Galliagh, three miles or so north of Derry, the outlines of the castle remaining to this day). Why they ended up in this area is puzzling: it can only be because they were guided there by clansmen, since Galliagh is well off the road by which de Luzon and his men would have travelled from the tip of the peninsula south towards Derry.

Some confusion arises because of the existence of two castles. Besides that of O'Doherty himself, there was another, apparently close by, in which lived 'an Irish bishop named Cornelius'. This can only have been Cornelius, Bishop of Down and Connor; the fact that he was a Catholic Bishop and thus of the same religion as the Spaniards, and also that he had a reputation for helping fugitives to hide from the English, may have persuaded de Luzon to go there. It is also possible, if less savoury, that a trap was laid for de Luzon, the Bishop being used as bait to bring the Spaniards within range of O'Doherty's castle, where a strong garrison of English troops awaited them.

This was certainly possible, but if it was the case, O'Doherty had played his cards uncommonly shrewdly. Fitzwilliam had already received a report dated September 18 which said in part that 'withall part of O'Dogherty's men have been familiar among the Spaniards since their landing, and it is said that

O'Dogherty himself hath been in speeches with them, which I think the rather to be true, for that he hath a fair target, a murrion, and a halberd of theirs which argueth to be received rather as a gift than to be had by any other means.' That his clansmen had hired boats to the Spaniards, helped to procure food, and guided them at least some of the way from outer Inishowen seems proof enough that whatever his outward loyalties, O'Doherty was prepared to help the Spaniards to a considerable degree. It is doubtful, therefore, that he had led them into a trap at the end of it all.

De Luzon was too old a hand to be caught by any tricks at this stage; when some distance from the castles he sent a messenger to Cornelius outlining their situation and asking for both help and advice. The Bishop's hands were tied, but he sent the messenger back with word that the Spaniards should fake an attack on his castle and that he would give it up to them under such conditions, believing that the English would think that de Luzon had taken it by force, thus freeing Cornelius from the suspicion of aiding the Spaniards.

De Luzon directed his party towards the castle and fired off a shot. Something checked him at this stage, however, and he became uneasy. He was on a stretch of boggy, marshy ground at one side of which stood the ruins of an old building, and he decided to use the shelter of its crumbling walls before going any further. But now a hint of betrayal had entered his mind; as his men crossed towards the ruin, a large force of mounted soldiers suddenly appeared. The English, their presence long feared and long rumoured, had come on the scene.

In fact, the 'two hundred soldiers' who now appeared out of nowhere to challenge the Spanish party were not English but Irish soldiers in English pay. They were led by Richard and Henry Hovenden (Hoveden or Oveden), two professional soldiers who were actually cousins of the Earl of Tyrone (they are sometimes also called foster brothers). Together with a Major Kelly (also Irish) they commanded mounted soldiers, all of whom were Irish. The force was there because of Fitzwilliam. He had had the Hovendens' report, written from Castle Berte on the 18th, telling him of the presence of the Spaniards in the area. Although he had not had time to reply to their first note before they met the Spaniards, they knew him well enough to know what his instructions would be, and so acted themselves. Their first note had said 'we are 150 men and will God willing be doing with the Spaniards as we may find our best advantage, though we are in doubt whether the country be true to us or not.' This was sent from Castle Berte just a couple of days before they met the Spaniards near Alliagh.

The Hovendens' position is in many ways typical not only of the Ireland of the day but of the Irish themselves. Here were two kinsmen of Tyrone himself, who was opposed in every fibre to the presence of Englishmen on his own soil. Tyrone was biding his time in the wings, watching every move – and remember that the *Valencera*'s survivors were the first from the Armada to land in Ireland. Yet while he must theoretically have sympathized with them for many reasons, his own avowed kinsmen the brothers Hovenden commanded *Irish* soldiers in *English* pay *against* de Luzon – an Irishism if ever there was one. If the Spaniards later on thought the Irish to be unreliable and unpredictable, they had sound grounds.

This was in many ways a historic moment in Irish history – the first meeting of a largish body of Spanish invaders with the forces of the defending occupiers. Many of the once great and now dying chieftains of Ireland, particularly those in the northwest, had waited years for this to happen. And now when it did occur, it was an anticlimax; a Spanish force spent, weak, and demoralized by successive hardships and privations, unable to do more than turn and wait for what might happen next.

What did happen was forseeable. Each force was sizing up the other and waiting for the first move. The Spaniards had by far the larger company, probably double that of the Hovendens, and were well armed and disciplined into the bargain. The bulk of them would have been trained soldiers of one of Spain's best regiments, the Neapolitan *Tercio*. But months of hardship and confined quarters had reduced them greatly. The Hovendens led troops which were, on later evidence, well trained and, above all, mounted. Boggy and marshy though the ground might be, a horseman was incalculably more effective than a tired man on foot. It has been alleged more than once that the

One of the two fifty-pound siege cannon recovered from the wreck of the Valencera *being lowered into a conservation bath by members of the City of Derry Sub-Aqua Club, which has conducted the excavation. (Colin Martin)*

Irish force had besides 200 horsemen a similar number of 'footmen, arquebusiers and bowmen'. There is little evidence of this; the brothers themselves admitted to '150 men' and later on to 'not being more than 140'. From what later occurred, there is no reason to doubt them.

Both sides now faced each other across a stretch of wet ground. Drums beat, the recognized signal for a parley, and spokesmen from each side walked cautiously forward into the space between the two forces. The Hovendens' description is probably the more accurate, apart from a few discrepancies (of which more later):

We came up with them [the Spaniards] in a village of Sir John O'Dogherty, called Illagh. We sent an emissary to learn who they were, and what was their intention in thus invading a part of the dominions of H M the Queen. They made answer that they had come with the intention of invading England and formed part of the Armada which had been beaten by the English fleet, and that they had been obliged by stress of weather to land in this place.

De Luzon and his men asked that they be allowed to hire a ship to take them back to Spain, a request naturally enough turned down by the Hovendens, who demanded instead that they surrender as prisoners of war. De Luzon replied that if this was the only alternative, then they would die rather than submit. The Hovendens took time to think about that, and then came back with the patently false assertion that if they did not surrender, three thousand English troops would arrive shortly and 'cut all their throats'. So far not a shot had been fired in anger. De Luzon still refused to surrender – probably he took the threat for exactly what it was. And so the talks ended in a form of stalemate; both sides turned away from each other.

By this time it was growing dark; the Spaniards did not know the country at all and to march off in darkness was an obvious folly against troops who doubtless knew their ground. There was nothing to do except wait for daylight, and they prepared to spend an uncomfortable and damp night; through the long hours of darkness sporadic attacks on their outposts punctuated the night but were repulsed with insignificant losses. When morning came at last, the Spanish force was still intact.

Once more the drums sounded for further talks. De Luzon, Captain Hieronimo de Aybar and Captain Beltran del Salto formed the Spanish deputation, Major Kelly and the Hovendens the English. Kelly's tone was noticeably tougher in the bright light of morning, but his terms for surrender seemed a great deal more lenient. If the Spaniards laid down their arms, he would ensure them all a safe conduct to Dublin and to Fitzwilliam, who he said, would then send them on to the Queen. De Luzon still held out for better terms, but in his heart knew that he had little recourse other than surrender. His men were very short of food and surrounded by an enemy force which would ensure that no supplies would reach them. He demanded that each man be allowed to keep his clothes and that the terms already offered by Kelly be adhered to; only then would he agree to surrender his arms. This was agreed to, and one by one every Spaniard gave up his sword or pistol.

Possibly no-one was more relieved than Kelly and the Hovendens; they had relatively few men, and while the Spaniards were obviously weakened, to take them by force would have taxed them to the utmost. But this was not enough: as soon as the Spaniards had handed over their arms, the soldiers stripped them of their clothes and left them naked; anyone who resisted was killed. De Luzon, furious at this instant breaking of an officer's word, demanded that the promises made by Kelly should be kept, but Kelly replied that the soldiers had disobeyed him and that he would make sure that all the Spaniards would be dressed at a castle several miles further on.

By this time a plan was evidently hatching in the Irish minds. De Luzon was told to get the men moving towards the castle where they would all spend the night, but when they had covered about a mile, Kelly announced that as the road was so rough and progress so slow they would all pass the night where they stood. The Spanish officers and gentlemen were separated from the remainder of the party and placed inside a square; they included de Luzon, the captains, del Salto, de Aybar, de Guzman and Manrique; Don Rodrigo Lasso, Don Antonio Manrique, Don Diego de Luzon and Don Sebastian Zapata, and several clerics. Some officers were left with the men; the latter spent the night without a stitch of clothing and in the damp cold of a northern September.

Once more an anxious, tiring night was spent by the Spaniards. De Luzon must have guessed that their Irish captors had little intention of keeping their promise of guiding all the Spaniards to Dublin: the separation of officers and gentlemen from the other ranks indicated that further treachery was likely. And so it was to prove. At first light, any officers left among the majority of the Spaniards were taken from their men and placed inside the square with the other officers. Then the rest of the Spaniards were ordered into an open field nearby; a line of arquebusiers on one side of them, and a line of cavalry on the other, ready and waiting, made hideously clear what was about to happen. The order was given; shots rang out and the cavalry charged. For a few minutes all was bedlam as the officers watched helpless from only a short distance away, and when the smoke cleared and the horses had been reined to a halt, well over half of the 350 Spaniards lay on the field. The others had fled in all directions, and about a hundred or so got away safely, many of them wounded. They were given refuge in the Bishop of Down and Connor's castle, and many later reached Scotland through the offices of the McDonnells of Antrim and O'Cahan of Dungiven. Many died in Ireland from the wounds received in the fighting.

This episode is one of the more brutal in the history of the Armada survivors in Ireland, more so perhaps because of broken promises than because of the fact that well over two hundred Spaniards were slaughtered. That the soldiers who did the killing were Irish, although technically English, underlined the horror of this massacre and left a permanent scar on the record of the native Irish in their dealings with shipwrecked Spaniards.

History differs from the Hovendens' account: their story of the 'battle' is vastly different from those of three survivors of it, Juan de Nova, Francisco de Nova and de Luzon himself. Of the massacre, the brothers reveal so little that one could be forgiven for imagining that it had never taken place,

seeing that they were more than six hundred men, we encamped at nightfall at a distance of a musket shot, we not being more than one hundred and forty. Towards midnight, we commenced skirmishing with them for about two hours, killing the *tiente de campo* and more than two hundred men besides, causing them moreover much loss in wounded, without our having lost more than one man.

This report to Fitzwilliam, written from Dungannon on the 24th some days after the massacre, is nothing less than a travesty of the real truth, but it elated him. Another threat had been erased.

O'Donnell now entered the scene; he had met the Hovendens shortly after the massacre, although how is not made clear. His son was held in Dublin Castle and evidently he was anxious to do what he could to ingratiate himself with Fitzwilliam to secure his release. The Hovendens told Fitzwilliam that

O'Donill and we have come with some of them [the senior officers among the Spaniards] to Dongainne [Dungannon] with the intention of bringing them to your Lordship, for which effect we beg you will be pleased to give orders that rations may be allowed them, as the prisoners are very weak and unable to march, and also should it appear proper to your Lordship that carts and horses be provided for their conveyance to Dublin. The chief of them [de Luzon] has a certain air of majesty, and has been [twenty-four years ago] in command of 30,000 men. Among the other prisoners are persons of quality.

Earlier O'Donnell had signified his willingness to side with the English against the Spaniards, according to the Hovendens' letter of September 18 to Fitzwilliam in which they alleged that O'Donnell

is willing to serve against them, and hath none of his country as yet come in to him, passing thirty horsemen; he hath sent for all his forces, but it is doubtful whether they will come to him or not.

On October 6, Patrick Foxe had informed Sir Francis Walsingham that

a great number of the Spaniards that were stript naked by the soldiers that serve under the leading of both the Hovedens [sic] are now come to the other Spaniards that landed in M'Sweeny's country, and thither brought by the Bishop of Derry, a most seditious Papist, and a man very like to procure great aid to the Spaniards if he can; O'Donnell is lately come up with a company of Spaniards that were taken prisoners, to the number of thirty, and is a suitor for the liberty of his son now pledge in the Castle of Dublin, in consideration that he lately hath served against the Spaniards.

However concerned about the welfare of his son, O'Donnell's behaviour in actively pursuing and capturing fugitive Spaniards is totally inexcusable: it quite probably amazed and delighted Fitzwilliam, who was unused to such willing co-operation from that quarter. As badly as O'Donnell behaved, however, the conduct of Hugh O'Neill, Earl of Tyrone, was even more reprehensible (O'Donnell at least had a plausible reason in that his son was captive in Dublin.) Tyrone was not the head of the O'Neill clan during the period of the Armada, this position being taken by Tirlach Lynagh O'Neill, by now an oldish man who had been the titular O'Neill for many years (his behaviour was exemplary). His way of greeting these Spaniards who had at long last landed in Ireland was nothing short of treacherous and represented a complete *volte face* on his part. The State Papers hold the bald facts which condemn him beyond argument: on October 21 he wrote to Fitzwilliam asking for 'munition and a commission of martial law', and saying that he would provide 'a month's victuals for my company to go against the Spaniards'. At this stage many of the Irish soldiers who had served under the Hovendens at the massacre near Derry had apparently run away, and Tyrone threatened 'severe punishment' for them and asked that Capt. (sic) John Kelly would join him to move against the Spaniards.

Nor was this all. Henry Hovenden, one of the brothers, echoed Tyrone's call for help and advised that he (Tyrone) should be supplied with munition 'that he may attack the Spaniards before they depart.' Tirlach Lynagh was infuriated by his kinsman's behaviour and promptly sent five hundred cattle to relieve the hungry Spaniards in Ulster and, it was alleged, prepared to make war on Tyrone in retribution, an allegation which Sir Richard Bingham, who as always appeared to be everywhere, passed on to Fitzwilliam with the comment that the report 'that T. Lynagh O'Neill hath entertained the Spaniards to make war on the Earl of Tyrone to be suspected.' Fitzwilliam, Bingham warned, should 'stand highly upon his guard, for between O'Neill, the Earl and the Spaniards he may too deeply engage himself.'

Bingham's fears that Tirlach Lynagh would make war on Tyrone may have stemmed from a report made two days earlier by William Taaffe to Fenton and George Bingham to that effect; the report had added that O'Donnell and his men had stayed with Tyrone to aid him against O'Neill. In the end, although O'Neill 'bitterly reproved' Tyrone, the whole affair fizzled out and nothing more positive was done.

We have left the survivors of the *Valencera* at the scene of the massacre near Derry; what happened afterwards is easily told. Many survived to reach Spain – that is, of those rank-and-file soldiers and seamen who had escaped the sword and ball of the Irish on the field of battle, if battle one can term it. Some, mostly wounded, were sent through the O'Cahans to Sorley Boy McDonnell in Antrim and he shipped most of them to Scotland, defying Fitzwilliam's express and explicit instructions to the contrary. The Bishop of Down and Connor arranged the passage of 'one hundred or so, who were unwounded' to the 'Island of Ibernia' (probably one of the Scottish Isles). They made their way to Edinburgh 'where the King was' and he in turn sent them to France, where thirty-two of them landed on December 27. Among them were de Nova and de Borja who had been sent on by Sorley Boy, and it was there, at Calais, that they met the Armada's chief navigator, Captain Marolin de Juan. Other Spaniards from the *Valencera* also made their more devious ways home, many through Scotland and on to France; but the total number who survived was pathetically small – how small we do not know, but at most in the low hundreds. Some stayed on in the north and were still there eight years later.

A party of roughly forty-two were kept prisoner by the Hovendens after the massacre, and these were marched first to Dungannon, from where the Hovendens wrote elatedly to Fitzwilliam with their twisted story of what had happened, and then later to Drogheda, there to be imprisoned. They were kept purely for ransom purposes, but only two are known to have survived for long enough to be ransomed. De Luzon himself was one, the other being Don Rodrigo Lasso; both were still prisoners in 1591, when they were in London, possibly in the house of Sir Horatio Pallavicini (Palavicino), a Genoese banker. It is probable that these two eventually reached Spain in exchange for the mysterious Monsieur de Nowe and Tyllyny, his son.

Of the remainder, little is known. Some died on the march to Drogheda: Hernando de Canavera, while crossing a river; Don Pedro de Salto (a son of Captain Beltran del Salto?) 'died before they surrendered' at fourteen years of age; Don Diego de Guzman, Don Antonio Manrique, Don Alvaro de Mendoza and Rodrigo Ponce de Leon were all so ill that they must have died early on. Three died in Drogheda: Don Diego de Luzon, a young brother of the Colonel, Don Sebastian Zapata and Sergeant Antonio de Bacia. Nothing is known of the others.

The list of prisoners in Drogheda includes the captain of the *Barca de Amburg*, whose survivors de Luzon had taken aboard the *Valencera* somewhere off northwest Donegal, sharing this act of mercy with the *Gran Grifon*. Beltran del Salto in all probability died in Drogheda, as also did Hieronimo Aybar, who had played a prominent role throughout, and the ship's captain of the *Valencera*, Horatio Donai. But all those who reached Drogheda were not officers or gentlemen, and it is the list of those other names, of drummers, ship's boys, servants, ship's clerks and even a humble barber, which perhaps strike the saddest chord.

IX

The Sheriff of Clare

OF all the provinces of Ireland to suffer from the colonial policies pursued vigorously by Elizabeth, Munster, comprising roughly the southwest corner of the island, was the major victim. There were diverse reasons for this; Leinster and the capital of Dublin were both perhaps even more influenced by England, but there were pockets of resistance, particularly in Wicklow, which continued to be a thorn in Elizabeth's flesh throughout her reign. Munster was different. The very fact that it more than any other province was singled out for a relentless policy of subjection, despoliation, and later on colonial settlement was owing primarily to its richness of land and comparative ease of access. It was a settled province in that for many hundreds of years the ancient clan systems had built up and maintained the land for agricultural use; Munster land is still the best in the world for cattle breeding and the Elizabethans knew its value.

The Desmonds (Fitzgeralds) were the primary landowners before the Crown took over. In 1585, for instance, the Earl of Desmond technically owned nearly 600,000 acres; by that time, the Desmond Rebellion against English authority had been crushed and these vast territories, rich and fertile, lay at the mercy of Elizabeth's wishes. Munster had been swept clean of any further sign of Irish restlessness and retaliation; the stage was set for its plantation. Within a few short years many younger sons of English landed gentry, invited by their queen, had come to Munster to receive lands under the plantation scheme, paying Elizabeth a rent of threepence an acre in Limerick and Kerry, and twopence an acre in Cork and Waterford. Their holdings by modern standards were enormous, ranging from 3000 acres to 12,000.

Although Ireland was in effect a foreign nation to English settlers, the attractions of what was more or less a free offer were enormous and there was for a time at least no shortage of eager planters seeking land in the province; there were ample and tempting conditions attached to their taking up the lands which even added further to the lure of Ireland. The lands were rent free until 1590 and for the following three years at half rent; imports from and exports to England were tariff-free for ten years; and perhaps most important of all their security of tenure and family would be ensured by

English garrisons. These Munster planters came to be known appropriately as the Undertakers. They included many prominent men of the day: Sir Thomas Norris, one of the famous Norris brothers, who had 6000 acres in Cork; Sir Walter Raleigh, with 12,000 acres in Cork and Waterford; Sir Warham St Leger, with 6000 acres in Cork; the Earl of Ormond, with 3000 acres in Tipperary; and Edmond Spenser, the poet-secretary of Lord Grey de Wilton, at one time Lord Deputy, who had 3000 acres in Cork.

The Munster plantation, however, was not a success. After the initial burst of interest the offers of Irish lands did not meet with the desired response. Life in Ireland held its own dangers despite assurances to the contrary, and finally just over half of the Desmond lands were taken by English planters. And the planters were to become, in the manner of many who settle in Ireland, more Irish than the Irish themselves.

There was one welcome effect from Elizabeth's point of view, however, and that was the comparative peace which followed the beginnings of the plantation and which enabled her increasingly to turn her attentions towards the wayward Ulster chieftains. The peace in Ulster was an uneasy one. The McDonnells of Antrim were held in check by a promise from James of Scotland; the O'Neill (Tirlach Lynagh) was aging and disinclined to war; but O'Donnell kept a shifting balance of freedom during the 1580s, leaving himself at all times room for manoeuvre, and the Earl of Tyrone was beginning to exercise the diplomatic talents which later made him the most formidable opponent of Elizabethan policies in Ireland during Elizabeth's reign. The peace of Munster allowed the English authorities to consolidate their hold on the territory with a more sophisticated system of administration and the garrisoning of strategic points. It was during this period that the Armada sailed against England, and later, that the first ships of the fleet came down on the coast of the province.

They created an instant panic, partly because their strength and intentions were unknown. The mere sight of so many vessels, great ships of war with towering masts and gun-ports bristling with cannon and decks swarming with armed soldiers, was enough to strike fear into every Englishman who gazed on them. But gradually the panic wore off; these Spaniards who had at first appeared so awesomely invincible were after all little more than shells of men weakened by deprivation and illness and who sought help and not war on the shores of Ireland.

But that first wave of panicky terror is understandable: the Armada ships seemed to be everywhere – in bays, in creeks, up the Shannon into the very heart of Munster, off the coast and around every corner came galleons, galleasses and merchantmen, with their hordes of small tenders. The improved English system of local government, with its network of sheriffs and spies, came into its own; from every corner of the province where ships were sighted came speedy and usually accurate reports, all rushed by road and mountain track to land eventually on Fitzwilliam's desk.

One of the first to sight and report the Armada ships off Munster was the Sheriff of the newly formed County of Clare; the territory had formerly been known as Thomond and the boundaries of the present-day Co. Clare follow remarkably closely those of the ancient Thomond. The Sheriff of Clare was Boetius Clancy, an Irishman loyal to the Crown, and a local administrator in English pay; Clare was at that time in the province of Connacht, having been included in 1584 by Perrott's shiring. It was annexed to Munster in 1602. Boetius Clancy was also a Member of Parliament for Clare in 1583 and 1613.

On September 16 Clancy sent a fast messenger to Bingham with the news that not only had Armada ships been seen close in to the Clare shore but that a boat had come adrift from one of them and he had captured it, empty. Spaniards off one ship had 'offered to land the last night in one of the cock-boats, which they could not do by reason of weather and the harbour [at Liscannor]. I do here watch with the most part of the inhabitants of the barony [of Kilmurry-Ibrickane, between Miltown Malbay and Doonbeg], and shall so continue till I learn further certainty, and as I shall learn I will advertize your worship.' Clancy enclosed with this message a piece of board which his men had found in the cock-boat that had drifted ashore; Bingham in turn sent it on to Fitzwilliam with the comment that there was 'some mystery hidden under the burne of three letters; but it should seem to be a mark under the K.P., the Catholic King's name.' He was right: the Spaniards had come to the shores of Ireland.

Clancy kept a close eye on the ships which crossed and re-crossed in the Atlantic. From the soaring and sheer Cliffs of Moher he could look down upon the Aran Islands, a few short miles out to sea at the mouth of Galway Bay. 'Last night two ships were seen about the islands of Arran, and it is thought that more sails were seen westward from the islands', he told Bingham. Closer at hand, however, on the southern side of the cliffs in the bay of Liscannor, was another Spanish ship; this was the vessel from which the Spaniards had attempted a landing only to be foiled by the weather, presumably as rough as usual. The galleass *Zuniga* remained there eight days, several times sending in men to obtain food and water, at all times heavily escorted by soldiers. On September 22 she weighed anchor and sailed off, finally reaching safety after an extraordinary series of misadventures (Chapter XI).

The *Zuniga* left behind a relic more interesting than the bit of wood or the cock-boat. On one of the trips ashore to take on supplies, the Purser, Petrus Baptista, had been taken prisoner, and among other matters revealed that the entire fleet was 'in great danger for want of bread, flesh, and water.' The myth of the invincible Spaniards was beginning to tarnish in English eyes. For the most part, as Clancy gradually discovered, the Spaniards tended to stay out at sea; his men watched the *Zuniga* while she was under the shelter of the cliffs in the bay but there were few signs of aggression. He must have regretted that the vessel could not be taken, but there was nothing he could do about it except to watch and wait.

The Cliffs of Moher in Clare, stretching northwards. Armada ships were sighted out at sea by lookouts on the cliffs, and the galleass Zuniga was seen close in, but escaped wrecking. Just to the south are Liscannor Bay, where she took on food and water, and Mutton Island and Doonbeg where the San Marcos *and* San Esteban *were wrecked.* (Irish Times)

Further down the coast from Liscannor, however, came electrifying news, first to Clancy (who appears not to have been present at the scene of the disasters, but further up the coast guarding against possible action by the men aboard the *Zuniga*) and later on to the Mayor of Limerick and Stephen Whyte, the alderman brother of Edward Whyte, clerk of the Connacht Council. It came in a report by Nicholas Cahan (Kahane), one of Clancy's own minor officials who controlled the area further south, down the coast from Liscannor. Cahan had already been involved in negotiations with a party of Spaniards on the shores of the River Shannon, where a small group of ships had sought shelter. Following these talks he had moved upwards along the coast towards Clancy and at Doonbeg had received momentous news. 'God hath cast to the shore of Donbegg a great ship from St Sebastian's, wherein were 300 men all drowned but three score or thereabouts,' he wrote elatedly. 'Another great ship [is] cast in at I Breckane and lost; they had both men and munition coming out of Flanders . . . we, the forces of Thomond, were all every day and night watching them, until they were all gone, which is a great loss for us in this barony . . . these two ships were lost at Tuesday . . .'.

The two ships 'of St Sebastian's' and 'of Flanders' were both lost on the

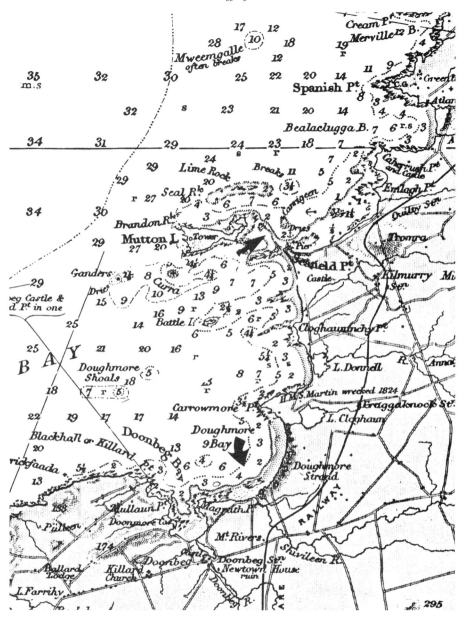

The southwest corner of Clare/Thomond, where two ships were wrecked. The San Marcos *hit a reef running out from Lurga Point on the mainland, directly east of Mutton Island in Malbay, while on the same day a few miles further south the* San Esteban *ran onto the White Strand north of Doonbeg.*

same day. Cahan wrote his report on the 12th (Old Style) (September 22 New Style); the Tuesday to which he referred would therefore have been Tuesday September 10, Old Style, or September 20, New Style. Both ships therefore were lost on September 20.

The ship of 'St Sebastian's' has long remained a mystery; the precise location of the wreck is variously given but appears to have been on the north side of Doonbeg Bay, on the White Strand, rather than on the south, which is more commonly accepted. Apart from tradition, which varies in the locality (a confusion perhaps caused by the wrecks of two large ships in quite a small geographical area), there is little more known of the wreck site.

From Cahan's own report, the size of the ship's company is known; 360 men was a substantial crew, implying that the vessel herself was large and probably of some note. Identification is helped further by the information that she apparently came from San Sebastian on the northern coast of Spain. This region, with a strong seagoing tradition, had supplied many ships to the Armada; they were in the Squadron of Guipuzcoa (that area of northern Spain along the Bay of Biscay which included San Sebastian) commanded by Miguel de Oquendo. There were twelve ships in the squadron, one of them a hulk (*Doncella*) and two others small tenders, the *pataches Asuncion* and *San Bernabé*. The rest were large oceangoing vessels of 291 tons up to 1200 tons.

If the ship wrecked at Doonbeg was from San Sebastian, there is little doubt that she was part of this Guipuzcoan Squadron; she was therefore one of nine

Looking northwest on Doonbeg beach, Co. Clare. On September 20 the San Esteban *was driven aground here; all but a handful of her complement of 264 were drowned. The survivors were later executed at Spanish Point, further up the coast.*

vessels, apart from the hulk and two tenders. Some are easily accounted for. The flagship *Santa Ana* reached Spain with Oquendo; the vice-flagship, the *Santa Maria de la Rosa*, sank in the Blasket Sound; the *San Salvador* caught fire in the English Channel and was towed into harbour by the English as a prize; the *Santa Cruz* reached Santander safely. This leaves five to be sifted through.

Four of these five reached Spain and Portugal; the *Santa Marta, Santa Barbara*, and *San Buenaventura* made it into home ports along the Guipuzcoan coast, while the *Maria San Juan* went all the way to Lisbon. This leaves us just one vessel, the *San Esteban*, which must therefore be the vessel wrecked at Doonbeg on September 20. Duro lists her merely as missing; but there is little doubt that it was this Guipuzcoan *nao* which was thrown onto the Clare coast.

The *San Esteban* displaced 736 tons and when she left Lisbon carried 26 guns and 264 men – some way short of Cahan's estimated 360. At Corunna, during the fleet reshuffle she was given just ten extra men, making a final tally of 274. But it is not necessary to take Cahan's figures literally; it is unlikely that he counted the bodies, or even that all of them came ashore. Furthermore, he was probably unused to the spectacle of so many dead: two hundred could have seemed three or four hundred. The survivors, thrown ashore at Doonbeg Bay half stunned and half drowned, posed little threat to the authorities; soldiers were waiting and all were taken prisoner. None were killed immediately as far as is known.

That Friday was a busy day for the Queen's officers. No sooner had they tidied up the situation at Doonbeg than word came from up the coast at Kilmurry-Ibrickane that another ship had gone aground a little way out to sea and that survivors were coming ashore.

Kilmurry-Ibrickane, the ancient barony, closely adjoins Doonbeg. It is landmarked by the still extant castle of Tromra, one of the many strongholds of the local chieftain Sir Turlough O'Brien, whose scattered family dominated the Thomond of their day, their lands extending over a huge area of northwest Munster. Tromra stands a short distance inland of a bleak and inhospitable coast, low-lying and desolate, with the equally low-lying Mutton Island almost directly to seaward.

This second ship had struck not the mainland but a reef close to Mutton Island, where she was breaking up. There are various rocks and reefs in the vicinity of the island and down the coast, but that in question is probably one directly inshore of Mutton Island, itself perhaps three-quarters of a mile off the mainland. At the point closest to the island, a long scar of bare rock reaches into the sea; it is a desolate and forbidding shoreline. It was probably at the seaward end of this reef running west from Lurga Point that this second ship was wrecked.

The seas were heavy that day – it was during one of the gales which caused so much havoc to many Armada ships – and the ship on the reef cannot have lasted long. The toll of dead and drowned was mounting as the crowds gathered on the mainland to watch. Just four bedraggled and exhausted

Tromra Castle near Quilty, Co. Clare; one of the castles of the O'Briens of Thomond, and still preserved, it may have sheltered survivors from the San Marcos, *wrecked nearby.*

sailors survived to reach the shore, where they were taken into captivity by a minor official named George Cusack. For many days afterwards wreckage and bodies came ashore along the coast, many dead Spaniards drifting ashore at Doolin and Ballaghaline further north up the coast, brought there by the swift currents along the shoreline.

What was this mysterious ship? Cahan himself says merely that she had 'men and munition coming out of Flanders' and that she was 'a great ship', meaning presumably that she was large. This limits the field of investigation only slightly; many ships in the fleet fit both of these isolated scraps of information.

There is, however, one possibly definitive clue to her identity. The sixty-odd survivors from the *San Esteban*, together with the four from the Mutton

Island wreck, were taken to Sheriff Clancy's castle near Spanish Point, north of Mutton Island. All were primarily soldiers and sailors, but among them (named in a brief list) appears the name of a Don Felipe de Cordoba. De Cordoba, a son of a prominent Spanish nobleman, Don Diego de Cordoba, was a gentleman adventurer who had shipped with the Armada at Lisbon, with his six servants. He now found himself, with some sixty of his fellow, but lower-born, Spaniards, within the cold walls of an English sheriff's castle.

Don Felipe de Cordoba had left Lisbon aboard the galleon *San Marcos*, a member of the Portuguese Squadron nominally commanded by Juan Martinez de Recalde but actually by the Duke of Medina Sidonia. The *San Marcos*, like all the Portuguese galleons, was one of the more significantly powerful vessels in the fleet; built for war and rough waters, they took the brunt of the fighting in the Channel and suffered terrible damage which resulted in two of these fine ships of war, *San Felipe* and *San Mateo*, meeting their end on the Dutch coast after the battle of Gravelines.

At Lisbon the *San Marcos* had 33 guns and 409 men, not including such menials as servants. As a member of the Portuguese squadron and one of the elite Armada fighting vessels, she doubtless carried a fair share of gentlemen and noblemen within her 790 ton bulk. Don Felipe was not the only person of high birth aboard; among the others were the Marquis of Penafiel, with no less than twenty-one servants (fourth highest number in the fleet); Don Enrique Enriquez de Guzman, a son of the Marquis of Navas; Don Garcia de Cardenas, a son of the Count of Pueblo; Don Alonso Tellez Giron, a son of the Duke of Osuna; Miguel de Gumarra, Alonso Ruiz, Alonso de Arquillos, and perhaps others. These few brought among them over fifty servants. The *San Marcos* also carried 292 soldiers; Francisco Perlines commanded 147 of these, Hernando de Olmedo another 46, while the remainder were of the company of Antonio Maldonado. There were 117 mariners. Probably well over 450 men were aboard, even allowing for wounds and illness. That just four pathetic wretches survived the wrecking of the *San Marcos*, within a short distance of the shore, a distance of which a good swimmer would think little, is a vivid testimony to the strength of wind and wave on that Friday in September.

Some doubt surrounds the fate of the survivors from the two ships. There is some evidence to support a theory that before the Spaniards were brought to Clancy's castle several were beheaded by soldiers from local garrisons, but this is disputable; the bulk of the prisoners were certainly incarcerated in the castle and later taken to a hill outside Spanish Point still called *Cnoc na Crocaire* (the Hill of the Gallows), and there hung before a crowd of natives and English officials, presided over no doubt by Boetius Clancy himself assisted by Sir Turlough O'Brien, Captain Mordaunt and a 'Mr. Morton'. Among those hung was Don Felipe de Cordoba; if there had been any intention to ransom him, it had been forgotten. The bodies were taken down and buried nearby in one common grave; their bones lie there today, in ground which is still known as the Spaniards' or Spanish Graveyard (*Tuama na Spainneach*). It is from the hangings at Gallows Hill and the subsequent burial of the victims nearby that present-day Spanish Point takes its name. No blame can be attached with any certainty to the native Irish who undoubtedly witnessed the wrecks, the captures and the hangings except perhaps to point out that no attempt was made to aid the Spaniards, of whom not one survived.

The two Clare wrecks are even yet of considerable interest. In a fairly highly populated area as was west Clare (Thomond), many items of interest were taken from the wrecks and existed for many years – even today there are items which could well have come from either the *San Esteban* or *San Marcos*. There is the magnificently carved door, possibly from a cabin of one of the wrecked vessels, which has done duty as a henhouse door on a Clare farm for many years; and then there is the superb table of oak with a mahogany top in Dromoland Castle, near Newmarket-on-Fergus, Co. Clare, to which is attached the Armada relic tradition. There are many, many tales still told by natives of possessions which their ancestors claimed came from the two wrecks: parts of masts, iron work, cannon balls of lead and stone, swords, knives and a dozen other smaller items. None of them can be verified, since most of the relics have long since disappeared, leaving behind only a strong verbal tradition, still vividly detailed.

Nicholas Cahan had a busy time in the days preceding the Tuesday of the Doonbeg and Mutton Island wrecks. He had been in the very south of Clare at the end of the previous week when reports had come that a group of seven ships, obviously of the Armada, had been seen off 'the Lupus Head' (Loop Head at the extreme southwestern tip of Clare, marking the northern tip of the Shannon River mouth which divides Limerick from Clare). Another group of four vessels was also seen off the head: possibly these were confused with each other. Cahan made post-haste for the area and arrived at Carrigaholt Castle, sheltered behind the long seaward jut of Loop Head. The castle, which still stands largely intact today, looks across the broadening Shannon at this point, with an excellent view of the best anchorage for large vessels in the entire lower reaches of this lengthy river (the longest in either Ireland or Britain).

The seven ships had anchored off Carrigaholt. Cahan sent off a terse note to Clancy with the bare information that 'seven ships from Flanders and Spain have arrived before Caryge-e-colle', a message which Clancy sent promptly to Bingham. It was September 15 when Cahan arrived at Carrigaholt, just five days before the two wrecks were to take place up the Clare coast. The ships remained at anchor in front of Carrigaholt. Though Cahan had no forces substantial enough to repel even a small party of Spaniards if necessary, these ships were not seeking confrontation; their sole object was to take on food and water, try to repair one hull which was apparently badly damaged and leaking heavily, and sail on the first fair wind for Spain. In other words, a breathing space.

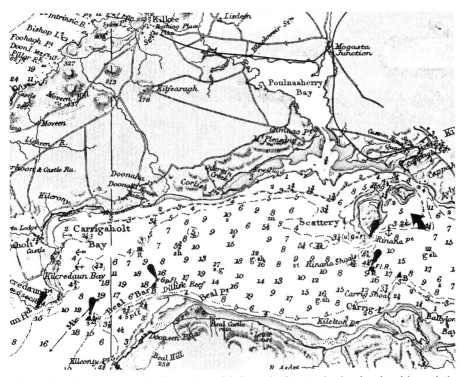

A day after the two wrecks to the north in Malbay, the Spaniards abandoned and burned the Annunciada *in Scattery Roads, near Kilrush on the River Shannon. She had been one of several ships sighted off Loop Head which had then anchored in Carrigaholt Bay. (This and preceding chart produced from portions of B A chart 2254 with the sanction of the Controller, HM Stationery Office and of the Hydrographer of the Navy)*

The Spaniards attempted landing in a small boat; Cahan and a local official, McSweeney, met them and a guarded discussion took place, both sides evidently playing for time and feeling each other out. This conference in all probability took place not at Carrigaholt but at Kilrush, directly upriver from Carrigaholt and on the Shannon, which here forms a sort of wide bay; Kilrush is on the same northern shore as Carrigaholt, and a short distance out into the river from the town is Scattery Island. Evidently it was near Scattery that the ships were: it is the best anchorage in the Shannon, protected from most winds and with room for manoeuvre where necessary. The State Papers called it 'Raviskeith' whereas the sixteenth century name of Scattery itself was 'Inishkeith'; there is no doubt that they are one and the same.

The fleet consisted of seven ships of which, according to Attorney General Sir John Popham (in a letter to Burghley of September 20, written from Cork), 'two are taken to be of a thousand tons apiece, two more of four hundred tons the piece, and three small barks', in other words, four large and three small vessels. A boat sent ashore to Kilrush tried to barter butts of wine for fresh water and it seems that some water at least was taken aboard, although the negotiations proved largely unsuccessful. One of the largest of the ships, according to Cahan, who saw her at anchor, was leaking badly 'and could not be mended'. All attempts at repair failed and eventually all her complement were transferred to the remaining vessels including the *Barca de Danzig* and the entire ship offered to the natives as payment for further aid. The offer was refused by Cahan; it appears that at least one party of Spaniards, desperate for food and water, then tried a forced landing but was easily repulsed. Cahan was doing his job well.

By now the wind was changing – the fair wind for Spain had, it seemed, come at last. The Spaniards were not prepared to wait much longer and began to weigh anchor and move out of the river towards the Atlantic. Before they did so, however, there was one remaining task; following strict Spanish practice they set fire to their abandoned ship. As they left Carrigaholt and Scattery behind, the big vessel burned to the gunwales and sank in the deep waters of the Shannon. On the 20th, the same day on which the *San Esteban* and *San Marcos* were driving onto the rocks just a few miles north up the Clare coast, the six ships sailed out of the Shannon and laid courses for Spain. The ill wind which drowned some seven hundred of their countrymen had brought them some benefit at least.

Cahan greeted their departure with relief. 'God be praised,' he wrote to Alderman Stephen Whyte and the Mayor of Limerick, 'those seven ships are gone but one ship they have burned and let her go to the shore.' Two days before he wrote that letter he had gone to Liscannor to help Boetius Clancy and was in time to witness the wrecks of the *San Esteban* and perhaps the immediate aftermath of the wreck of the *San Marcos*, both of which took place a short ride across the land from Kilrush. A couple of days later he was back in Kilrush, from where he sent his joyous report.

The ship which the Spaniards burned and sank at Scattery has usually been identified as the *San Marcos* – wrongly so. All the evidence points to her being not the *San Marcos* but the *Annunciada*, yet another ill-fated member of Don Martin de Bertendona's Levant Squadron.

The *Annunciada* was, like many ships in the Armada, a Ragusan vessel. Sixteenth century Ragusa-Dubrovnik, the forerunner of the modern Yugoslavia, had a formidable and often ignored naval tradition and supplied many ships to the Armada, far more than has been hitherto revealed. Ireland took a heavy toll of Ragusan ships; Dr John de Courcy Ireland, whose unique work in this specialized field of maritime research has brought to light the large role which Ragusan ships played in the Armada, has estimated that of all the vessels wrecked around Ireland several at least must have come from the shipyards of this thriving Adriatic republic. The *Annunciada* was a 700 ton converted merchantman, of Mediterranean build, carrying 24 guns and 275 soldiers and seamen. Like most of her squadron, in fact like most of the

Mutton Island, off Co. Clare, seen to the west from Lurga Point on the mainland. The long line of broken water running towards the island marks a reef on which foundered the San Marcos *during a gale on September 20. Most of her complement of some 400 perished; the survivors were later executed at Spanish Point nearby.*

Mediterranean or southern-built vessels, she had suffered greatly in the heavy weather and it was this probably more than any other factor which had caused her to leak so badly that she had to be abandoned and left to burn. All her crew and where possible the guns were removed at Scattery.

The English State Papers give the name of the captain of the ship burned in the Shannon as Doliste de Ivella and this name gives the vital clue to the ship's identity. Ivella is quite patently not a Spanish name but instead a corruption of a Yugoslav (Dubrovnik) name, Iveglia. With that established, we are on firmer ground, though Ragusan nomenclature is every bit as difficult as deciphering Spanish names. It is fairly clear that Doliste de Ivella is at least an English corruption of the name of a famous Ragusan seaman and shipowner, Ohmucevic Iveglia. The *Annunciada*'s Ragusan name was the *Presveta Anuncijata*; formerly she had been captained by another Ragusan, Nikola Olisti-Tasovic, who may have been with the Armada but on another Ragusan ship. Doliste de Ivella may quite possibly be a corruption of Olisti-Tasovic also (Iveglia, Ivella; Olisti, Doliste).

The *Annunciada* had brought arms and ammunition together with part of Don Alonso de Luzon's Regiment of Naples from Taranto to Spain, and later joined the rest of the Armada vessels assembling at Lisbon. She appears to have come through the Channel fighting relatively unscathed, but at Calais was damaged, possibly through a collision in the confusion after the fireships episode, and from then on was escorted by a little fleet of five tenders. These and other facts emerge from the deposition of Sergeant Alonso de Pares who had been aboard the *Annunciada*: according to him the vessel had sprung several bad leaks and was accompanied right around Scotland and down the west coast of Ireland by her attendant *pataches* and on reaching the mouth of the Shannon had put in for repairs, her officers realizing that she could go no further and was in imminent danger of sinking.

Modern Yugoslav authors have alleged that the survivors on the *Annunciada* were transferred in the Shannon to another Ragusan ship, the *Sveti Jerolim* (666 tons) which apparently failed to reach Spain. The *Sveti Jerolim* was commanded by Captain Peter Ohmucevic-Grguric, and since both he and Iveglia are known to have returned safely to Spain and indeed to 'have won distinction in later years fighting the English under the flag of Spain', it is unlikely that they were transferred to the *Sveti Jerolim*. All the evidence points instead to the entire complement of the *Annunciada* having been divided among the *pataches* and an *urca*, the *Barca de Danzig*, which later reached Spain, and which had joined the ships in the Shannon on the 13th, the day after the little group had first entered the river mouth.

Several Ragusan and one Italian account claim that Ohmucevic Iveglia was aboard the *Annunciada*, and the English State Papers appear to confirm this in giving the name Doliste de Ivella. Iveglia certainly survived to prove such a thorn in Elizabeth's flesh in later years that she wrote to Sultan Murad asking him 'to punish the town of which he [Iveglia] was suzerain that produced such a pest'. Iveglia is commemorated by a tomb in the Dominican Church in Dubrovnik.

It thus appears reasonably certain that the ship burned and abandoned in the Shannon was the *Annunciada*; it needs further evidence to consolidate this opinion, but it seems unlikely that this will ever be forthcoming. As in so many instances surrounding the identification of Armada ships wrecked around Ireland, absolute proof is elusive. In the final analysis, however, it seems there can be little doubt that it was not the *San Marcos* but the exotically-titled *Presveta Anuncijata*, Mediterranean built, Ragusan owned, and Spanish chartered, which burned and sank in the muddy brown waters of the River Shannon on September 20, 1588 as her crew sailed safely off to Spain.

X

The Drowning of the Saints

BY the fourth week of September the English authorities in Ireland were appealing frantically to London to send extra men and ammunition to resist any threat or possibility of invasion from the seemingly countless Armada vessels being sighted every day along the entire seaboard from Kerry to Donegal. The numbers of sightings may have been exaggerated: obviously many ships would have been seen several times, and their presence on the Irish coast multiplied in error as they moved down the coast. On the 19th, for instance, Vice-President Thomas Norris was writing to London that '140 sail were on the coast', a report which coincided with (or may have been inspired by) a similar one from Alexander Brywer and others to the Privy Council that there was 'a great fleet of Spaniards on the coast', this stemming from another report from Limerick a day earlier (18th) that '140 ships of the Armada, as it is thought, are beaten by stress of weather to the coast.'

In Dublin, Fitzwilliam and the Council were properly alarmed by such information; grimly they addressed a letter to the Privy Council in London in which they stressed that if the Spaniards should invade Ireland 'small hope of any assistance was to be had in the Pale against the Spaniards.' They sought arms and ammunition for 6000 men, a clear indication that they thought the existing forces in Ireland inadequate for the task which might face them.

Bingham, one of the first to be involved with the shipwrecked Spaniards, had already appealed to Fitzwilliam along much the same lines. 'I would wish (if it could so please your Lordship)', he wrote from Athlone on the 18th, 'that we had some lasts of powder with lead and match in the store here, for it is the thing we shall greatly want if stirs arise, and being there, it is as safe as in any other place, and hereof I beseech your Lordship to consider.' He felt that 'it were very convenient to levy a band of footmen of this country people, I mean such as have been soldiers, for is service come on we shall lack them . . . here is store of idle men. . . .' This idea was not acted upon; it might have eased Bingham's position, and his acute shortage of soldiery, if Fitzwilliam had seen fit to do so.

On the 20th Fitzwilliam and the Council were again urgently seeking help from London – they had 'neither men, money nor munition to answer these extraordinary services.' Evidently, in view of the reports now flooding in of more and more and yet more Spaniards they felt that the situation was becoming desperate.

The Privy Council had its own difficulties; it was now trying to cope with the disbanding of England's own Armada fleet, facing at the same time mounting pressure and dissatisfaction over its treatment of the fleet's sailors, many of whom were in as poor condition, if not worse, as the Spaniards. But the urgency of the need to reinforce Ireland's defences had at last sunk home, and they passed the requests from Dublin on to Elizabeth.

The Queen at least acted. A force was to be raised, embarking in the River Severn and proceeding from there to either Cork or Waterford. The task of organizing it was given to Sir Richard Grenville, one of the more prominent men of his day (a few years later he was to gain a permanent place in history with his historic fight against great odds in the *Revenge* in the Azores, which resulted in his death).

We require you [Elizabeth told Grenville] that upon the north coasts of Devon and Cornwall, towards the Severn, you make stay of all shipping meet to transport soldiers to Waterford, and to give charge that the same ships be made ready with masters, mariners, and all other maritime provisions needful, so as upon the next warning given from us or from our Council they may be ready to receive our said soldiers, which shall be three hundred out of Cornwall and Devon, and four hundred out of Gloucestershire and Somersetshire. We have also . . . some other further intention to use your service in Ireland with these ships aforesaid, whereof Sir Walter Rawley, knight, whom we have acquainted withal shall inform you, who also hath a disposition for our service to pass into Ireland, either with these forces or before they shall depart.

Elizabeth wrote that letter to Grenville on the 24th, and on the following day instructed the Lieutenants of the relevant counties concerned in setting up this force of seven hundred 'for putting men in readiness to march to Ireland within an hour's warning'. She had taken some action, but confined it to organizing a force, having it ready and prepared, and with ships waiting to take it to Ireland at short notice. So far, however, she seemed unwilling to actually send the troops until it became absolutely necessary (concern for her limited pocket was evident here: a long campaign in Ireland, even with a force of seven hundred soldiers, was a costly expense she could not really afford).

Fitzwilliam was still not satisfied and continued to pester Walsingham. On the 26th he asked the Secretary of State to 'hasten five or six ships from Bristol to the Irish coast to destroy the forty [how the number had shrunk] sea-beaten vessels returning to Spain.' But on the same day Sir Henry Wallop of the Council was writing to Burghley saying that the threat to Ireland from the Spaniards appeared to be almost totally diminished; there was, he assured Burghley, 'no fear of any hurt by foreign invasion this year.'

The 'sea-beaten vessels' had in the meantime had a rough time of it; the logbooks and other reports and depositions from those who endured the hardships of the long voyage home to Spain, sparsely detailed as they are, nonetheless tell a grim tale of privation and a desperate fight for survival. Apart from the endemic weaknesses caused by bad food, sickness, wounds, cramped quarters and the thousand and one horrors attendant on long voyages in the sixteenth century, the weather had been terrible, the fleet buffetted and tossed about by unceasing gales and headwinds. Sea-beaten they were – and who would blame them.

One of the more closely detailed accounts of this voyage around Scotland and Ireland and back to Spain comes from the paymaster of the Castilian Squadron, Marcos de Aramburu; but while his seamanlike log-keeping and observations on weather are fascinating in themselves, his account is of special value since he witnessed the sinking off Kerry of another Armada vessel, the *Santa Maria de la Rosa*.

Aramburu's classic narrative 'Account of what happened to Marcos de Aramburu, controller and paymaster of the galleons of Castile in the vice-flagship of those under his charge' begins not off Kerry but deep into the Atlantic close on a third of the way to Iceland from the northwest of Ireland, near Rockall, a remote speck of storm-washed rock, barren and inhospitable and some 250 miles from the Donegal coast. He was aboard his own ship, the galleon *San Juan Bautista*, the vice-flagship of the squadron which was itself commanded by Diego Flores de Valdes. The *Bautista* was a slightly bigger galleon than many of her squadron, at 750 tons; she carried 24 guns and some 243 men.

The paymaster does not mention why she had drifted apart from the main body of the fleet by the time the Armada had turned the corner around Ireland and sailed south for Spain; the ship was apparently undamaged – at least Aramburu makes no mention of any shot holes or storm damage. In the early days of September, however, he had gradually brought the *Bautista* closer in towards the Irish coast, navigating with a care and accuracy which were a feature of his ship-handling. On the 11th they sighted land, the first for many days, to the east. In the early morning light, with visibility shortened by heavy spray from a strong blustery wind, the pilot thought that the distinctively shaped outlines were the small islands of the Ox and Cow (now the Bull and Cow), which are off Dursey Island at the head of the Kenmare River which divides Cork and Kerry. It was not a bad guess, but it was wrong.

The *Bautista* continued down along the coast, now trying to gain searoom; she was some miles off the coast and while her position was hardly perilous, care was called for. Like all square-riggers the galleon had difficulty in sailing into a headwind; the southwesterly blew straight onto her bow making the shore a lee one. However, the pilot seemed confident that he knew the coast and Aramburu was content to keep his distance, although progress was slow.

Gradually the wind began to veer to the south sou'west and they gratefully tacked a little out to sea, by this time becoming wary of what might lie ahead. For the rest of that day and all the next the *Bautista* beat roughly southwards, but in the late afternoon of the 12th the wind freshened and began to blow hard from the south, so strongly that sail had to be furled and the ship allowed to run before the gale. That night 'there was a most violent storm with a very wild sea, and great darkness on account of the heavy clouds.' All night wind and rain pushed the galleon back to the northward as she drifted almost helplessly before it. When dawn broke on the 13th there was no land visible. They had no idea how far north they had been blown; Aramburu's later estimates of his position are clearly in error.

That morning the wind shifted to the northwest and the *Bautista* resumed the voyage south. A curious course was laid, presumably by the pilot; instead of sailing southwest to escape possible hazards that might lie to the eastward towards the land, they sailed southeast, a heading which was maintained for all that day and night and held on the 14th also, as the wind gradually freshened once more and backed into the west. Now and then, on the 14th, the sailors caught fleeting glimpses through driving rain and heavy seas of the shape of another ship, probably from the Armada, but they failed to come close enough to identify her.

On the morning of the 15th, with the wind gusting to gale force from the west, they again saw land; two large islands appeared ahead through the mist and rain, and to port a long line of land that could only be the mainland. As the day wore on and the land grew more distinct, it took on identifiable form. They could not now doubt their position; the two large islands were of the Blasket group off Kerry and the mainland was the massive hump of the Dingle Peninsula, topped by Mount Brandon at 3127 feet.

Aramburu's ship was now in deadly danger, for which he could blame his pilot for the initial error in identifying the land seen on the 11th as the Ox and Cow off Dursey. By his account of the 11th and 12th he had sailed almost directly out to sea, or as near to such a course as was possible. Then came the gale that blew the *Bautista* back to the north in one night to an unnamed point in the ocean from where, with a helpful wind, it took her two and a half days to sail south to a point some thirty-five miles short of where they had been on the 11th when land was first sighted.

There is no doubt that the land which the pilot had previously identified as the Ox and Cow cannot have been those two conspicuous landmarks. Admittedly the weather was 'murky and cloudy' and the ship some three miles off the coast. It has been postulated that what they saw on the 11th was Inishtooskert and Inishtearaght, the two most outlying islands in the Blaskets. This still leaves very much in the air the problem of how a ship which was blown off course and backwards should take three days to recover the ground lost in one night, and with a following wind, more or less. It is possible that the Skelligs were mistaken for the Ox and Cow (there is some resemblance), but the Skelligs are west nor'west of Kenmare Bay, and if they were indeed the land sighted on the 11th, then the gale which blew the *Bautista* back on the 12th must have been of awesome strength.

Aramburu had little time to worry about where he had been for the last couple of days. He was now hemmed in against the land by the wind on their starboard side and by the islands ahead, caught on a lee shore in a trap from which there seemed little hope of escape. It would be next to impossible to try to weather the Blaskets, and without expert pilots he could not sail through the Blasket Sound between the islands and the mainland. He turned north nor'east as soon as he realized the situation, trying to backtrack along his course to clear the northwestern flank of the peninsula and perhaps gain shelter in Brandon Bay. The chances were slim of making even the shelter of Smerwick Harbour, just around the corner, let alone reaching Brandon Bay further up along the coast, but it was all he could hope for. A stroke of good fortune came now, for standing out from the land was a great ship and a tender, the same ship that they had sighted on the day before but had not been able to recognize in the distance and bad weather. She was much nearer now, and her identity unmistakeable: the galleon *San Juan* of Portugal, the vice-flagship of the entire Armada, commanded by the *Almiranta-general* or second-in-command, Don Juan Martinez de Recalde.

In sharp contrast to Aramburu, Recalde knew precisely where he was and

Juan Martinez de Recalde, Almiranta-general *of the* Armada and in command of the galleon San Juan of Portugal.

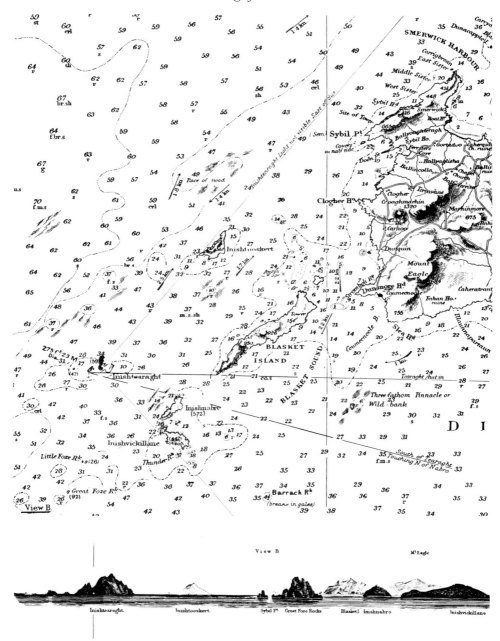

The Blasket Sound, at the tip of the Dingle Peninsula off southwest Kerry, where the Santa Maria de la Rosa *sank after striking Stromboli Reef. The wreck was found in 1968. View B shows the topography from the southwest. (Produced from portions of BA chart 2679 with the sanction of the Controller, HM Stationery Office and of the Hydrographer of the Navy)*

what he was doing. He had been here before in 1580, when he had helped to escort the Papal force which entrenched itself in Smerwick, only to surrender and be slaughtered by the then Lord Deputy, Grey de Wilton. This time Recalde had brought his *San Juan* in towards Smerwick to take on food and water: he was there by design, Aramburu by accident.

We turned towards him despairing [wrote the Castilian paymaster] and we ignorant of the coast, of any remedy, and saw that being able to double one of the islands, towards another stretch of land which he saw before him, he turned east. We stood to windward of her and followed, thinking he had some information. He kept approaching the land and ran into the Port of Vicey, through an entrance between low rocks, about the length of a ship, and anchored. We came in behind him with the tender.

In this brief and laconic passage Aramburu sketches just the merest detail of an extraordinarily daring and skilful piece of seamanship and navigation. Recalde's pilot was 'a Scotchman whom he had on board his ship, whose vessel the Duke had taken', but whoever the pilot, the seamanship had been vintage Recalde. The admiral had been ill and in his bunk for some time (he was sixty-two and the privations of this wearing voyage were taking their toll of his health and strength), but on the day they reached the vicinity of Smerwick he had struggled from his bunk to come on deck and guide the *San Juan* in; 'the admiral . . . came not out of his bed until this day week, in the morning that they ran upon the shore.'

To understand what Recalde had achieved one has to know the Blaskets and to appreciate the extreme dangers which they offer to sailing vessels even in calm weather. There are six islands in the group, the biggest the Great Blasket and the smallest Beginish ('the small island'); the other four are Inishtooskert, Inishvickillane, Inishtearaght and Inishnabro. They lie in a scattered clump off Dunmore Head, the most westerly headland in Ireland, at the tip of the Dingle Peninsula, and are separated from the mainland by a deep, rock-strewn and tide-torn sound.

Recalde had entered the sound not through the top or bottom, but from the western side, threading a delicate course between rocks, islands and reefs, with a strong tide-rip to add to the difficulties. The *San Juan* and the *Bautista* had met somewhere to the northwest of Inishtooskert, the most northerly of the islands. Recalde, having probably investigated his chances of entering Smerwick but deciding against it, was steering southwest in order to clear Inishtooskert to the west. With Aramburu he had succeeded, doubling the island to windward and then turning east towards the land and the other islands. This move must have seemed certain disaster to Aramburu; it was, however, the only one left. Perhaps the *San Juan* could have weathered the other islands further to the southwest – Inishtearaght (the most westerly of the group), Inishvickillane and Inishnabro – but Recalde could not be sure of that. And other hazards besides those three islands could mean the end of his ship;

there were the Foze rocks, Great and Little, and a maze of tidal streams. In turning east once he had doubled Inishtooskert he was doing what he thought safest, although it must have appeared anything but that.

The three vessels had a clear run to the east from Inishtooskert almost as far as the Great Blasket's northern tip, but once within range of the big island there was a nightmare of tangled rocks and reefs, some clear of the water, some awash, some hidden beneath the waves. To negotiate these safely was the last hurdle. To starboard as they neared the Great Blasket was the small islet of Carrigfada ('the long rock'); to port, amid a cluster of jagged rocks, were Ballyclogher and Wig Rocks; and between these two and Carrigfada threaded a narrow channel, which Aramburu says was about as wide 'as the length of ship' but which is closer to being two hundred yards, with up to forty feet depth of water running through it even at low tide. A deep, narrow channel, especially tricky in the heavy seas then running, it was nevertheless a clear, hazard-free passage into the shelter of the Great Blasket.

Recalde had calculated nicely; he brought his ship through the channel without any hesitation, Aramburu and the tender following. Once through they were in a small sound, with Carrigfada and Illaunboy giving some shelter to the northeast; through this they ran on in deepish water between Beginish to the northeast and the tip of the big island to the southwest until they had the tall shoulder of the latter tucked in astern. Only then, with the Great Blasket breaking the worst of the wind and seas, did the ships drop sail and anchor.

Today this is a passage which in bad weather no yachtsman in his right mind would even begin to contemplate. In a gale and rough seas, with a clumsy sailing ship of over 1000 tons, Recalde's feat was little short of miraculous. But need he have chosen this exposed passage into the shelter of the sound? The simpler way was down through the northern end of the sound, entering near Clogher Head and moving south past Dunquin on the mainland in ample room and deep water. However, to attempt this in a west wind would have been fatal; with the wind on the beam the ships might very well have failed to luff up against it, and if this happened there could only have been one result.

Although Recalde had chosen the safest anchorage in the sound, this was not saying a great deal; in fact there is no anchorage anywhere near the Blaskets in which a large sailing vessel might be safe in bad weather. Sidney Wignall, who organized and led the expedition which discovered the remains of the *Santa Maria de la Rosa* in the sound in 1968, and who dived for many months during which he covered almost every inch of the sound, says of it simply that 'there is no holding ground for either ancient or modern anchors in Blasket Sound.' John Grattan, the professional diver who supervized the diving team's operations, opined that it was the most dangerous place he had ever dived in; any vessel which anchored in the sound in bad weather was 'courting disaster'. Wignall and his team found that, contrary to what the charts of the area showed, almost the whole of the sea bed from the beach on the Great Blasket (opposite which Recalde and Aramburu had anchored) across the sound to Dunquin on the mainland 'consists of bare rock, semi-bare rock with a sprinkling of sand, or a sandy bottom that lay only a few inches deep over bedrock.' This is the very worst sort of ground on which ships can anchor, simply because the sand, if present at all, is not of sufficient depth to afford a good grip for the anchor flukes: in any sort of wind there is a danger of dragging.

For the moment they were safe; the Great Blasket sheltered them from the prevailing southwesterlies, and the only winds to which the vessels would be exposed were those from the north – which could only help them on their way home. The Spaniards had now time to draw breath, take stock of their situation, and begin if possible to take on fresh water and food from the mainland, there being little on the island.

Their arrival in the sound had not gone unnoticed. An English official was stationed in the nearest large town to the Blaskets, Dingle on the mainland, some ten miles from where the ships now lay. In all probability James Trant had had the ships under surveillance for some time, and he now hurried to the cliffs on the mainland overlooking the sound from where he could see them clearly. By the 20th, Attorney General Sir John Popham was writing to Burghley with the news that 'two great ships and one frigate [lie] at the Blasquets in the Sound there.' But a great deal had happened in the five days since the Spanish ships had slipped by Inishtooskert and anchored by the islands.

Some Spaniards had been captured from a party sent ashore in one of Recalde's cock-boats to the mainland. They had hoped to get water and food and had been sent off just after the ships had anchored – the matter was evidently urgent. But the eight men had hardly landed when a force of English soldiery sent from Dingle by Trant came out of concealment, and taking them by surprise, easily captured them and brought them into Dingle. Four of these prisoners, all common sailors from their depositions, were examined in Dingle; probably all those taken prisoner were examined also, but if so there is no surviving evidence. But the statements of the four are of great interest for they give a clear picture of the state not only of their own ship, Recalde's *San Juan*, but of the entire fleet, and moreover contained a great deal of information on the Channel battles.

The four were Emmanuel Fremoso, Emmanuel Francisco, John de Licornio and Peter O'Carr. The first two were Portuguese, Licornio a Biscayan, and O'Carr a Fleming. Fremoso's statement is longer than those of the remaining three; perhaps he was both more intelligent and lucid than they, or less determined to keep to himself any information which he might possess. He intimated that the *San Juan* had been short of food and other provisions for some time, apparently having expected replenishment from the Duke of Parma, and then speaks of the repeated storms and gales which the fleet met and which scattered it into a dozen or more different groups. 'There are now remaining in the Admiral's [Recalde's] ship near about five hundred men . . . the men being very sick and one of the pilots. There are eighty soldiers and twenty of the mariners in the admiral's ship and they do lie down and die daily, and the rest are very weak and the captain very sad and weak.'

Here Fremoso seems to imply that Recalde had come upon that part of the Kerry coast by accident rather than design: the *San Juan* was 'so near the coast before they found it, that by means of the strong westerly wind they were not able to depart out of it.' On balance this seems at least arguable; Recalde knew this part of the coast, and had to find food and water, and it is more than possible that he thus made almost directly for Smerwick. The statement paints a graphic picture of the state of the *San Juan*'s provisions for the wretched men aboard: 'There is left in this Admiral but twenty-five pipes of wine, and but very little bread and no water but what they brought out of Spain which stinketh marvellously, and the flesh meat they cannot eat, the drought is so great.' And a direct rebuttal of the English fear that the Spaniard's motives in attempting to land on Ireland were aggressive rather than defensive: 'the admiral's purpose is with the first wind to pass away for Spain.'

Francisco's evidence was largely corroborative. He is, though, more specific about actual damage to the *San Juan*, all of it sustained apparently during battle. 'The Admiral [ship] was many times shot through, and a shot in the mast, and the deck of the prow spoiled . . . the Admiral's mast is so weak, by reason of the shot in it, as they dare not abide any storm, nor to bear such sails as otherwise they might do . . . and further, the best of that be in the Admiral's ship are scarce able to stand, and that if they tarry where they are any time, they will all perish.'

Licornio says little of interest, but O'Carr, the Fleming, was able to give a great deal of detailed evidence (with many incorrect facts and figures, incidentally). He confirmed the shortage of food and the appalling quality of what little remained on board the galleon; 'they have bread sufficient; their beef is corrupt; water they want; many of them are sick.' O'Carr also remarks on Recalde's failing strength. 'The Admiral, after such time as the fight was at Calais, came not out of his bed until this day week, in the morning that they ran upon the shore . . . this Admiral is of Biscay either of Bilbao or Auerede and of fifty-seven years of age, and a man of service.' Recalde was indeed from Bilbao, but was sixty-two years old; ill as he was, he had been responsible for saving his vessel.

It is in O'Carr's testimony that there appears the first mention of the Prince d'Ascoli (Antonio Luis de Leiva, to give him his fuller title). He merely says that 'there is a bastard son of King Phillip [sic] of twenty-eight years of age in this fleet, in a ship with the Duke, called the Prince of Asculagh in Italy. The Prince passed from there in a pinnace about Calais.' The Prince d'Ascoli (or Asculagh, Ascula, Ascolo, Ascoli, Ascule, Asculy *et seq*, to illustrate the abandoned variety with which the Spaniards made a stab at spelling proper names) was an important figure in the Armada, being the first of the

Commanders of the Fleet, a position close to the very highest command. An illegitimate son of Philip II, he took his title from the ancient Italian city of Asculum and had the somewhat dubious distinction of having the second highest number of personal servants (thirty-nine) in the Armada.

The Prince had sailed from Lisbon aboard the Duke's *San Martin* but had left her at Calais while the fleet was anchored, for a reason which he explained in a letter to Philip. During the fireships engagement at Calais, Medina Sidonia 'directed some of us who were most in his confidence to go in *zabras* and carry instructions to the other squadrons. By the Duke's orders, I took with me Captain Marco, as I had done on other occasions, and sailed towards the rear squadron. In the interim the flagship sailed away.' Following this and several other episodes, the Prince claimed that he eventually reached Dunkirk, having failed to enter Calais, and there found the Duke of Parma who refused to allow him back to the Armada, by this time out of sight. It was from Dunkirk, on August 12, that he wrote to the King, by which time the fleet was off Scotland.

The eight Spanish prisoners were taken by the English on the 15th, the day the ships entered the sound. Recalde's first attempt to land on the mainland had ended in failure and he did not try again that day. On the following day the three vessels tried to make their anchorages as secure as possible. Recalde was short of a heavy anchor (his own were apparently lost at Calais, a fact which Emmanuel Fremoso appears to confirm in his testimony, saying that 'each of their ships lost three anchors at the same place [Calais]', presumably including the *San Juan*). Recalde gave Aramburu two cables and a light anchor, receiving in return a heavy anchor from the *Bautista*. When the heavy anchor was bent onto another cable the Admiral seemed satisfied that this would stop possible dragging, which he obviously feared. Aramburu had his own heavy anchor so the *Bautista* also seemed secure.

They had good reason to be nervous of their anchorages. The Blasket Sound is an area of primarily bad weather, with gales and storms being common; the ships had come during the autumn equinoctial gales and already both captains had had sufficient experience of Atlantic weather to be wary. Their uneasy sanctuary was in one of the bleakest and most remote corners of western Europe, among almost inaccessible islands surrounded by rocks and reefs and separated from the mainland by a stretch of water notable for navigational hazards.

The Blaskets, wild and desolate though they are, have an almost intangible charm of their own. The sound itself, which runs loosely from around Clogher Head in the north to southwards of Dunmore, is roughly ten to twelve miles long, but generally the term 'sound' is understood to refer almost without exception to the stretch between the islands and the mainland, which is about three miles wide at its broadest point. Of the six islands, the Great Blasket is easily the largest, an elongated, knobbly bulk running roughly southwest from tip to bottom, about $5\frac{1}{2}$ miles long, rising to a 961 feet high pinnacle about two-thirds down its length. Its northeast side is fronted by a

Clogher Head at the northern end of the Blasket Sound, with the Great Blasket dimly visible in the right background. (Pat Langan)

beach, the famous White Strand, and faces across the sound directly towards Dunquin on the mainland. Today the remains of a village rise above the White Strand, for until quite recently the big island was inhabited. It was opposite this village, several hundred yards offshore, that the three Spanish ships had anchored.

Like most remote inhabited islands, the Blaskets have produced a remarkable people – hardy, spirited and attuned to every mood of the sea. They have also produced some equally remarkable literature and folk tradition; Maurice O'Sullivan, a native of the Blaskets and the author of the unique *Twenty Years A-Growing*, by any standards a literary classic, describes the Great Blasket intimately as one who spent his formative years there, and is especially revealing on the islander's attitude to wrecked vessels, of which there must have been many over the centuries. Writing of a wreck and its cargo which floated ashore onto the island, he exclaims, 'Great King of Virtues, it was a marvellous sight – tins, barrels of flour, big black boxes, big white boxes, big boxes of bacon . . . everything was in confusion – boxes and chests of every shape and colour, not an inch of the sand but was covered in wreckage. . . .' T H Mason, in his evocative *The Islands of Ireland*, wrote after a visit there during the 1930s that 'much flotsam and jetsam is thrown up by the sea. During the war, the islanders were well off, for in addition to getting high prices for their sheep and wool, they obtained a lot of wreckage.' Of the outlying island which the ships had doubled to get into the sound, he wrote; 'Inishtooskert . . . appeared like some reptilian monster, dark and threatening, with its jagged profile silhouetted against the sky and its body in shadow, straddling across the ocean.' Grim, bleak, forbidding, inhospitable – all those epithets, and many more, fit the Blaskets and their sound.

By the next day the Admiral had clearly decided that fresh water and food must be obtained if possible. Although Aramburu does not say so, the Spaniards had already been onto the big island; from the cliffs James Trant had seen them land there, reporting that 'They go ashore every day on the island to refresh themselves and to take water.' But the water on the island was clearly not enough.

Remembering his lost eight men, Recalde now sent out a party of fifty, mostly arquebusiers, who tried to land but were baffled by the mainland's impregnable coastline (there are few safe places at which a small boat could land) and also by the presence of the 'two hundred men' whom James Trant had 'watching upon the shore every day'. Later they were apparently more successful, taking on water from the mainland, most probably at Coumenoole Strand, south of Dunmore Head, where a stream enters the ocean.

On the 18th Recalde continued to take on water, this time from the big island itself; for the remainder of the day and probably for the next three days the ships continued to load whatever few provisions they could obtain. The weather had stayed reasonably calm, an unusual state of affairs at that time of the year; and then, on the 21st, it changed with dramatic swiftness.

'*Comenzo a entrar el viento Oeste con una terribilisima furia, claro con poco aqua*', wrote Aramburu – 'the wind began to blow from the west with terrible violence, clear but with a little rain.' Recalde's suspect anchor would not hold and the *San Juan* began to drift down onto the *Bautista*. Aramburu could do little to avoid collision; the two great ships hit, the *Bautista*'s lantern and some of her mizzen tackle being smashed before Recalde could bring the big galleon under control again. But now both ships began to drag together. The danger of their anchorages had now become all too clear in the violent gale. A succession of anchors might have held the ships, but they were short of anchors; all they could hope for was that by some chance the anchors would find a hold or that the wind would ease in time for them to work their way clear of the cliffs on the mainland, now coming hideously close to the east.

There now entered the sound, while Recalde and Aramburu were fighting to save their ships, a fourth vessel – the *Santa Maria de la Rosa*, vice-flagship of the Guipuzcoan Squadron. They had not seen her enter; Aramburu thought later that she might have entered the sound by 'another entrance, towards the northwest', the direction from which Recalde had turned away almost a week ago. It is probable that the *Santa Maria* had been blown by the westerly gale from somewhere northwest of Inishtooskert and had come into the sound at the top, somehow managing to keep clear of the mainland as she sailed down the sound.

The Blasket Sound from the north, with the Great Blasket in the background and the mainland at Dunmore Head, on the Dingle Peninsula, at the left. Recalde in the San Juan *led his tender and Aramburu's* San Juan Bautista *into the Sound from the right, through the maze of rocks and reefs which lies north of the Great Blasket. The* Santa Maria de la Rosa, *which entered later, was wrecked to the left of the Great Blasket, at a spot hidden by the long promontory. (*Irish Times*)*

It has often been suggested that the *Santa Maria* must have hit a rock as she entered the sound; damaged she certainly was, for she fired a distress gun and then another as she came down the sound towards the other vessels. Possibly she was blown into the sound through the gap between Inishtooskert and the Great Blasket itself, and if so it is highly probable that she did indeed hit somewhere in the maelstrom of hazards; it is also possible that she could have hit Young Island, north of Beginish; but whatever happened, the *almiranta* was in dire straits when she appeared and drifted down towards the *San Juan* and the *Bautista*. There were now three vice-flagships in the sound: those of the Portuguese, Guipuzcoan and Castilian Squadrons.

The *Santa Maria*, also (and confusingly) known as the *Nuestra Senora de la Rosa*, was a considerable ship by Armada standards, displacing 945 tons, and carrying 26 guns and some 297 men. Before Corunna, the *Santa Maria* had suffered damage to her mainmast in a storm and this was repaired in July at Corunna. She was a southern or Mediterranean vessel, with all the proven frailties of that design in rougher waters, and even at that early stage had shown her disadvantages as a tough ship of war. The Guipuzcoan was apparently sound by the time the fleet sailed from Corunna, but during the Channel battles she suffered terrible damage, being 'shot through four times and one of the shots was between the wind and the water, whereof they thought they would have sonke, and most of her tackle was spoiled with shot.'

By the time the *Santa Maria* entered the Blasket Sound she was far from being seaworthy; she had not been so at Corunna nor after the Channel engagements, though she had come staggering through those misfortunes. But this last westerly gale had proved the final and unyielding barrier; whether the *almiranta* had hit a rock on entering the sound seems largely immaterial: her days were run. 'She had all her sails torn to ribbons, except the foresail,' wrote Aramburu. 'She anchored with a single anchor, as she had no more. And as the tide which was coming in from the southeast beat against her stern, she held on until two o'clock, when it began to ebb, and at the turn she commenced drifting, about two splices of cable from us, and we with her.'

The tide in the sound today ebbs south sou'west at a brisk 2.2 knots; it is safe to say that in 1588 it was not much different. When the *Santa Maria* had come in, her drift was halted by a flood tide going almost directly northwards, and even at the slack of the flood she was relatively safe. But when the tide had turned and begun to drain from the sound with increasing speed, her single anchor was not enough: even the other two large vessels, whatever about the small 40-ton tender, found it hard to keep from shifting with several anchors down. Under those conditions the *almiranta* could not hope to hold.

As ominous as matters seemed, however, neither Aramburu nor Recalde can have been prepared for what now happened. 'In an instant' wrote Aramburu in words which have lost not a trace of their frightful and poignant impact, 'we saw she was going to the bottom while trying to hoist the foresail, and immediately she went down with the whole crew, not a soul escaping – a most extraordinary and terrible occurrence.' As the other Spaniards watched, the *Santa Maria* sank like a stone in the rushing waters of the sound; they spread wide to receive her and then closed. A welter of spray broke over the grave and settled; spars and barrels, hatch covers, tackle, planks, all the pathetic flotsam of shipwreck floated on the surface. Drowning men called for help as the racing currents bore them out to sea.

Neither Recalde nor Aramburu could do anything to help, although they cannot have been more than a stone's throw from the scene. They faced their own dangers; 'we were drifting down on her to our perdition' wrote Aramburu. The strong tide was pulling at their vessels, the anchors scraping across the rocky bottom of the sound unable to get a grip.

One man managed to save himself by struggling onto some floating planks and had lain exhausted, until some quirk of the current bore him to the mainland at Slea Head, possible somewhere in the vicinity of Coumenoole Strand, where he was taken by English soldiers. They brought him to Dingle; and there he told the full story of the wreck. This sole survivor was John Anthony of Manona, or Genoa, a son of the *Santa Maria*'s pilot, Francisco de Manona. Examined first on the 21st, the same day that he had come ashore, his deposition of that date is scrappy and largely uninformative. But sparely detailed as it is, it reveals a vital scrap of information: 'in which shippe of principal men there were drowned . . . the Prince of Ascule, base sonne of the King of Spaine. . . .'

What Manona was saying electrified the English. A son of Philip's (albeit illegitimate and thus without pretence to the Spanish throne) was nonetheless a personage of great importance; here was a survivor saying that no less a person than the prince had been aboard the *Santa Maria*, and that he too had been drowned. We had left D'Ascoli in Calais; how could he have regained the fleet, that is if his letter to Philip was genuine? The note seems incontrovertible: Manona must have been wrong. But he stuck to his story and insisted repeatedly that the prince had been on the *Santa Maria* at the time of her sinking.

It was only during the second examination, four days later, that his English inquisitors wormed out the full story.

The Prince of Ascule, the King's base sonne [said Manona], came in the company of the Duke in the Duke's ship called the galleon of St Martine, of a thousand tonne, but at Callice [Calais] when Sir Francis Drake came near them, this Prince went to the shore, and before his return the Duke was driven to cut his anchors, and to depart, whereby the Prince could not recover that ship but came into the said ship called *Our Lady of the Rosarie*, and with him there came in also one Don Pedro, Don Diego, Don Francisco, and seven other gentlemen of account that accompanied the Prince.

The English were still not satisfied, and a third examination of Manona was made on the 27th, consisting largely of questions about the Prince. Manona never wavered; the Prince had been aboard the *Santa Maria* and that was that. What was more, he could describe D'Ascoli with apparent precision:

a slender made man of a reasonable stature of twenty-eight years of age, his haire of an acorne colour stroked upwards; of a high forehead; a verie little beard marquelotted; whitely faced with some little red on the cheeks. He was drowned in apparel of white satten for his doublet and breeches after the Spanish fashion cut, with russet silk stockinges. When this Prince came into their ship at Callice, he was appareled in blacke rased velvet laid on with brode gold lace . . . this Prince's men, for the most part where in the ship that this examinate was in, from their coming out of Spaine; and when they were at Callice the Prince passed in a little Phelocke [cock-boat] with six others from shippe to shippe to give order to them, and some said that he went to the shore at that time.

To say that this is mystifying is simplifying the matter: it comes to a straight choice between Manona and the Prince's letter. Later historical research has apparently thrown little light on whether or not, if the Prince did stay at Calais, he played any important role thereafter. If we plump for Manona's testimony, it is because of his insistence, not once but several times, that D'Ascoli was aboard the *Santa Maria*; he had no reason to lie about it and his description of the prince and how he came to join the Guipuzcoan *almiranta* sounds convincing. Certainly his English interrogators were convinced; James Trant reported that 'in a mighty great ship of 1000 tons, wherein was Il Principa Dastula, base sone of the King of Spain. The name of the ship was the *Santa Maria de la Rosa* and as soon as ever they cast anchor they drive upon a rock, and there, was cast away into the middle of the sea, with five hundred tall men and the Prince, and no man saved but one, that brought us this news, who came naked upon a board.'

Manona's description of how the wreck occurred is important.

This ship broke against the rockes in the sound of the Bleskies a league and a half from land upon the Tuesday last at noon, and all in the ship perished saving this examinate, who saved himself upon two or three planks, the Gentlemen thinking to save themselves by the bote, it was so fast tied as they could not get her loose, thereby they were drowned . . . as soon as the ship broke against the rock, one of the Captains slew this examinate's father [the pilot], saying he did it by treason.

Many points in this statement must be examined with great care, and several are wrong: the ship was not 'a league and a half' (some 4½ English miles in other words, although a Spanish league was 4½ miles) from land when she sank but at the narrowest point of the sound; nor did the wreck occur on Tuesday but on Wednesday the 11th, O.S. (the 21st, New Style). But these are largely irrelevant; what is vital to the wrecking incident itself is that the *Santa Maria* sank because, claimed Manona, she 'broke against the rockes.'

The Great Blasket seen to the southwest from near Dunmore Head. The Santa Maria de la Rosa *struck Stromboli Rock, underwater to the left of the large rock in the centre of the picture and about halfway between the Great Blasket and the mainland. The sole survivor was washed ashore near where this picture was taken, examined by Crown forces and executed. (Bord Failte)*

The only rock or reef in that part of the sound which has any bearing on the wreck is the Stromboli Rock, or Reef, about a third of the way across the sound from the mainland, between the Lure (a long rock projecting southwest from the tip of Dunmore Head) and the eastern tip of the Great Blasket. A look at the map indicates exactly where this reef is, although the Admiralty charts do not give its precise position. Stromboli is undoubtedly the rock on which the *Santa Maria* perished, and its surroundings are perhaps the most dangerous waters in the sound. The 1968 expedition which found the wreck of the *Santa Maria* also discovered that this relatively small area took the full force of the ebbing tide, and that the tide ebbed in just over half the time it took to flood. Thus the area around Stromboli amounted to a very considerable tide-race; evidently the *Santa Maria*, anchored there at the turn of the tide, was swept onto the reef by the mounting force of the strong ebb forcing her southwards. She had tried to anchor – had indeed stayed anchored from midday to two o'clock 'when she commenced drifting', at a point northwest of the rock itself, perhaps about midway across the sound, and close to where the other vessels were anchored and trying desperately to stop dragging their anchors across the sound.

The most logical sequence of events hereafter is that Aramburu's *Bautista* began to drift on a roughly similar course to the *Santa Maria*; Aramburu writes that he was drifting down on her 'to our perdition.' While the *Santa Maria* sank, evidently having struck Stromboli, Aramburu managed to avoid a similar disaster by quick action;

it pleased Our Lord for that passage in case of such a necessity we put a new stock to an anchor which had but half a stock and which Juan Martinez gave us with a cable [in the exchange of gear on the 18th]. We dropped this anchor and her head came round; and we hauled in the other anchor and found the stock with half the shank, for the rest was broken, and the cable chafed by the rocks over which we were lying.

Their foresight undoubtedly saved the *Bautista*; her original anchor had not only dragged but had broken, and the cable had undoubtedly been chafed by the sharp rocks which make up Stromboli Reef and its surrounds. Aramburu saved himself and his ship, but he must have come perilously close to following the *Santa Maria* to the bottom.

Stromboli Rock as shown on the Admiralty charts does exist, but in 1968 divers found that it was not what they called the 'true Stromboli'. This was 'further to the west and its summit, a mass of sharp rock flakes, stretches menacing fingers to within seven or eight feet of the surface at low water.' The Stromboli Rock designated on Chart 2790 was so named after being struck by the British gunboat HMS *Stromboli* in 1858 while on survey work in the sound; the ship appears not to have suffered, but some eight or nine feet of the rock was knocked off its tip.

The *Santa Maria* struck the 'true' Stromboli – the reef rather than the rock. The impact on the lightly built hull of the heavy Guipuzcoan, already holed with shot and strained by gales, was enough to push what must have been a gaping hole in the hull towards the stern. The *almiranta* was swept past the reef already sinking; then, some distance southeast of the 'true' Stromboli, she sank immediately, going down by the stern. Although those aboard tried to launch the cock-boat there was no time.

This sequence of events is not just supposition. The extensive work by the Wignall team of divers over a number of seasons has pieced together a theory which is not easily disproved. The key points were of course the finding of the wreck itself, in over a hundred feet of water some two hundred yards to the southeast of the reef, and the discovery on the bottom of the sound of a series of anchors, all of which fit in with the accounts of those who witnessed the wrecking. Rusted with salt and age, these anchors confirm all the evidence of Aramburu. Four were found which were almost certainly from the Armada ships (another was uncertain). Two were opposite the White Strand on the Great Blasket, where Recalde and Aramburu had first anchored on coming into the sound, south of Beginish and southeast of a rock called Barnagh Rock. They were lost on the 21st when the *San Juan* and the *Bautista* dragged and the *San Juan* collided with Aramburu's vessel. New anchors had been bent on and the ships brought up. The two anchors found near Barnagh Rock were within two hundred yards of each other; both were badly corroded but not sufficiently to conceal the fact that one was only a half anchor, broken off along the shank, while the other had only one fluke and no shank-ring. Further across the sound, on a line southeast of the original anchorage,

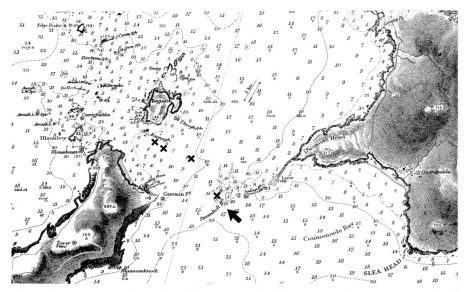

The positions of anchors found in the Blasket Sound, which have helped in the reconstruction of events. Great Blasket Island on left. (Reproduced from portion of BA chart 2790 with the sanction of the Controller, HM Stationery Office and of the Hydrographer of the Navy)

another anchor was found, on an almost direct line with Stromboli Reef, and about halfway between the reef itself and the Beginish. The anchor with one fluke and its ring missing was probably the *San Juan*'s, lost just before she dragged and collided with Aramburu's ship. The collision had probably also broken the *Bautista* loose from her own anchor: hence the two anchors quite close together, southeast of Barnagh Rock. The anchor in the next position, halfway between Beginish and Stromboli, is less easily explained, but is not in any case a vital link in the chain of events.

Near the reef a huge anchor was found, and there was a smaller one some fifty feet away. The big anchor, about seventeen feet long, had lost a fluke and was fouled in the reef, as was the smaller one. The first was in all probability the 'single anchor' of the *Santa Maria* and had caught when she dragged onto the reef. Manona's father, the pilot, had then cut the cable, hoping to free the ship, and had been slain for this act. The smaller anchor was probably that which Recalde had given Aramburu on the 18th, and to which he fixed a new stock; Aramburu, trying to keep the *Bautista* from following the *Santa Maria*, had dropped it in desperation and it had found a grip on the reef, holding the ship against the powerful current but perilously close to destruction. Somehow, in the hours that followed, probably on the flood tide, he was able to claw cautiously away from the danger area to a safer anchorage elsewhere.

Here the question of depths of water over the rocks enters the picture. The *Santa Maria* would have drawn between 18 and 20 feet; Stromboli Rock has a charted depth over it of 15 feet at low water and about 25 feet at high water; Stromboli Reef (the 'true' Stromboli) comes to within seven or eight feet below the surface at low water, according to the diving team, which would mean that it was covered at high water by some 18 to 20 feet of water.

The *Santa Maria* struck the reef shortly after high water, when the ebb was running hard. It takes just over four hours to pour out through the narrow neck of the sound around Stromboli and it is safe to assume that by the time the ship struck, the water had dropped perhaps a foot or so from its highest level. The reef is sharp and dangerous at its tip and quite capable, in a gale, of ripping open the bottom of a wooden ship swept onto it sufficiently to cause instant flooding and sinking. This is undoubtedly what happened. For a few moments the *Santa Maria* was held by her one anchor, and released only when the pilot, hoping somehow to save the ship from pounding on the reef, cut the cable.

Manona's testimony that the ship struck a rock was confirmed by James Trant ('they drive upon a rock'); by Henry Wallop ('by striking upon a rock'); and above all, by the suddenness of her sinking. All the evidence, above and below the water, combines to present an unassailable theory as to her wrecking.

We have seen how Aramburu had managed to avoid a fate similar to that of the *Santa Maria*; earlier, he had been observant enough to notice that when the Guipuzcoan had entered the sound 'by another entrance nearer the land, towards the northwest', she had been accompanied by another, un-named vessel, commanded by Miguel de Aranivar, which presumably anchored up-tide of Recalde and Aramburu and managed to hold there. At four o'clock, by which time the initial speed of the ebb had slackened and Aramburu was beginning to breathe again, another ship entered, 'the ship *San Juan*, of Fernando Horra'.

The identification of this hitherto mysterious ship has taxed the ingenuity of many. She was also in a poor way when she came into the sound, with 'the mainmast gone . . . and the foresail blown to shreds'. She let go her anchor and came to near the others, but because of the furious gale they could not offer help or even communicate with her. On the following morning, the 22nd, Horra lowered his longboat and conferred with Recalde and Aramburu, making known his 'distressed condition'. Evidently he thought his ship so unseaworthy that the only course open was to leave her and take ship with the others. 'As it [the condition of Horra's ship] was seen to be hopeless', says Aramburu, 'Juan Martinez decided that I should take the whole of the company of Gonzalo Melendez, and distributed that of Diego Bazan among the tenders.' Recalde wanted the guns from Horra's ship also, but gave up after trying several times to salvage them. What happened to this ship, deserted by crew and captain, is not known; that she does not lie in the Blasket Sound is reasonably certain following extensive investigations, but her condition was so bad that she cannot have got far.

What was this mysterious '*San Juan* of Fernando Horra', often known as the '*San Juan* of Ragusa'? For centuries her identification has remained unsolved, but in fact it is simply achieved. The vital evidence lies in Aramburu's testimony that he and Recalde took off her 'the whole of the company of Gonzalo Melendez and distributed that of Diego Bazan among the tenders.' Both Melendez and Bazan clearly commanded companies of soldiers aboard Horra's ship, and both are listed by Duro as being aboard the *San Juan* of 'Diego Flores' (Diego Flores de Valdes, commander of the Castilian Squadron); '*escuadra de Diego Flores; la San Juan, capitan Gregorio Melendez, con los capitaines Melgarejo y Diego Bazan*'.

Aramburu's familiarity with this ship is worth noting; he knew the captain, Fernando Horra, identifying the ship by referring to its captain, an allusion which betokened acquaintance, which was natural in that both were in the same squadron. But this still does not clear up the matter, as there were no less than three *San Juan*s in the Castilian Squadron. Aramburu's own vessel, the galleon *San Juan Bautista*, we can rule out immediately. There was the galleon *San Juan*, wrecked at Streedagh Strand in Sligo, as already shown. This leaves the third and final *San Juan*, a *nao* or merchantman with the appellation *Bautista*: this is our ship, Though there were two *San Juan Bautista*s (St John the Baptist) in the squadron, whereas Aramburu's was a galleon, Horra's was a merchantman. There is further proof in that Duro lists the *nao Bautista* as lost, and in a following document confirms that Diego Bazan was in a ship lost off Ireland '*la compania de que es capitan D. Diego de Bazan, hijo del Marques de Santa Cruz, pasa a esta nao de la suva, que era la San Juan Bautista, de la escuadra de Diego Flores, que se echo a fondo en Irlanda.*' Thus more confirmation that Diego de Bazan, here listed as a son of Santa Cruz, was aboard the *San Juan Bautista* (the *nao*). No further proof than this is needed.

The discrepancy of Duro's 'Gregoriò' and Aramburu's 'Gonzalo' (Melendez) can be disregarded in the light of Spanish name spellings. Duro lists Gregorio once, and Gonzalo when he quotes Aramburu's own account, but elsewhere settles for a safe 'G. Melendez' – evidently he took the easy way out. But it is no matter, as there is no other Melendez listed among the Armada personnel, and it is therefore safe to assume that Gregorio and Gonzalo were the same person.

What happened to the abandoned *nao* has never been explained. Recalde did not set her alight and leave her, as was the invariable custom when the Spaniards were forced to leave a ship. That she was in the sound on the 21st is confirmed by James Trant's letter of the 21st, but we also know that she was there at least until the following day by Aramburu's own account. Trant does confirm that there were five ships in all in the sound; three great ships (Recalde's *San Juan*, Aramburu's *Bautista*, and Horra's *Bautista*) and two tenders. Miguel de Aranivar, that mysterious man, had evidently departed. Was his own ship perhaps not a great ship after all, but a Castilian Squadron tender? Aramburu, himself the Castilian paymaster, again refers not to the ship's name but to that of her captain, and this familiarity could be because Aranivar's ship was of the same squadron. Both Trant and Edward Whyte confirm that there were two tenders, one of them 'a barque which came in since that time [the 15th]'. Aranivar had entered with the *Santa Maria* or at least at the same time. Probably his ship was one of the Castilian tenders, of which there were two, both 75 tons displacement, the *Nuestra Senora del Socorro* and the *San Antonio de Padua*, with forty-five and sixty-six men aboard respectively. Both of these *pataches* (tenders) are listed as lost by Duro, and although this need not mean literally that both were wrecked, it is reasonably firm but not conclusive evidence that it was the case. Aranivar did not lose his ship in Blasket Sound, since no mention in any source is made of another wreck. It must remain a mystery, like so many other shadow ships.

There is, however, another possibility of identifying Miguel de Aranivar's vessel, a theory which I would not consider were it not for the quality of the scholarship of the man who put it forward. Garrett Mattingly (*The Defeat of the Spanish Armada*) writes that a hospital ship left Dingle Bay with Recalde, and later, seeking refuge in one of the Channel ports, ran onto the rocks at Bolt Tail in Devon, becoming the only Armada vessel actually to be wrecked in England. Now the history of the Bolt Tail wreck is well known since most of her complement got ashore and were held captive for some time locally. She was the *San Pedro Mayor*, a 581 ton member of the *Urcas* Squadron, but nowhere does anyone prove that she was a hospital ship, although this is perfectly possible, the hospital ships being included apparently in that particular squadron.

Mattingly unfortunately died in 1962; he gives as sources the Irish State Papers (those calendared and printed by Laughton), Spotswood Green, Cyril Falls, Duro, Herrara Oria and Hume (Cal. Span. IV). In none of these is it stated positively, however, that the *San Pedro Mayor* was one of the Blasket vessels.

It is easy to disprove the theory altogether from two contemporary accounts by Aramburu and James Trant, both of whom were in the middle of it all. Trant's letter of September 11 (21) mentions 'three great ships' and again, having mentioned Recalde's ship, repeats that 'the other two are great ships also', going on to add 'they have two small barques.' Later on, he mentions that one of the great ships 'has her main mast broken' – a clear reference to Horra's ship.

The timetable here is everything. Recalde enters first, followed by Aramburu and Recalde's tender: three ships in. Then enters the *Santa Maria de la Rosa* and at the same time Miguel de Aranivar's ship: five in all. The *Santa Maria* then sinks: back to four. But a couple of hours after she sinks, Horra's vessel arrives, which brings us back to five. These five were the ships that Trant writes of. The three great ships were Recalde's *San Juan de Portugal*, Aramburu's *San Juan Bautista*, and Horra's *San Juan Bautista* – a merchantman as opposed to Aramburu's galleon. That leaves the 'two small barques', one Recalde's tender and the other the ship of Aranivar, which infers that she was small. It could not, therefore, have been the *San Pedro Mayor*.

When Recalde and Aramburu had completed the transfer of Gonzalo Melendez's and Diego de Bazan's troops, sailors, officers and other personnel from the 650 ton *nao*, all the Spanish ships must have been crowded indeed. The two tenders had taken their share, but they were small vessels and had little room. The *nao* had had 285 men on board at Lisbon, but this, like most of the listed Spanish complements, is probably an underestimation. In the meantime Aramburu was growing anxious of his own situation; he had already been lucky to avoid wrecking, and now, with at least a hundred more men crammed into the *Bautista*, he was in a hurry to be away; besides, food and water were still short. Recalde reluctantly agreed to let him leave for Spain, and on the morning of the 23rd Aramburu sailed on the wings of a light easterly wind. It was an ebbing tide and he first attempted to lower exit from the sound, taking advantage of the stream. But he had barely moved when the wind dropped, and for a while it looked as though the current would sweep the *Bautista* onto the Great Blasket – 'we were very near being lost.' The wind sprang up again, and changing tack he manoeuvred the galleon under topgallants out through the narrow passage between the rocks and reefs on the northwest of the sound.

He was still not clear. The wind frustratingly dropped once more, and again the struggle to avoid danger began. It was successful, but only barely; the men had been at it all day and night was coming on, and Aramburu decided to drop his one remaining anchor (he had had to abandon the smaller one lodged in the reef). An hour into the night the wind again shifted and blew from the southeast, and the *Bautista* once more began the alarming drifting with which they had had to contend during almost the whole of their stay in the sound. Using the anchor, he brought the vessel's head around and set sail in a last desperate effort to clear this graveyard of ships. It was pitch dark and blowing hard, and Aramburu had managed to enmesh himself in perhaps the most treacherous maze of danger along this part of the coast. Avoiding rocks, reefs and islands by a hairsbreadth, the *Bautista* shot a narrow passage between them all with more luck than judgement, and suddenly she was free.

Aramburu's narrative, understandably enough, is vague and difficult to follow in that he does not tell us how he managed to get the *Bautista* out of the sound. To say this is understandable is an understatement; it was blowing hard, and darkness added to the confusion of tacking and anchoring and drifting and tacking again, with shifting winds and heavy seas and a running tide tying it all into an inextricable knot.

We can thus only guess at how he did escape. Probably the *Bautista* followed roughly the same route as that by which she, and Recalde, had entered, except that the outward run began, I think, from somewhere to the east of Young Island, further up the sound. With the wind as it was, it seems doubtful that he could have made it back out from opposite the White Strand (and his narrative does appear to hint that he was considerably further north than that point) through a channel whose dangers any chart makes all too

White Strand, on the northeast side of the Great Blasket, and the western entrance to the Blasket Sound, seen from the village above the Strand. The San Juan, *piloted through the rocks and islets lying off the northern end of the island by Recalde, was the first of six ships to enter the Sound.*

clear. Did he sail through between Young and Beginish Islands, threading blindly a narrow channel studded with rocks and reefs, most of which would have been south of him, and past Kilbreedagh and Hen Rocks, with Stookeen and the Crows to the north? I think he did; but that is guesswork.

It is interesting to follow his own words here, which we pick up from the time he set sail finally: 'with a dark and cloudy night we tried to get out to windward of the reefs [in other words, by the route by which he had entered] but the current would not allow us; rather it was carrying us to our destruction. We turned and tried by an opening between the islands. The wind was freshening still more; there was a sea on, with heavy clouds and violent showers. . . . It pleased Our Lady,' he finished this passage feelingly, 'to whom we commended ourselves, that we should get out, sailing all that night to the west, so that by morning we found ourselves eight leagues from land.'

Aramburu's subsequent adventures are too lengthy to describe here; he beat back and forth off the southwest tip of Ireland for days before he got a wind slant which allowed him to weather it and sail for Spain, where he eventually made landfall at Santander. As for Recalde, he left with the *San Juan* and the tenders on the 27th, also reaching Spain, where at Corunna a few days after his landfall on October 7 he died, worn out by the voyage and the sickness which had kept him in his bunk for much of the journey home. Aramburu survived to lead a distinguished career in Philip's navy, being present at the battle with the *Revenge* in the Azores in 1591. John Anthony of Manona was less lucky: despite going through three examinations – an undoubted euphemism for torture under interrogation – and being kept alive for as long as it took to give all the information he had to his interrogators, he was killed by them. Also killed were the eight men taken from the landing party off Recalde's *San Juan*, including Fremoso, Francisco, Licornio and O'Carr. Probably they expected little mercy, knowing the exigencies of warfare, but their ending is sad nevertheless.

The significance of the loss of the *Santa Maria de la Rosa* lies not in any single facet of her wrecking but in a number of them. She probably (for there must remain some doubt) carried a son of the King of Spain, whether 'base' or not; just one man survived her sudden death; as Aramburu might paraphrase his own words, 'a most extraordinary and terrible occurrence'. The eye-witness accounts of her sinking are detailed and graphic – and more valuable in the light of the scarcity of similar material on other Armada wrecks around Ireland. Most significant of all, some fairly substantial remains and artifacts have been found, almost exactly where it was predicted that she must lie. In the future excavation of this fascinating wreck lies a wealth of stored information.

The mystery of what she carried may one day be cleared up. Manona testified that there were 15,000 ducats in gold coin and a further 15,000 ducats in silver coin, but this remains to be seen; he may have been spinning the tale to keep himself alive. If so, he failed.

XI

Myths and Mysteries

ONE of the largest and most intractable problems facing any researcher brave enough to tackle contemporary material on Armada wrecks in Ireland is the difficulty of identifying ships. In most cases ships that were wrecked or foundered around the Irish coast are either not named at all in the various records or else wrongly named; only in isolated instances, and then all too rarely, is fact sufficiently capable of verification as such; the number of reports where ships are named correctly is tiny in comparison with the total.

There are many reasons for this. Spanish names differed radically from the simple names usually applied to Irish or English vessels, and their translation into approximate names which would be understood or remembered by Englishmen or Irishmen was a haphazard affair. A fair illustration is the *Santa Maria de la Rosa*, otherwise and more commonly known as the *Nuestra Senora de la Rosa*, or in English, *Our Lady of the Rose*. In contemporary records there is scarcely a single instance where this exceptionally well documented vessel's name was given correctly; time after time she was described as *Our Lady of the Rosary* or *Nuestra Senora de la Rosario*. There was such a ship in the Armada, but she was the flagship of Pedro de Valdes, commander of the Andalusian Squadron, and captured by Francis Drake in the Channel just after the beginning of the running battle between the fleets and brought into an English port as a prize.

Usually, however, the ships were not named at all in accounts, and were often left completely unidentified; occasionally a scrap of information was given which might provide a flicker of light, as for instance in the case of the *San Esteban*, wrecked off Clare, and described in the State Papers as 'of St Sebastian's'. But even these clues are rare enough.

In many cases identification can only be guessed at through lists of prisoners which the English kept. Usually the names were wrongly spelt; 'de Suazo' becomes (phonetically) 'de Swasso', and so on. Phonetics in fact plays a large role in the identification of ships and also placenames and surnames; for instance 'Mac Win land' which is McSweeney's land, and 'Manglana' which is MacClancy. There are many examples of this throughout contemporary records; the historian and researcher must wade through them as best he can.

The Irish hardly ever kept records: most of them were illiterate, and in any case could scarcely have cared less about the name of a ship or its commander. Their primary concerns were with plunder and little else, and it is only in the northwest and north, where the Gaelic clan system still preserved within it the elements of civilization and kindliness, that we find real contact between native and Spaniard and a consequent and welcome growth of recorded fact and substance concerning ships and their crews.

The English records were better, but not by much. Their system of spies seldom seems to have garnered names of ships; even the sheriffs and agents, right up to the provincial governors, seem afflicted by a similar carelessness. 'Three Spanish ships' were reported in Killybegs; 'twenty-four Spaniards were taken in the Bay of Tralee'; the coroner of Clare parleyed with Spaniards who came ashore, but he neither took their names nor those of any of the seven ships which lay a couple of hundred yards away before his eyes. The ship of '700 Spaniards' was 'drowned with 200 or 300 men in her' – she is unnamed (this was the *Valencera*); eleven ships were in a creek in Donegal – again unnamed; a ship of 1000 tons was wrecked in Clew Bay and sixteen of her men came ashore – again there is no name, even though it would have been simple to ascertain it. A ship came right up to Galway and landed seventy men, all of whom were captured and imprisoned, yet no-one thought to inquire as to her name. Two ships were wrecked off Clare: they are described as 'of St Sebastian's' and 'out of Flanders'; seventy-two Spaniards were taken in Tirawley from a ship wrecked on the rocks – again neither ship nor men are named; three ships were 'cast away' at Sligo and their wreckage lay for weeks on the beach there, yet no-one identified them nor thought of asking the many prisoners who were taken and executed. A 'ship at Pollilly' sailed without anyone knowing her name; 'three great shippes . . . rode at anchor' in the Blasket Sound; and so on and so on, to the point of distraction.

It need not be thought that these lists were made by men who knew no better. The Secretary of the Council, Geoffrey Fenton, a usually meticulous and conscientious reporter of events, gave a detailed list of no less than seventeen ships, all of the Armada and lost in and around Ireland, a list which included estimates of men drowned and killed, and of ships which escaped wrecking. Not a single ship is named in that list.

The lists of prisoners did, however, yield names which can be traced back through contemporary Spanish lists of Armada personnel, which often gave the ships to which these men were attached. Even these lists are questionable; the fairly extensive reshuffle of ships and personnel at Corunna, meant that a list of men attached to certain ships which was made at, and referred to, the Lisbon assembly might not be as accurate afterwards. By and large, however, these Spanish lists are one of the few reliable sources.

More often than not, the sole method of identifying a vessel is to comb the lists of lost ships and ships returned from the Armada. There is a solid core of

Irish wrecks where identification is irrefutable: these include the *Girona, Valencera, San Juan of Castile, La Rata Encoronada, Duquesa Santa Ana, El Gran Grin, Santa Maria de la Rosa*. Then there is a less persuasive list of wrecks which have been more or less satisfactorily identified, but where identification is very much open to question; this includes such vessels as the *Juliana, Lavia, Falco Blanco, San Marcos, San Esteban, Annunciada* and *San Juan Bautista*. The remainder of ships which are tentatively named have the slimmest foundation for being so; they include the *Santiago, Ciervo Volante, Santa Maria de la Vison, Concepcion* and the two *Trinidads*. All else is darkness, often total.

There is little doubt, too, that very often wrecking incidents were confused and even duplicated in reports; in at least one instance a ship which was said to be wrecked in one place was in fact apparently in another. There is little hope of untangling such contradiction. The remoteness and difficulty of communication in some out-of-the-way corners of Connacht or Ulster meant that the only evidence of a wreck would come by word of mouth.

Tradition is an excellent and trustworthy guide to wreck sites. It is unreliable and inaccurate on other details. More often than not a tradition which has been handed down through the centuries concerning the actual site of a wrecking incident is right: in not a single instance have I seen it proved wrong, and therefore it must be respected quite as much as (if not more than) the contemporary record. Tradition rarely names ships, and when it does it does it wrongly, a judgement which applies to almost every pronouncement of the legend. But on the *placement* of wreck sites it is more or less infallible. Too often historians have downgraded the accuracy with which these wrecks are remembered; it is a curious aberration of judgement which ignores the fact that native folklore and memory have a long recollection of local events, and while it may distort it cannot alter the kernel of truth which is the centre of such legend.

The historian who attempts to sift through the immense and disparate collection of contemporary reports and ancient tradition faces equally immense difficulty. It is eased, however, by a close study of the wreck sites themselves, where very often a geographical detail missing from a report can illuminate an otherwise mysterious puzzle. Tides, currents and the variations of weather and sea conditions around the coasts is another and equally important factor. It is only when all the widely varied and often apparently irrelevant pieces of information and knowledge are gathered and sifted through that the overall picture begins to appear.

This chapter lists all the possible wrecks which have not already been identified in this volume; it does not claim to be accurate. Perhaps further research may throw up new factors which may change what is written here, but for the moment, the judgements however slight are made with every known factor taken into account, and using that as a basis, a possible – indeed the most probable – theory of events is built up. These sequences are offered without real conviction, but they are the most logical in that they are supported by the greatest weight of evidence available, however slight this may be.

It is very possible that the number of wrecks given is incorrect, but it is certainly not very far from the truth – perhaps by a couple of ships more or less. Vessels could be wrecked on the coast of Ireland and never be heard of; there are remote areas of Mayo (perhaps screened from view by the great rising cliffs of Erris/Tirawley) or Donegal, where a ship could be lost at night on some remote headland and be just scattered timbers and floating bodies the day after. But such a theory lies beyond proving.

For simplicity's sake the possible wrecks, apart altogether from those already dealt with in earlier chapters, are listed from the north of the country to the south, from the top to the bottom. They are marked on the relevant map, which helps to make sense of a complicated story; every available fact has gone towards the manufacture of the proffered theory, and in that sense at least there is some credence to be attached to their possible fate.

Lough Swilly

A large, long and narrow inlet of the sea, Lough Swilly splits north Donegal into two distinct territories; to the east is the Inishowen Peninsula, the scene of the wreck of the *Valencera*, which itself is likely to be responsible for an apparently misleading statement in the State Papers that there was a wreck in Lough Foyle, which is to the east of Inishowen and separates Donegal from Derry.

The State Papers (Ireland) give several fleeting allusions to a Spanish ship or ships being burned in Lough Swilly itself. On October 20, in a letter to Fenton and George Bingham, William Taaffe refers to 'two Spanish ships burned', which is echoed in a further communication dated October 29 from John Crofton, Thos. Mostion (Mostyn?) and Richard Dogherty to Sir Richard Bingham, that 3500 Spaniards had sent for succour 'having burned their broken ships'. On the whole the evidence seems to imply that an Armada ship was burned in Lough Swilly, but I am inclined to doubt it. By and large it must regretfully be discounted, though such an event is far from being impossible.

The Rosses

This is the collective name given to an area of land in western Donegal situated between Gweedore in the north and Dungloe in the south. It is an area of unparalleled beauty and rare attraction scenically, wild and unspoiled. Here we are on much firmer ground in the sense that there is absolutely undeniable evidence of not one but two wrecks in the locality. Both are in the

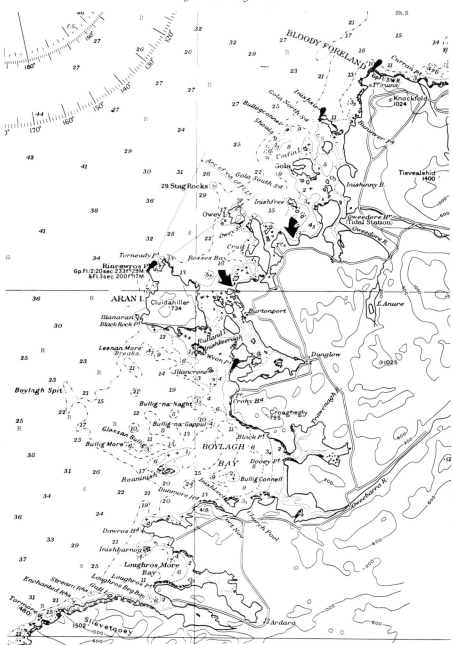

The area of the Rosses in western Donegal, in the Dungloe/Burtonport/Kincasslagh district, where two ships from the Armada were wrecked. The upper site is that of what may be the Juliana; the lower is a smaller vessel. (Produced from portion of BA chart 2723 with the sanction of the Controller, HM Stationery Office and of the Hydrographer of the Navy)

vicinity of Arranmore roads, between Arranmore Island and the mainland. There are countless rocks and islands in this intricately channelled seascape and it seems obvious that the two vessels knew very little of their whereabouts in attempting to gain shelter along this coastline. The more northerly of the two wrecks is near Mullaghderg in Inishfree Bay, just north of the tiny village of Kincasslagh. It lies in some thirty feet of water, on a sandy bottom whose surface frequently is churned up by strong tides and currents; sometimes the bones of the wreck are visible above the sand and at other times obscured. Many dives have been made on the site and occasional items raised, among them a swivel gun now in a private collection in Ballyshannon. The outline of the vessel is about seventy feet long, a keel length which would appear to indicate a displacement of some 700–800 tons, from the proportions of other Armada wrecks. The first known attempted excavation and investigation was made in the late eighteenth century, when a group of young men, with several good swimmers and expert divers, managed to reach the vessel underwater. It would appear that at that time at least part of her upperworks were still preserved, although this is apparently not now the case. Lead ingots were brought to the surface and an unspecified number of 'pretty made and pretty shaped' brass guns, which were taken ashore, melted down and sold as 'three cartloads' of scrap metal at 4½d a pound. Some iron guns were found, which were left on the bottom, and also coins, whose existence in the locality of the Rosses is verified up to the latter years of the last century. The brass cannon bore the arms of the King of Spain. Boyle, the leader of this expedition, later testified that the lead ballast was 'a yard long, triangular, the sides being pointed towards the end, setting thicker in the middle' – a typical piece of Armada ballast.

Following this first effort, little was done until over a century later, when in 1895 another expedition was organized and a small steamer, the *Harbour Lights*, chartered as a survey vessel. Two weeks' work resulted in a blank record; the sand, which still covers the wreck on most days, proved an impassable and impossible barrier to further investigation and the attempt was called off.

Since then there have been a number of attempts on the wreck, particularly in latter years, when more sophisticated diving equipment has made investigation somewhat easier. Many of these have been frustrated through the accumulation of sand which so often covers this wreck, but items have been brought up and will continue to be: an entirely unsatisfactory situation where one might hope for, and expect, a more responsible attitude towards a wreck of almost incalculable historical importance and whose investigation should surely be left to a scientific and properly and authoritatively controlled expedition.

There is little doubt that this is an Armada wreck, since there is evidence other than a strong local tradition to support such a theory; of tradition there is not a scrap. Patrick Bonner, the schoolteacher on Arranmore Island and a respected and knowledgeable local historian with a deep interest in the Armada, has this to say of the local tradition: 'folklore is silent on the Armada story, at least here in the Rosses. My ancestors have lived at Cloughglass (site of the second and more southerly of the two wrecks in the area) since the seventeenth century and I have never heard even the slightest echo of the Armada saga handed down. . . . they knew nothing of the wreck until 1853 (when an anchor was found) and then . . . it meant nothing to them.'

Bonner gives as a possible explanation of this mystifying lack of tradition the view that the area of the Rosses was largely unpopulated in 1588. 'There was a new influx of people to the Rosses in the seventeenth century (1609, 1654 and after 1690) and the newcomers knew nothing of what happened there in the century previous to their coming – hence the great difficulty in filling what one could describe as the great vacuum. The population of the Rosses prior to the Plantations must have been very small indeed [the Ulster Plantations, particularly under Cromwell, which forced many natives from the richer lands of east Ulster across to the barren western half of the province].'

It is with the identification of the Mullaghderg wreck that the real difficulties are encountered. The first possible clue to emerge stems from a letter in the Spanish State Papers and written by members of a party of eight shipwrecked Spaniards from the Armada appealing for aid to enable them to reach home. The letter was written in 1596, eight years after the ships were lost around the coast, and reveals that the small party was in the northwest with O'Donnell and Tyrone and had apparently helped to train native soldiers for the Ulster chieftains, by then becoming increasingly militant against English rule. Among their names are those of survivors of three wrecks, the *Lavia*, wrecked at Sligo, the *Trinidad Valencera*, wrecked in Inishowen, and yet a third Levant Squadron vessel, the *Juliana*.

This is the first intimation that the *Juliana* was wrecked in the general area of the northwest. There are gaps in the overall picture of the Donegal wrecks, such as the two unidentified vessels at Killybegs and a remote possibility of a third unnamed wreck at Donegal town itself. But the *Juliana*, unlike the two wrecked at Killybegs, was of considerable size, displacing 860 tons and carrying 395 men and 32 guns on leaving Lisbon. This rules her out as being one of those at Killybegs.

The remaining possible wrecks in Donegal are few, and the inference is thus strong that the *Juliana* was wrecked somewhere along that county's coast. Had she been wrecked further south, her survivors would have been either executed or hustled along the escape net from Sligo to Antrim; in Donegal they were largely remote from such aid, and furthermore, the wrecking of such a ship might very well go largely unnoticed among the creeks and cliffs of this wild coast.

The *Juliana* was certainly lost – there is no doubt of that, as the Spanish State Papers make clear, some of her survivors were in Donegal in 1596 and again a year later. The ship was probably at least seventy to eighty feet in keel length (the *Santa Maria de la Rosa*, at 945 tons, had an estimated keel length of around ninety feet) and such a length would undoubtedly fit the wreck at the bottom of the sea near Mullaghderg. This wreck is also the only unaccounted-for one in Donegal which appears to fit the known facts. There is thus a strong inference, but alas little else, to suggest that the Mullaghderg wreck is that of the Levantine ship *Juliana*. The local name for this ship is traditionally given as 'The Most Blessed Trinity', but there is no ship in the lists which matches the description.

The Cloughglass wreck, which is north of Burtonport and south of Cruit Island, opposite Arranmore Island, is equally well known locally but again apparently unidentifiable. Its size is noticeably less than that of the Mullaghderg wreck, which suggests that it is the remains of a tender or despatch vessel rather than either a front-line ship or a hulk.

Apparently nothing was known locally of this wreck until 1853, when the coastguards at Rutland Island, in the straits between Arranmore Island and the mainland, found an anchor on a strand at Cloughglass known as *Cul Tra* – the back strand. It is stated variously that it was found by the local residents and by the coastguards themselves, but the consensus appears to support the fact that one or more of the coastguards were involved in its discovery. The then chief coastguard officer, Mr Richard Heard, instigated a search which had the support of Admiral Sir Erasmus Ommanney, CB, a high official in the service who was then on a tour of inspection in the area. This anchor went to adorn the railings of the United Service Institution in Whitehall, London.

Once again the wreck has been the scene of many dives by amateurs, and there is plenty of evidence that many items of great historical value have been removed from it. A local farmer whose tractor was hired by some of these divers testifies to the fact that it was driven away from the site of the wreck with 'the full load of my tractor, mostly cannon and things like that.' This is nothing short of vandalism and depredation and can merit only the strongest condemnation. The wreck, close in to shore and in fairly shallow water, is vulnerable to the attentions of even casual divers, and although there is not a great deal of it left, what little remains deserves at least the careful and scrupulous attention of marine archaeologists.

It may be possible some day to identify the Cloughglass wreck. Although this vessel appears to have been one of the smaller ships in the Armada and as such not of as great an importance as, say, the *Juliana*, it is none the less fascinating for that.

Killybegs

This picturesque fishing harbour was the base from which the galleass *Girona* with Don Alonso de Leiva aboard set out on her last voyage, an attempt to reach Scotland, which ended on the coast of Antrim. It was also the scene of two other, if minor, wrecks of Armada vessels.

The first report of Armada ships near Killybegs is contained in a report in the State Papers dated September 15 and written by Sheriff George Bingham to his brother Richard, which mentioned that three Spanish ships 'bore down towards the harbour of Calebeg [Killybegs].' The most complete version of these three ships is given much later, in a report by Henry Duke on October 5: 'Three of the Spanish ships coming into the harbour of the Killibeggs in M'Sweeny's country, one of them was cast away a little without the harbour, another running aground on the shore brake to pieces. The third being a gally and sore bruised with the seas, was repaired in the said harbour with some of the planks of the second ship, and the planks of a pinnace which they had of M'Sweeny.'

The 'gally . . . sore bruised with the seas' was of course the *Girona*. Clearly one of the ships sank outside the harbour, while the other somehow managed to wreck herself within it, the timbers from this second and presumably more accessible wreck being used to repair the *Girona*. Again there is not the slightest shred of evidence as to the possible identity of these two small vessels: small they undoubtedly were, and therefore of relatively little significance. However this does not change the fact that two Armada ships were wrecked at Killybegs – the only town or village in Ireland which can boast (if that is the proper word) of such an event.

Donegal Town

'There is another ship at Donegall,' wrote Patrick Eulane to Sir Henry Bagenal, Marshal of the Army, 'and it was saved by means of a coal-boat that was sent to them from the shore, but they lost their mainmast, and they cast out 120 great horses and sixty mules.' Eulane's report was dated October 24 and is the only reference in the State Papers to this ship. Spotswood Green also mentions it, quoting a similar source as well as a reference in the Carew Papers to what could well be the same ship, which Carew reports was lost 'in O'Boyle's country'. These are the only two references which I have been able to find in relation to this event.

There are a few extractable facts, scanty though they are. If the ship 'cast out 120 horses and sixty mules', then she was a supply ship, a hulk or *urca*, and a fairly large one at that. 'O'Boyle's country' technically should refer to the Dawros/Rosbeg area of west Donegal where the *Duquesa Santa Ana* was wrecked, and I would oppose Spotswood Green's contention that Carew's reference was to a possible Donegal wreck. Besides, Eulane makes no reference to the ship at Donegal being actually wrecked but says merely that she was 'saved', which would imply that she survived and was able to continue her voyage, albeit without her mainmast. I have a strong feeling that this vessel is tied in with another possible wreck at Inver, in Broadhaven, Co. Mayo, and will continue this theory below. It is also possible that this vessel picked up some companions of Captain de Cuellar (Chapter VII) at Donegal, but this is very doubtful.

Streedagh Strand, Co. Sligo

The third ship of the trio wrecked at Streedagh (Chapter VII) has never been identified. However, there is more than a possibility that she was yet another Levant vessel, the smallest of the squadron, the 666 ton converted merchantman *Santa Maria de la Vison*.

The evidence for this supposition is contained in the same list of prisoners, given in the contemporary papers in Trinity College, Dublin, which contains the name of Manuel Orlando, master of the *Lavia*, almost certainly also wrecked at Streedagh. Besides Orlando's name there is a 'Vicenzio Debartulo', and both are described as 'Venitian Captains'. The name 'Debartulo' is paralleled in the full Armada lists by only two similar names, those of Nicolas de Bartolo, captain of the galleon *Florencia*, a vessel commandeered from the Grand Duke of Tuscany's minuscule navy and which reached Spain safely; and Juan de Bartolo, captain of the *Santa Maria de la Vison*. No Vicenzio or even Vicenzo is listed. It appears fairly certain that the Vicenzio Debartulo and the Juan de Bartolo, master of the *Santa Maria*, are the same man, the obvious conclusion being that the *Santa Maria* was wrecked somewhere along the northwest coast of Ireland and within the sphere of power of Sheriff George Bingham of Sligo, whose prisoner her captain became. If this was indeed the case, then the list of ships wrecked along that part of the coastline must be scrutinized carefully. Once this is done the limits are clearly set, for with the exception of the third and unnamed ship at Streedagh, there is no other plausible evidence to suggest that the *Santa Maria* was wrecked anywhere other than on the Sligo beach.

To support this one could with some justification cite the strong local tradition in and around Streedagh, a tradition held to this day, that one of the three ships wrecked there in 1588 was called the *Santa Maria*. At the same time this is largely meaningless: while it is tempting to accept the tradition as further proof, the fact is that all around those parts of Ireland where Armada ships were lost tradition gives similar names to nearly every such wreck, almost as though the Spaniards could think of no other name for their vessels. Tradition, usually almost infallible on actual sites of wrecks, must be doubted as to nomenclature, at least in this case. But there is ample if circumstantial evidence to support the theory that the third ship at Streedagh was the *Santa Maria de la Vison*.

Tirawley, Co. Mayo

As a district, Tirawley no longer exists. It formerly referred to that remote area of north Mayo whose formidable coastline caused so much hardship to the Spanish vessels trying to weather it from the shelter of Donegal Bay. Somewhere along this coast was lost a vessel of considerable size, and her wrecking was marked by a singularly distasteful episode of brutality. Edward Whyte's letter to his brother Stephen, dated September 22, gives the gruesome details briefly. 'There was about that time, one other great ship cast away in Tirrawley and that there are three noblemen, a bishop, a friar, and sixty other men taken by William Burke of Ardnearie; and all the residue of that ship are slain and drowned, insomuch as he writes that one Melaghlen McCabb, a Galloglass, killed eighty of them with his galloglass axe.'

Unfortunately there is neither mention of the vessel's name nor of the spot where she was wrecked, so once more we must guess at the truth. Tirawley covered a very wide area and had a long coastline; William Burke, one of the Burkes of Mayo who, unlike the remainder of his wild kinsmen, appears to have been on reasonable terms with Governor Bingham, lived at Ardnaree, near Ballina. It has sometimes been stated that he handed over his sixty-five prisoners to Sir Richard Bingham, but there is clear evidence elsewhere in contemporary reports to confirm that instead they were turned over to George Bingham in Sligo. He, in company with a cousin, Francis Bingham, Robert Coker and Captain Greene O'Molloy, had been entrusted by his brother with the task of rounding up all prisoners in the baronies of 'Owles and Erris' (roughly the coast extending from Clew Bay around to Ballina) and it was while undertaking this task that the prisoners from the Tirawley wreck were put in his custody by William Burke.

This was a fairly sizeable vessel judging by her complement. Whyte later amended the number of prisoners which Burke took to seventy-two; together with the eighty men who were hacked to death by the singularly bloodthirsty McCabb, the initial figure is in excess of 150 men, and it is fair to assume that many were also drowned while coming in to land. In other words, a ship's complement of perhaps 250–300 is not an unreasonable assumption. Geoffrey Fenton is more helpful. He lists this vessel as 'in Tyraughlie one shipp, 400 men [lost]', and while his figures might well be questioned the inference nonetheless is that this ship was a big vessel, as was her complement. But we are still no nearer to solving the mystery of her identity; the State Papers, in common with all other contemporary sources, yield no further significant details.

That the ship wrecked in Tirawley was of some importance might be deduced from the fact that she carried a bishop aboard; few of the lesser vessels bore the same distinction. He must have been Irish to have been on the voyage in the first place, for while there were hundreds of Spanish clerics with the fleet, none were bishops. So it was an Irish bishop in all probability who ended up in George Bingham's tender clutches. His fate cannot have been pleasant.

We have now considerably reduced the number of possible Armada vessels wrecked around Ireland; most of them are at least tentatively identified, with the exception of three which are still outstanding, at least in the northwest of the country. These three are the ship at Donegal which was rescued by a turf-boat; the Levant ship *San Nicolas Prodaneli*, which we know was wrecked in Ireland somewhere in this vicinity, and finally the 600 ton hulk *Santiago*, which the Spanish State Papers say perished off Ireland. (Unfortunately, they say no more.) It can be taken for granted here (and proved later in the course of this chapter) that the Tirawley wreck was not a front-line but a more minor ship. She was not a tender (her complement was too large): therefore she was a hulk, or supply ship. It is to the squadron of *urcas* therefore that we must next turn.

At first sight this is a daunting task; there are no less than twenty-three. A fair proportion, however, can be disposed of at once on varied grounds, such as their safe return to Spain, their too small size, and other reasons; among this group are the *Perro Marino, Paloma Blanca, Ventura, Santa Barbara, Santiago, David, Gato, Esayas* and *San Gabriel*. This leaves a total of fourteen; which is still formidable.

From these we can eliminate the flagship *El Gran Grifon*, wrecked on Fair Isle; the *almiranta San Salvador*, which returned safely to Spain; the *Falco Blanco Mayor*, captured by the English in the Channel in January 1589 while on her way back to Hamburg; the *Castillo Negro* and the *Barca de Amburg*, which both foundered in the northern seas somewhere off Donegal/Antrim; the *Casa la Paz Chica*, which returned safely to Spain; the *San Pedro Mayor*, the only Armada vessel actually wrecked on English shores (in Devon); *El Sanson*, which got back to a Galician port; *Barca de Danzig*, which ferried at least some of the *Annunciada*'s complement from the Shannon back to Spain; the *Falco Blanco Mediano*, wrecked off Connemara; the *Santo Andres*, which returned; this makes a further twelve to be deducted from the original twenty-three and leaves us with just two of the *urcas* yet to be accounted for.

Both vessels show some similarities; while the *Casa de Paz Grande* of 650 tons was considerably larger than the 400 ton *Ciervo Volante*, they carried similarly-sized crews of 225 and 222 men respectively. Of contemporary record there is little enough, but what there is might well be significant in that while the Spanish State Papers make no mention whatsoever of the *Casa*, they list the *Ciervo Volante* as being lost, without going further. At least one historian has placed the wreck of the *Ciervo Volante* at Scattery Roads in the Shannon, but from what I can see there is little evidence to support this, all the facts pointing to that vessel being the *Annunciada*.

On the spin of a coin, almost, we must choose the *Ciervo Volante*; she was lost somewhere, and probably around Ireland, and she does not fit in with any wrecks around the coast other than the Tirawley one; she was big enough and

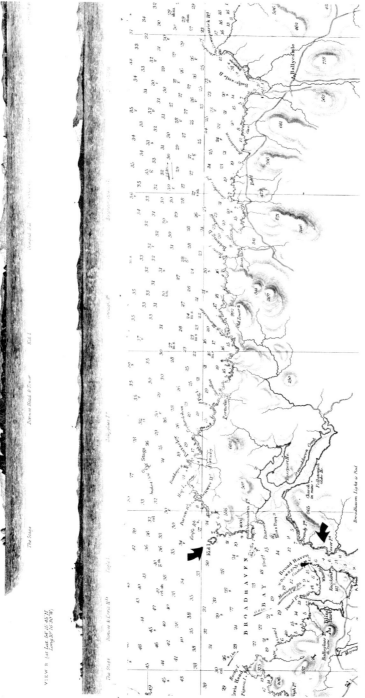

Tradition and contemporary reports place three Armada wrecks on the north Mayo coast. That in Tirawley can only be located somewhere between Benwee Head and Dunpatrick Head. The other two are thought to be at Inver, deep inside Broadhaven Bay, and off Kid Island, close to Benwee and at the entrance to the Bay. The profiles of the Tirawley coastline are drawn from the north and northwest. (Produced from portions of BA chart 2419 with the sanction of the Controller, HM Stationery Office and of the Hydrographer of the Navy)

had enough men on board to fill even the macabre demands of Melaghlen McCabb, and had a sufficiently large complement to match Edward Whyte's estimate of survivors and dead. Her total complement of 222 is nowhere near Fenton's estimate of 400, but then the Secretary was proved wrong elsewhere, and Tirawley being remote, news from there could have been distorted by the time it reached his ears, although apparently he did visit the area at some stage during the panic over the Armada. The *Ciervo Volante* is named almost without conviction, and with the dubious advantage of the weight of the Spanish Papers. But this is really the slimmest possible evidence to identify the *urca* in Tirawley. As to the wreck site there are various claims, from near Belderg Harbour in the west of Tirawley to somewhere near Ballina. One can say no more than that the wreck probably lies somewhere between those two points.

Broadhaven, Co. Mayo

In connection with Armada wrecks Broadhaven is less well known than most areas around the Irish coast. This is a strange aberration, since there are traditions of not just one but two Armada ships in the vicinity of this bay, which lies on the northward side of Erris Head itself. Erris Head to the west and Benwee Head to the north flank the approaches into Broadhaven, which from being a broad and spacious bay guarded by magnificent cliffs and mountains and by the sentinel crags of Kid Island suddenly fans out into three winding inlets which cut south and southwest deep into the wide, low bogs of the Erris Peninsula.

Broadhaven, which joins Blacksod Bay at Belmullet through a short canal which cuts through the isthmus at that point, is less familiar to Armada historians for two reasons, its remoteness from the normal channels of sixteenth century communication and the scarcity with which even the broad outline of the area around Erris is mentioned by contemporary Armada documents.

Even if there were no records of any sort to indicate that there were Armada wrecks in and around Broadhaven, its very geographical position would lead one to expect them there. Any ships falling into Donegal Bay from the north or northwest would find themselves embayed by the great westerly thrust of Mayo crowned by the intimidating Erris – one of the wildest sea capes in the world. Trying to weather this and failing, they would naturally fall back towards Broadhaven; once pushed back towards the bay there could be little chance of escape in a wind from the north, for between Erris and Downpatrick Head, about thirty miles to the east, there are at least twenty miles of the finest cliffs in Ireland – fine, that is, in the scenic sense. To a sailing vessel the cliffs represent an awesome threat.

Tradition strongly supports the suggestion that there were two Armada

*The Mayo coast north of Broadhaven Bay. The peculiar shape of the rocks, known locally as Stacks or Stags, is a feature of this formidable coast. Erris Head, west of Broadhaven, was a prime factor in the loss of many Armada ships, which failed to weather it and were blown onto the coast. Tradition places one such wreck near these cliffs. (*Irish Times*)*

wrecks within Broadhaven Bay; one at Kid Island off Benwee Head and marking the entrance to the bay. If a vessel did strike Kid Island there could be no hope of any escape; the cliffs are sheer not only on the island but on the mainland. Here even a great ship might sink without ever being seen, since the cliffs on the coast rise from the inland bogs to their highest point where the land meets the sea, effectively screening a great deal of the expanse of Broadhaven Bay, especially from the east, southwest and west. There is not a solitary piece of documentary evidence connected with this supposed wreck from any contemporary source; any argument for its existence rests solely on tradition, which is strong in the area. If a ship did sink there, it is likely to have been a small one, possibly a tender of some sort. Other than that, we must leave the story to the folk-tellers.

The other wreck is slightly better documented, but yet with slim evidence. There are several points not entirely circumstantial and centring around this wreck which suggest that it may have been that of the *urca Santiago* (600 tons and 86 men) which the Spanish State Papers assert was lost off Ireland. The Irish State Papers contain two references to the fact that an Armada ship was wrecked in the inner recesses of Broadhaven close to a townland called Inver, on the eastern side of the inlet which runs south and then west from the lighthouse at Knocknalina inland towards Belmullet. Local tradition can point out the site of this wreck without hesitation, and taking into consideration the accuracy with which tradition locates most wreck sites

Inver, Broadhaven Bay, Co. Mayo. Forming one side of Erris Head, this is a sheltered inlet off Broadhaven, the bay in which several Armada vessels may have been wrecked. A ship which sank near Inver may have been the Santiago *; her crew marched overland to the Mullet Peninsula, southwest of Broadhaven, and embarked aboard the* Duquesa Santa Ana, *herself wrecked subsequently in Donegal.*

around Ireland, there is no reason to doubt the accuracy of the Inver legends.

The crew of this vessel is reported to have joined the complements of the *Rata* and *Duquesa Santa Ana*, which at the time had assembled at Tiraun (Torane), on the other side of Erris and south down the Erris Peninsula itself, the *Duquesa* being anchored in Elly Bay (Pollilly). The first mention is contained in Geoffrey Fenton's first note to Burghley of September 29, when he briefly mentions the fact; it was repeated on October 10 by Edward Whyte, writing from Athlone to Walsingham. Both Whyte and Fenton were reliable witnesses and we must accept what the State Papers say on the matter in the absence of other reports.

James Machary, a survivor of the *Duquesa*, makes no mention of a third crew joining at Tiraun; neither does Gerald Comerford, agent of the Crown in the Erris area. But this does not necessarily mean that the crew of the Inver wreck did not join the *Duquesa*; if the ship's complement was small, it would cause little enough comment among men whose main attentions were elsewhere.

The interesting fact about this wreck is that it is known still in the area as the 'bare ship' – *an long maol* – signifying that she was mastless when she was wrecked. The unnamed ship which had to be assisted into Donegal by a turf-boat was also mastless: could they be the same? Add to this coincidence the fact that the *Santiago* was an *urca*, as was the Donegal vessel. We have already accounted for all the *urcas* with the exception of the *Santiago*: her listed crew of eighty-six was small enough, and likely smaller still by the time she was wrecked. Finally, the Spanish State Papers say that she was wrecked in Ireland, and there is the added factor that no other known wreck around the country fits such a vessel as the *Santiago*.

It may never be proven, but there is plenty of circumstantial evidence to suggest that the *Santiago* made landfall at Donegal town, where she was saved by a turf-boat and where it was noted that she had lost her mainmast. Somewhere in Donegal Bay her men threw out the cargo of horses and mules to lighten her and enable her to beat out to sea again, at which point presumably the native boat came to assist. After this, declining to enter Donegal Town itself, the *Santiago* drifted on down the bay, still mastless but perhaps with a jury rig which would at least keep her under way. She managed to beat as far as Broadhaven, but failing to weather Erris ran into the shelter of the bay and went aground at Inver. While there, her men heard of the presence of the *Duquesa* some twelve miles away and leaving the ship at Inver (probably sunk or beyond repair by that time) walked south and crossed the isthmus at Belmullet to join Alonso de Leiva at Tiraun.

Although most of the pieces of this theory fit, it is offered more as a possible and satisfactory solution than as a reconstruction of fact, though it is reasonable to assume that the (second?) wreck in Broadhaven was that of the *Santiago*.

Curraun Peninsula, Co. Mayo

That there was a wreck at the Fynglasse (modern Toorglass) area of the peninsula, at a point where the land mass of Curraun bulges seaward between Mulrany and Achill, is well documented and indisputable. The element of doubt, however, is in whether, as is often claimed, this was the *Gran Grin* which had earlier missed Clare Island and drifted on to ground on the mainland. There are in my opinion sufficient grounds for believing that the *Gran Grin* was wrecked on Clare Island; and certainly the balance of the evidence of the State Papers suggests such an answer. If we can accept this, then the problem of identifying the Fynglasse wreck remains.

It has been suggested in Chapter III that the Fynglasse wreck was that of the Levant Squadron vessel *San Nicolas Prodaneli*, one of a possible two dozen Ragusan ships which sailed with the Armada. Her loss is affirmed by Spanish records, and was an almost inevitable result of her being of frail build similar to her squadron sisters. A hint of the truth may emanate from a report by Bingham to the Queen on December 13, in which he complained of being upstaged by Fitzwilliam over a matter which is of no concern at this point. Bingham also says, however, that 'my brother George Bingham had one Don Graveillo de Swasso and another gentleman by licence, and some five or six Dutch boys and young men, who coming after the fury and heat of justice was past, by entreaty I spared them, in respect they were pressed into the fleet against their wills . . .'.

There is no 'Don Graveillo de Swasso' in any of the Armada lists of personnel. There is, however, a Don Gabriel de Suazo listed as a captain of infantry aboard the *San Nicolas* at Corunna; the phonetics of both names are so similar as to leave little doubt that de Swasso and de Suazo are the same person. If, then, de Suazo was the man taken by George Bingham, it would mean that the *San Nicolas* was wrecked somewhere in the northwest of the Sligo Sheriff's territory. George Bingham had been sent by his brother on a tour of Erris and Owle (Fynglasse lay in the latter barony) to mop up whatever remained of Spanish survivors and to commandeer whatever cannon, etc were salvageable from the various wrecks. It is very conceivable that he found de Suazo and his companions either earlier or during this tour of Owle.

The *San Nicolas Prodaneli* was originally a Ragusan ship, named by the Spaniards after her captain (and possibly part-owner) Marin Prodanelic, a prominent Ragusan seaman. He was aboard the *Sveti Nikola* (her true name) when she was wrecked and presumably perished. The Levant vessel displaced 834 tons and carried some 355 men, together with 26 guns. The inference that she was wrecked in Ireland is strengthened by a letter dated February 1589, from Marin Ranjina, a Ragusan in Lisbon, to Prodanelic's brother in Dubrovnik which refers to the wreck of the *San Nicolas* in Ireland. 'Ever since I saw your brother . . . with the rest of the Armada, I have been uneasy, but in no case did I think to send you such . . . sad news. Now I see from Peter Ivelja's letter that the uncertain rumours have been confirmed and I have learned that he perished on the cliffs of Ireland, and of all those that were with him scarcely a dozen have been saved.'

There are striking links between this letter and the Fynglasse wreck. The place where the ship is commonly said to have struck is surrounded by cliffs ('the cliffs of Ireland'?), while only sixteen men survived the Fynglasse wreck, compared with 'scarcely a dozen' who, according to Ranjina, survived the wreck of the *San Nicolas*. One of these was undoubtedly de Suazo. Once more we are left with insufficient evidence to prove anything concrete; yet there is a very strong argument to support the contention that it was the *San Nicolas Prodaneli*, formerly the Ragusan *Sveti Nikola* of Marin Prodanelic, which was wrecked inside Clew Bay on the Curraun Peninsula.

Tralee, Co. Kerry

An area of considerable mystery is a description which would fit the sea around Tralee. For many years, starting with Spotswood Green's theory in 1906, successive historians have accepted that at least two ships were wrecked thereabout; in fact there is substantial doubt as to whether even a single vessel was lost, let alone two. Men from an Armada ship at Tralee are recorded as being the first on Irish soil, but there is no evidence of any worth to suggest that she was wrecked rather than captured or surrendered. The latter seems the most probable.

On September 19 the Vice-President Thomas Norris of Munster wrote to Walsingham enclosing the examination of the twenty-four Spaniards taken at Tralee; by that time they had been murdered by Lady Denny, wife of Sir Edward Denny, a noted planter (often referred to with some puzzlement as an 'undertaker', a term which contrary to its normal meaning was commonly used to describe English planters in Munster; Denny had vast stretches of land near Tralee). Sir Edward was absent in Dublin but his wife did her duty in English eyes. Not a man survived. Norris' letter gives the full details. 'There were twenty-four Spaniards taken in the Bay of Tralee, all of Castile and Biscay, which were executed because there was no safe keeping for them . . . three of them offered ransoms for their lives, promising that they should find friends in Waterford to redeem them, whose names they would not tell.' All else contained in the report referred to the general Armada campaign.

The bark thus appears to be either Castilian or Biscayan and was probably one of the *pataches* or *zabras* attached to both squadrons as tenders. There were six tenders with the squadrons, varying in tonnage from 70 to 96 and all having similarly sized crews, with the exception of the Castilian *patache, San Antonio de Padua*, which had sixty-six men aboard (she can be ruled out with some certainty). All five remaining vessels had crews varying from forty-two to forty-six men.

The Spanish State Papers are not particularly helpful; three of the five vessels are listed as lost, the other two not being mentioned at all. Tenders had a habit of being carelessly recorded in accounts of ships lost or returned, since they were after all of somewhat minor importance, but it is no help whatsoever when it comes to identifying these little ships. It appears to have been accepted practice that if there was no record of a ship, particularly a tender, she was commonly accepted as lost. But we do find that many small vessels listed as lost managed to return to Spain or were left in various countries having borne messages there and failing to rejoin the fleet for one reason or another. The Spanish State Papers say nothing of either of the Biscayan *pataches Isabella* and *San Esteban*; we will therefore tentatively rule these two out of our calculations.

Of the three left, any one could be the bark taken or lost at Tralee. They are the *La Maria de Aquirre* and the *Miguel de Suso* of Biscay and the *Nuestra Senora del Socorro* of Castile. The *Miguel* was smaller than the other two at 36 tons and carried 46 men; and *Maria* displaced 70 tons and carried 43 men. The *Socorro* carried 45 men and was the largest of the three at 75 tons: she may have accompanied Recalde on his voyagings among the Blasket Islands. It has been theorized at least twice that the Tralee ship was the *Socorro*; I have found not a shred of evidence other than supposition to support this. The lost ship could well have been one of the three mentioned – but which?

There is another possible route through this apparent impasse. So far we have accepted that the vessel was of the Castile or Biscay Squadrons, but this is after all an assumption founded on the fact that the survivors described *themselves* (or, more precisely, were described) but *not* the ship as being of Castile and Biscay. The thread of this argument is that the ship need not be either Biscayan or Castilian: she could have come from a different squadron, probably that of the *pataches* and *zabras*, who made up a squadron of twenty-two commanded by Don Antonio Hurtado de Mendoza.

A further clue may well lie in the number of crew – twenty-four. Possibly this had been reduced since Lisbon or Corunna by the usual deaths, but we are reasonably safe in assuming that her original crew cannot have been much in excess of thirty men. If we extract from the squadron led by Hurtado the names of all *pataches* and *zabras* having crews of this size, we find ourselves with a list of six, all with crews of twenty-two to thirty-one in the Lisbon roster.

After Corunna this list showed radical changes. It may well be that the *pataches* and *zabras*, insignificant enough in themselves, provided a form of reserve from which Medina Sidonia and his senior commanders and other officers could choose replacements and replenishments for the front-line vessels; a detailed and specific study of the Corunna muster and its intricacies is beyond the scope of this book but might well show hitherto unrevealed facts bearing on such a theory. Be that as it may, of the six possibles selected from the Lisbon muster the crews of all but one were substantially reduced by an overall figure of about twenty-five per cent. The remaining vessel, the *zabra La Trinidad* which at Lisbon had a crew of twenty-three (just one below the figure of the Tralee ship) had it raised at Corunna to twenty-four – the magic figure. Her tonnage is not given in any of the records but was in all probability in the region of the forty tons or so given by Edward Whyte.

We are now left with two distinct arguments, one which gives us three possible ships, the other which yields just one. Neither suggests vessels common to both. If only because it provides at least an outright answer, the *zabra Trinidad* is put forward. There is the slimmest evidence for so doing, but of all the vessels which might have been taken at Tralee, she seems the most likely. The closest perusal of the crew's examination fails to show that the ship herself was from either Castile or Biscay, and the fact that the men themselves were from those areas proves nothing; the *Trinidad*, for all we know, could have been from neither.

There is also the added factor of the size of her crew: effectively, she is the only small tender either in her own squadron or the Biscayan and Castilians to come near the specified figure of twenty-four. And there her case must rest.

As to the other wreck, usually said to be of a large Biscayan ship sunk somewhere in Tralee Bay, there is little or nothing to confirm the story, apart from a strong contradictory tradition. There is a possibility that a Castilian ship, the *Trinidad*, which had kept company for some time with Marcos de Aramburu's *San Juan Bautista* while moving south down the coast of Kerry,

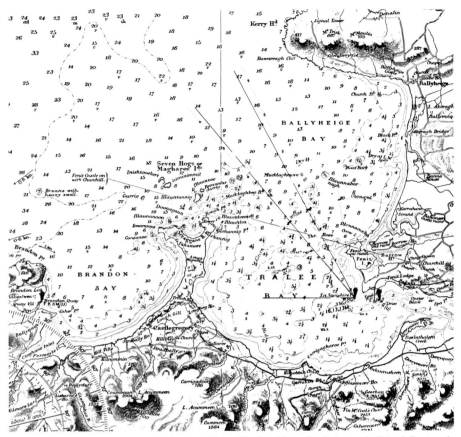

The deep indentation of the coastline between Kerry Head and Brandon Point on the Dingle Peninsula would have been a hazard for ships attempting to beat to the southwest, and contemporary reports suggest that it may have claimed at least one Armada ship. The Blaskets lie at the western end of the peninsula. (Produced from portion of BA chart 2679 with the sanction of the Controller, HM Stationery Office and of the Hydrographer of the Navy)

may have been blown inshore sometime around the night of September 12. She never reached Spain and must have sunk somewhere between Kerry Head and home.

The fate of this ship is interesting. Aramburu observed on September 2 that she was 'taking much water onto its bow', which implies that the 872 ton vessel was finding it difficult to press on for Spain. Until she disappeared forever from Aramburu's view, the two big ships kept in intermittent and distant contact. Aramburu's log last mentions her on the night of the 12th: The ship *Trinidad* was sailing close to us, under foresail and mainsail [this in spite of a strong gale and heavy seas]; but after midnight we lost sight of her, though we showed our lantern.' This was also the night on which Aramburu's

Bautista was blown far back along her course; presumably, if the *Trinidad* was not wrecked she also was blown back, in which case she would have likewise resumed course southward on the morning of the 13th, when the gale died down to be replaced by a welcome following wind.

Aramburu does not mention the *Trinidad* again. On the 15th he met Recalde and his tender, and on the same day all three anchored in the Blasket Sound. But he does mention that on the same day again 'we saw another ship to leeward close to the land. God will have been pleased to come to her aid, for she was in great danger.' If the *Trinidad* had survived the tremendous gale on the night of the 12th (and who is to say that she did not?) it is entirely possible that she had roughly paralleled Recalde's course over the following three days, in which case she too would be near the Blaskets. The *Trinidad* would not have had the benefit of the navigational lead which Recalde gave to Aramburu and which saved him and his ship from perishing, and thus could have taken the passage through the Blasket Sound along the leeward or mainland side of the islands – a hazardous one for those who do not know it, but in reasonable weather navigable with close knowledge and care. The ship which Aramburu saw on the 15th trying to navigate the sound receives no further mention.

Was she the *Trinidad*? On the face of it there is every chance that she was. There is absolutely no single shred of evidence to suggest that she was wrecked in the Bay of Tralee, but a great deal more to connect her with the next mystery ship, which was wrecked somewhere around Valentia Island. The story of a large Biscayan wrecked near Tralee must regrettably be left there; quite simply, there is not enough evidence to support the theory.

Valentia Island, Co. Kerry

Valentia Island is a scooped-out shovelful of land tucked into a rough niche at the corner of Kerry, between Doulus and Portmagee, and on the opposite side of Dingle Bay to the Blasket Island group, a part of Munster which in the sixteenth century was also a part of what became known as Desmond, an area of land controlled by the great Desmond family, the Fitzgeralds. There is no doubt whatsoever that a large Armada ship was wrecked in 'Desmond', which could be said broadly to refer to that part of Kerry south of Dingle Bay, which would of course include Valentia Island but which was far south of Tralee Bay.

Geoffrey Fenton in his list says merely, as is his wont, that there was wrecked in 'Desmond, one shipp, 300 men.' No word of survivors or the vessel's name. In 1845 a Spanish astrolabe, dated 1585, was found in Valentia by some fishermen; it is now in the National Maritime Museum in Greenwich. There is the added fact of a tradition, if not a very strong one, of a wreck at Valentia of an Armada ship.

Valentia Island, Co. Kerry, with the mainland in the background. Hereabouts an Armada ship went down, possibly one of the many Trinidads *in the fleet. A sixteenth century astrolabe was found here during the last century, probably from the unknown vessel. The fishing boat in the centre gives an idea of the height of the cliffs in the background. (Bord Failte)*

Could the Castilian ship *Trinidad*, surviving the passage through the Blaskets, have struggled across the mouth of Dingle Bay in the howling gale which had forced Recalde and Aramburu to run for their lives on the 15th, and once across the bay been unable to weather Valentia Island and foundered nearby? Geographically, and taking into account wind, tides and the probable state of the vessel herself, this theory does provide an answer which is acceptable. The Spanish State Papers list the *Trinidad* as lost; the area of that loss must have been either off Kerry or in the open ocean between Ireland and Spain; her crew (302 at Lisbon) matches Fenton's estimate of 300; and as Fenton intimates, there were no survivors. From the Blaskets across the mouth of Dingle Bay to Valentia is hardly fifteen miles; leaving the Blasket Sound sometime during the afternoon of the 15th, the *Trinidad* could very well have been wrecked some fifteen miles or so southwest of there later that night, when the gale was still blowing and the weather was foul. I believe this to be the case.

Zuniga

There is nothing – or little enough – of either myth or mystery over the *Zuniga*. One of the four Neapolitan galleasses and a sister ship of the *Girona*, this vessel had of perhaps all the Armada the most trying and difficult times.

She was not wrecked: that final fate she at least escaped. But everything else happened to her. Apart from that, she is one of the better-chronicled ships in the fleet and for that reason highly interesting. Of the other ships in that misfortuned Neapolitan Squadron the fate of the *Girona* needs no retelling. Hugo de Moncada, who commanded the squadron, had lost his life and his ship, the *San Lorenzo*, as far back as Calais. Only the *Napolitana* survived unscathed.

Under Captain Juan de Saavedra, the *Zuniga* left Lisbon with a complement of around 290; probably she carried considerably more as that figure (given in the Lisbon muster) does not account for servants, adventurers, medics, priests or others. The total was in all probability well over three hundred. Apart from Saavedra's seventy-six Neapolitan soldiers, Andres Berdugo captained another fifty-nine, and Juan Perez de Loaysa 118. These three appear from all accounts to have been the principal officers aboard. The galleass carried fifty guns of various sizes including at least two full culverins.

We hear little of the *Zuniga* during the Channel battle; as the other galleasses played as small a part in the actual fighting this is hardly surprising, and yet from later information it does appear as if she suffered some damage at least. Along with most of the fleet, she passed between the Orkneys and Fair Isle on August 19, later sighting the northern coast of Ireland, probably somewhere east of Malin Head if not that landmark itself. For the next fortnight we hear little of her, swallowed up as she was by the wide spaces of the Atlantic as the fleet wallowed westward. But on September 2 she appealed to Medina Sidonia for help: she had damaged her rudder and had suffered elsewhere too; that fortnight had seen tremendous gales which were undoubtedly her undoing.

The hard-pressed Duke had his own problems, however, and could find little time or inclination to help the *Zuniga*; every ship must press on, only the fittest surviving. And so the galleass struggled on for another five days before appealing again for aid, this time to Recalde on the *San Juan de Portugal*. The Biscayan *Almiranta*, sick and dying in his bunk, his vessel in sore straits, could offer only advice: sail on for Spain.

But it was too late for the *Zuniga*. Her rudder would not hold out for that length of time, and like all the ships she was short of food and water. So she turned her bows in for Ireland, possible with Recalde's navigational advice for he knew the lower coastline well. A week later we find her off the coast, probably somewhere around Tralee Bay or possibly even further south, behind a long headland which she could not weather in her almost rudderless condition. As the wind grew into a sou'westerly gale she dropped back before it along the coast, fetching up in the shadow of the great Cliffs of Moher, and dropped anchor at Liscannor on the coast of Clare only a short distance north of where two of her compatriots were to be wrecked.

From September 14 to the 22nd the *Zuniga* stayed at anchor off Liscannor. The wind was constant if not always unfavourable, and she was in no fit state to head on for Spain. Besides, it must have seemed an ideal chance to take on food and water in an area of the coast which, although they could not have known it, was not at all heavily protected by Crown forces. That the galleass took on food and water is known; and that she took it by force is probable if not proven – one of the few ships of the Armada known to have done so (in the Shannon off Scattery Island, and in the Blasket Sound).

If English forces were thin on the ground at Liscannor, they were not entirely absent. Boetius Clancy, then High Sheriff of Clare (Chapter IX), was there to tell Bingham in a note of September 16 that:

one ship is anchored in an unusual harbour, about a mile westward from one of Sir Turlough O'Brien's houses called Liscannor; the said ship had two cock-boats, whereof one brake from the ship and landed, and it is not like our English cock-boats; it would carry twenty men at least, and it is painted red, with the red anchor, with an earthen vessel like an oil 'prock', and the small board which this bearer shall deliver your worship was also therein found. What the vessel is I do not know; they offered to land the last night in one of the cock-boats, which they could not do by reason of the weather, and the harbour.

Two days later Bingham passed on the message to Fitzwilliam, together with the piece of board taken from the *Zuniga*'s cock-boat which Clancy had had sent to him; there was, Bingham mused, 'some mystery hidden under the burne of three letters; but it should seem to be a mark under the K.P., the Catholic King's name.'

Much more important evidence, however, was to 'brake from' the galleass. A day or so after Clancy's man had commandeered the cock-boat, they took prisoner the ship's purser, Petrus Baptista, apparently while he tried to bargain with them for provisions. For some curious reason the purser was examined before the Bishop of Kildare, an unlikely circumstance which remains unsatisfactorily explained, but which probably accounts for his survival (one of the handful to have survived examination). Baptista probably told his interrogators all he knew, which was not a great deal; it did, however, confirm what Fitzwilliam must by now have suspected, that the entire Spanish fleet was in complete flight, its spirit broken and its ships and crew in a bad way – 'in great danger' as the captured purser had it, 'for want of bread, flesh and water.'

Baptista's future is tantalizingly obscured and only a few scattered hints here and there in the Irish State Papers reveal his fate. In 1591, for instance, we find someone of his name serving the Lord Deputy (still Fitzwilliam at that time, not yet succeeded by Sir William Russell); a year later the name is mentioned again in a dispatch from Burghley, which would seem to indicate that the former Spanish purser was now a paid servant of the Crown. From there on, we know nothing.

Back as Liscannor, the *Zuniga* continued to take on food and water and repair the rudder. On September 22, with a favourable wind, they slipped anchor and bore away for Spain. The wind freshened to a near gale and they weathered the southwest corner of Ireland with ease, running strongly as far as Cape Finistère before the wind changed, in the fickle fashion it appears to have reserved for the struggling Armada. These galleasses were uncomfortable in any sort of headwind and sea; the wind, changing now to sou'west, drove them back up the English Channel (but not back towards Ireland, where assuredly they would not have escaped a second time). On October 11, battle-scarred but still afloat, the ship limped into Havre de Grace.

Not far from Havre was, of course, Calais, the graveyard of Moncada's *San Lorenzo*; the wreck was there still and from some of her intact timbers the *Zuniga*'s men began to repair their damaged vessel. There too they picked up fifty-six survivors from the *San Lorenzo* and another twenty or so who had somehow escaped from Ireland and made their way as far as Calais and Havre. Some of the stores from the *San Lorenzo* were also brought aboard the *Zuniga*, and work began in earnest to complete the last leg of the long journey home.

Time was against them, as well as the winter which had now set in, and it was April before the galleass, patched up and with not an inch of space left on her for another soul, sailed from Havre on what all those aboard felt must now be the final stretch. But there was always the wind, and the Channel is a stormy stretch of water in April: once more the *Zuniga* met rough seas and strong headwinds and was blown back until she scraped into Havre again, battered .and torn, having lost some of her equipment, but still indomitably afloat.

By then there must have been some of the company who feared that they might never reach Spain in their patched-up, leaking, overstretched, ramshackle wreck of a ship. Unrest among the crew grew into open mutiny, soon quelled however. More repairs were carried out, but nature had not yet finished with the galleass. At that time Havre (as were many of the adjacent ports) was given to silting, an ever-present problem in a time when dredging methods were inadequate and equipment for dredging even more so. As the *Zuniga* lay at her moorings the silt gathered around her and spring petered out into summer. By the middle of the season, when she should have been en route for home, the ship still lay in harbour, anchored by silt, helpless and unable to move.

From that point on, we lose track of the *Zuniga*. We do not know if she ever reached Spain: probably she did, to great rejoicing. She is listed as lost by the Spanish State Papers, but that is accounted for by her long absence following the arrival home of the surviving ships of the Armada some eight months before. No-one in Spain knew that she had survived until a *relation* reached there from Havre, detailing all the repairs which were then being done.

It is in one sense at least curious that we know so little of her subsequent movements, for she is among the best documented of any of the Armada. The three accounts – the *relation*, and others by Juan de Saavedra and Purser Pedro de Igueldo – are irritatingly vague on the points we would like to know more of, and as irritatingly precise on those which matter least. De Igueldo's position in all this is also obscure, for he was the Chief Purser in the fleet and it is doubtful whether he was indeed aboard the *Zuniga*. We do learn, however, that she was more or less rebuilt; and that she had had to throw overboard two culverins during the gale that drove her once more back to Havre. And that, more or less, is that.

If the *Zuniga* did reach home, then it was a remarkable survival and an even more remarkable achievement. Overriding this extraordinary series of mishaps is a sense of admiration at the fortitude of men who, though constantly losing, kept on trying – a fortitude which appears again and again during the campaign.

Epilogue

A S he had seen in the first, so Sir Richard Bingham saw out the last of
the Spaniards from the Armada to land in Ireland. By the end of
October, some six weeks after the first sightings, the threat to English rule
was over and Bingham was able to write jubilantly to Sir Henry Wallop on
November 3 that 'the Spaniards have departed, leaving but a few begging sick
men.' Those scattered pathetic few were the remnants of a once-great force
that at one time exceeded six thousand men; Philip's great enterprise, a threat
to Ireland as much as it was to England, failed in Elizabeth's western colony as
surely as it had done off England's shores.

Throughout the State Papers of those frenetic weeks of September and
October there runs a changing note; first of suspicion and unease as the news
filtered through of the Invincible Armada bound for England's shores,
emotions understandable in the harsh light of Ireland's well-recognized
vulnerability; then fear, real fear, as the reports began to speak of ships off the
coast and later of actual landings by Spaniards. For three or four weeks
perhaps that fear was at its height; and then as the English realized that the
Spaniards' real intention was to reach their homeland as quickly as possible, it
began to wane.

Fitzwilliam and Bingham were the two men primarily responsible for the
growing confidence of the English administration in Ireland that it could cope
with these shipwrecked wretches, who came to land in search of food and
water and not for invasion and war. In Munster and Connacht their hands
reached into every hidden corner and plucked forth shivering Spaniards from
the darkest and most remote recesses. Hardly a man survived in the two
provinces who had come ashore from a wrecked Armada vessel; from Kerry
to Clare, from there to Galway, from Galway up to Tirawley where Melaghlen
McCabb waited on the shore with his gallowglass axe, the Spaniards were
butchered without mercy. It was the only way for English rule to survive; a
survival of the fittest.

Only in Ulster, the last great stronghold of the Irish chieftains, was there a
continuing need for anxiety. As long as Alonso de Leiva and a force of some
two thousand Spaniards remained on Irish soil, surrounded and aided to a

206

degree by native clans of questionable loyalty and often outright opposition to English rule, there was danger of the most serious kind. The clans could rise, and if that happened and an alliance of native and Spaniard grew and blossomed, Ulster would fall; and once that happened, the whole of Ireland was in peril.

The departure from Killybegs on October 26 of the galleass *Girona* and some thirteen hundred men was the real turning point as far as Fitzwilliam and the Irish Council were concerned. Only when the large force of armed Spaniards had left could they breathe once more; but had they been able to read de Leiva's mind for at least a month beforehand, they would have realized that Ireland stood in no danger from these invaders. Their heart was gone, drowned with their ships; and they thought only of homes and families and the faint chances of seeing both once more. Fitzwilliam's journey through winter rains and floods of the middle of November and into December told him all he wanted to know; 'there yet remaineth in that province [Ulster], as it is said, one hundred or thereabouts, being most miserable, both in body and apparel, and few or none of them Spaniards', he wrote to the Privy Council on January 13, his labours over and his troubles eased. That was Ulster; of Connacht, Bingham had over three months earlier been able to report that 'this province stands clear and rid of all these foreign enemies, save a sillye poor prisoners'; they had done their work well, and without a hand raised in England to help. They had not needed it.

As to the Irish themselves, their consciences cannot have been as clear. Hardly an Irishman had stirred to aid the Spaniards, whose tread on Irish soil they had for so long importuned and eagerly awaited. When the time had come, sadly and perhaps typically they had stood aside and allowed it to pass. In Munster and Connacht, while the Spaniards were allowed their lives, they were given little else; their money, their arms, jewels, even clothes, were taken. Here and there some were sheltered, but on threat or promise even they were handed over. On Clare Island and at Alliagh in Inishowen, Irishmen put hand to sword and murdered as lustily as Fitzwilliam could wish.

Even in the isolated, less dominated North matters were little different. The Earl of Tyrone, the O'Neill (Tirlach Lynagh) and the O'Donnell stood aside with the rest of their countrymen, except in the case of O'Donnell, who actually took arms against them. Shamefully and to his eternal discredit, Tyrone exercised his tongue rather than his considerable sword. It was left to two clans, neither strictly Irish, to help the Spaniards actively, and to those two Scottish-origin clans on Irish soil, the McDonnells of Antrim and the MacSweeney's of Tirconnell, many a shipwrecked fugitive owed his life. Tirlach Lynagh did send five hundred cattle to the shipwrecked Spaniards, according to one report, and if so, he can be slightly exonerated.

As the last few were being hunted down in the woods and bogs of Ireland by relentless English soldiery, the remnants of Philip's Most Felicitous Armada were nearing the end of their long voyage, homing in on the northern ports of Spain like wearied carrier pigeons, wings drooping and energies exhausted. It was a forlorn and silent fleet which straggled into Santander, the ports of Galicia and Guipuzcoa, or Lisbon; and even then its troubles were not over. Those ports into which the ships had limped as into long-sought havens were not prepared and were short of food and medicines; as the weather-beaten ships lay at anchor in their home waters, festering with scurvy and typhus, with men dying by the score each day, it was difficult to believe that this was home.

It was only when they reached home that two of the Armada's major figures, Recalde and Oquendo, released a slipping hold on life; the aging Biscayan had gone back to his bunk once his ship had cleared the Blasket Sound on the wings of a fair wind for Spain and stayed there until he died, embittered and saddened; Oquendo gave up silently, lying feverish in a Spanish port as his men died in droves alongside him. The Duke of Medina Sidonia lived; sick as he was, he slipped home almost secretly, enclosed in a covered carriage, to his orange groves in San Lucar. What his thoughts were back among his own Andalusian hills we do not know.

In Ireland, the gigantic wave which the Spaniards had raised on the surface of English rule subsided in the aftermath of their departure; in a few weeks it was as if nothing had ever happened, that the vision of great ships looming like awesome birds of ill omen along the coastline was a mere dream. The old Gaelic chiefs, their chance gone, returned to the internecine squabbling which was their principal pastime; it was their inability to co-operate which had lost them this one great opportunity as surely as it was to lose the final chance to smash English rule and re-create the Ireland of which they were now at last becoming relics. Kinsale and 1601 changed everything; Spanish help would be no more. Ireland could have fallen during the Armada period, had de Leiva been more resolute, had O'Neill and O'Donnell thrown caution into the wild Irish sky, had Philip grasped the true state of things – but these are the imponderables which create and motivate history. The danger to England ensuing from a Spanish occupation largely escaped Philip; it did not escape the shrewd Elizabeth or her faithfully efficient henchmen, Fitzwilliam and Bingham, that flail of Connacht.

In the end, it all came to naught. The bones of Spanish sailors hidden under golden sand at Streedagh and Ballycroy and Rosbeg, wedged in rock and reef in the Rosses and the Blaskets and Lacada Point, buried peacefully in the still and fertile soil of Clare – those bones serve as a silent yet eloquent monument to the lost enterprise of Philip II, King of Spain.

Appendix I

COMPOSITION
OF THE SPANISH ARMADA

It is not possible to say precisely how many ships were in the Spanish Armada; the two most commonly accepted totals are 128 and 130. There were two main counts or musters, the first at Lisbon in May before departure, the second at Corunna where the Armada reorganized its scattered forces. Both musters, taken primarily from Duro (whose arithmetic is notoriously unreliable) are given here.

Lisbon muster

Squadron	Classes of ships	Ships	Men
Portugal	Ten galleons, two tenders	12	4623
Biscay	Ten merchantmen, four tenders	14	2800
Castile	Ten galleons, four merchantmen, two tenders	16	4177
Andalusia	One galleon, nine merchantmen, one tender	11	3105
Guipuzcoa*	Ten merchantmen, two tenders	12	2608
Levant	Ten merchantmen	10	3527
Pataches y zabras	Twenty-two *pataches* and *zabras*	22	1093
Urcas	Twenty-three *urcas* (hulks)	23	3729
Naples	Four galleasses	4	1341
Portugal (galleys)	Four galleys	4	362

Other men: 2088

Totals: 128 vessels; 29,453 men

*Duro lists twelve *and* fourteen vessels for this squadron, but names only twelve.

Broken down into classes of vessels, the Lisbon muster showed that the fleet originally comprised: 21 galleons, 43 merchantmen, 4 galleys, 4 galleasses, 23 hulks, 22 *pataches* and *zabras*, and 11 tenders. Duro's figures for personnel simply do not tally; rather than compound his numerous errors his estimates have been taken.

Corunna muster

Squadron	Classes of ships	Ships	Men
Portugal	Nine galleons, two *zabras*	11	3705
Biscay	Nine merchantmen, four *pataches*	13	2374
Castile	Ten galleons, three merchantmen, two *pataches*	15	3808

Andalusia	Ten merchantmen, one *patache*	11	2809
Guipuzcoa	Ten merchantmen, one hulk, one *patache*, two pinnaces	14	2936
Levant	One galleon, eight merchantmen	9	3297
Urcas	Nineteen hulks	19	2844
Pataches y zabras*	One merchantman, two hulks, eleven *pataches*, seven *zabras*	21	850
Naples	Four galleasses	4	1336
Portugal (galleys)	Four galleys	4	341
Carabelas	Nine tenders	9	125
Feluccas	One felucca	1	42

Totals: 131 vessels; 24,067 men

*Here listed as under the command of Agustin de Ojeda, as opposed to the Lisbon muster command of Don Antonio Hurtado de Mendoza.

The Corunna muster was more hastily compiled than that at Lisbon, hence the many discrepancies. Basically they are similar, except that the Corunna list gives an additional three ships; one of the hulks (*urcas*), the *David*, could not sail, which reduces the later total to 130.

Again, Duro's figures have been taken, but there are some terrible errors in his counting: for instance, the Guipuzcoan total of men is given as both 2936 and 2536, a difference of 400. But to try to amend all these would, as I have said, compound his errors even further. So they are best left as they are.

Principal Spanish Commanders

Don Alonso Perez de Guzman, Duke of Medina Sidonia, C-in-C; Portuguese Squadron
*Don Juan Martinez de Recalde, Biscay Squadron, and second in command
Don Diego Flores de Valdes, Chief of Staff, and Castilian Squadron
Don Pedro de Valdes (cousin), Andalusian Squadron (captured by English)
*Don Miguel de Oquendo, Guipuzcoan Squadron
Don Martin de Bertendona, Levant Squadron
*Don Hugo de Moncada, Naples Squadron (galleasses)
Don Diego Medrano, Galleys of Portugal
Don Juan Gomez de Medina, *Urcas* Squadron (wrecked on Fair Isle)
Don Antonio Hurtado de Mendoza, *Pataches y zabras* Squadron
*Don Alonso de Leiva, commander of land forces and designate C-in-C of Armada

*Died either during or shortly after campaign.

Appendix 2

ARMADA LOSSES IN IRELAND

Ship	Squadron	Tons	Guns	Men	Principal Officer	Where wrecked	Date
Girona	Naples	700?	50	289	Fabricio Spinola, Captain	Lacada Point, Port na Spaniagh, Co. Antrim	Oct. 28
Trinidad Valencera	Levant	1100	42	360	D. Alonso de Luzon	Glenagivney Bay (Kinnagoe), Inishowen Peninsula, Co. Donegal	Sept. 16
Barca de Amburg	*urcas*	600	23	264	Juan de San Martin, Captain	at sea north of Malin Head, Donegal	Sept. 1
Castillo Negro	*urcas*	750	27	273	Pedro Ferrat, Captain	foundered at sea NW of Donegal	Sept. 4(?)
Juliana	Levant	860	32	395	D. Fernando de Aranda	Mullaghderg, Arranmore, Co. Donegal	
unknown	*zabra?*					Cloughglass, Arranmore, Co. Donegal	
Duquesa Santa Ana	Andalusia	900	23	357	Don Pedro Mares, Captain	Rosbeg, Loughros Mor Bay, Co. Donegal	Sept. 26
unknown	*zabra?*					outside Killybegs Harbour, Co. Donegal	
unknown	*zabra?*					inside Killybegs Harbour, Co. Donegal	
San Juan	Castile	530	24	276	D. Diego Enriquez	Streedagh Strand, near Grange, Co. Sligo	Sept. 25
La Lavia	Levant *Almiranta*	728	25	274	D. Martin de Aranda, Judge Advocate	Streedagh Strand, near Grange, Co. Sligo	Sept. 25
Santa Maria de la Vison	Levant	666	18	307	Juan de Bartolo, Captain	Streedagh Strand, near Grange, Co. Sligo	Sept. 25
Ciervo Volante	*urcas*	400	18	222	Juan de Peramato, Captain	Tirawley, formerly north Mayo barony	Sept. 22(?)
Santiago	*urcas*	600	19	86	Juan Hernandez de Luna, Captain	Inver, Broadhaven Bay, Erris, Co. Mayo	Sept. 21(?)
La Rata Encoronada	Levant	820	35	419	D. Alonso de Leiva, C-in-C designate	Fahy Strand, Ballycroy, Blacksod Bay, Co. Mayo	Sept. 21

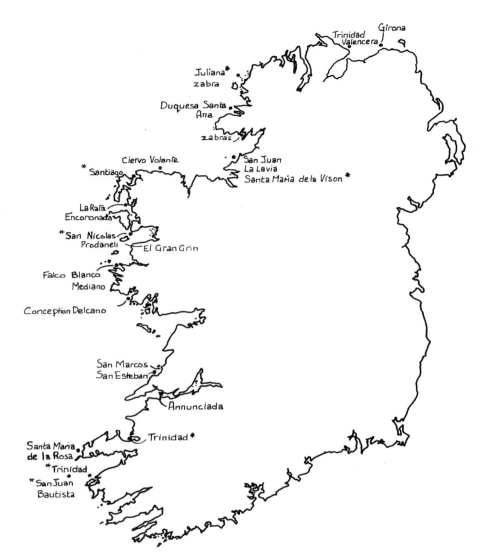

The sites of twenty-four wrecked Armada ships around the coast of Ireland; not included are those of the Castillo Negro and Barca de Amburg, both of which foundered off the NNW coast some miles out to sea. Asterisks indicate tentatively identified wrecks.

Ship	Squadron	Tons	Guns	Men	Principal Officer	Where wrecked	Date
El Gran Grin	Biscay	1160	28	329	D. Pedro de Mendoza; Capt. Andres Felipe	Clare Island, Clew Bay, Co. Mayo	Sept. 22(?)
San Nicolas Prodaneli	Levant	834	26	355	Marin Prodanelic, Captain	Toorglass, Curraun Peninsula, Co. Mayo	Sept. 16
Concepcion Delcano	Biscay	418	18	225	Juan Delcano, Captain	Duirling na Spainneach, Ards, near Carna, Co. Galway	Sept. 25(?)
Falco Blanco Mediano	urcas	300	16	103	Pedro de Arechaga, Captain	Freaghillaun South (Island), Ballynakill, Co. Galway	Sept. 25(?)
San Marcos	Portugal	790	33	409	Marquis of Penafiel	On reef between Mutton Island and Lurga Point, near Spanish Point, Co. Clare	Sept. 20
San Esteban	Guipuzcoa	736	26	264		Doonbeg, Co. Clare	Sept. 20
Annunciada	Levant	703	24	275	Ohmucevic Iveglia, Captain	Scattery roads in River Shannon	Sept. 20
Trinidad	zabras		2	24		Tralee, Co. Kerry (taken)	Sept. 18(?)
Santa Maria de la Rosa	Guipuzcoa	945	26	297	Prince D'Ascoli, son of Philip II	Stromboli Reef, Blasket Sound, Co. Kerry	Sept. 21
San Juan Bautista	Castile	650	24	285	Fernando Horra, Captain	SW of Blasket Islands, at sea (?)	Sept. 24(?)
Trinidad	Castile	872	24	302		Valentia Island, Co. Kerry	Sept. 15

The total number of ships lost in Irish waters was twenty-six. In losses per squadron, they were:

Levant: seven
Urcas: five
Castile: three
Zabras: four
Biscay: two

Guipuzcoa: two
Portugal: one
Andalusia: one
Naples: one

Every squadron in the Armada lost at least one ship in Ireland. It is important to note that owing to the impossibility of identifying the *zabras* lost around the Irish coast, the figures of ships lost per squadron are uncertain as each squadron with the exception of those of the Levant, *urcas* and Naples, had *zabras* attached. The squadron of galleys, which never reached Ireland, has not been included in this table.

The remarkable havoc caused to the Levant Squadron (seven ships lost) is worth noting. Another of this squadron, the *San Juan de Sicilia*, was lost in Tobermory Bay in Scotland, and the only Levantine vessels to reach Spain were the flagship *La Regazzona*, and the *Trinidad de Scala*. The Levantine ships, all converted grain-carriers and merchantmen, were of a much lighter build than many of the Armada ships and could withstand neither the rigours of war nor the rough western ocean.

It is worth noting too that the poorest sailers in the fleet, the *urcas*, also lost a high proportion of ships; they found it difficult to make progress in the heavy weather conditions around Ireland. At the other end of the scale is the single ship lost from the magnificent Atlantic galleons of Portugal; the *San Marcos* was not wrecked, but abandoned and burned in the Shannon after being found beyond repair.

Losses of Men

Because it is next to impossible to give an exact indication of such a figure, the course taken here is to give two tables; Table A showing the number of men on the relevant wrecked ships as given in the Lisbon muster, and Table B showing the probable losses in men drowned, killed, or taken by the English in Ireland. This latter table also includes figures for possible and probable survivors.

The figures in Table A were changed by the reorganization at Corunna and by deaths from wounds, disease, etc, so that by the time the ships were wrecked around Ireland each complement, with the exception of about three ships, would have been reduced, sometimes substantially, from the Lisbon muster. Table B tries to correct this insofar as possible, but it is a monumental task and no guarantee of great accuracy can be given. Table A also assumes that the average complement of men per *zabra* was in the region of fifty-three, based on a mean figure from the Lisbon muster and taking into account all thirty-three *zabras, pataches* and other small tenders listed in the fleet.

Table A

In Co. Antrim (one ship)*	289 men
In Co. Donegal (eight ships)	1808
In Co. Sligo (three ships)	857
In Co. Mayo (five ships)	1411
In Co. Galway (two ships)	328
In Co. Clare (three ships)	948
In Co. Kerry (four ships)	908
In the Seven Counties (twenty six ships):	6549 men

*The *Girona*, which then carried 1300, from two other vessels together with her own company.

These figures broken down do not reveal several factors affecting the totals for each county; in an overall sense, however, this is largely irrelevant.

Table B

(i)	Men lost (based on Lisbon muster)	6549
	Others (servants, clerics, hospital staff etc)	500
	Total men lost	7049
	Deduct 20% for losses at sea or in battle	−1409
	Remaining in fleet	5640
	Extra men in certain vessels (*Girona*'s rowers, et al)	300
	Total of adjusted figures	5940
	Total number of men lost from the Armada in Ireland: 6000 approx.	

(ii) Taken off foundering ships and brought to Spain (*Annunciada* and the
    nao San Juan Bautista)   560
Other survivors, notably from *Valencera*, three Streedagh wrecks,
    and others   200
Total survivors safely returned to Spain (though many did not
    live long afterwards)   760
          (rounded off at 750)

(iii) Men shipwrecked   6000
   Survivors   750
   Total definitely lost in Ireland   5250
     drowned or killed by shipwreck   3750
     executed by English forces   1500

   Summary: ships lost   26
        men lost   5250
        survivors returned to Spain   750

(iv) *Some contemporary estimates:*
   Geoffrey Fenton, Secretary to the Irish Council: 16 ships, 5394 men lost.
   Sir Richard Bingham, Governor of Connacht: 15–16 ships, 6000–
    7000 men.
   Robert Adams, cartographer: 17 ships, no estimate of men.
   John Strype (later period): 17 ships, 4791 men.

EXCAVATED ARMADA WRECKS
IN IRELAND

It is only within the last decade or so that serious archaeological attention, in a practical sense, has been given to the many Irish wrecks, which has meant the discovery and partial excavation of three of prime historical and archaeological interest. They are the *Girona* in Antrim, found in 1967; *La Trinidad Valencera* in Donegal, whose remains were discovered in 1971; and the *Santa Maria de la Rosa*, found off Kerry in 1968. There have been other wrecks which have been investigated but not by officially recognized means, and these include the *Juliana* and an unnamed small vessel in the Rosses in Donegal; the *Duquesa Santa Ana*, also in Donegal; and the *Concepcion* off Connemara. Several attempts also have been made on others but with little success.

Of all the wrecks around Ireland not already investigated, the *Juliana, Santiago, San Nicolas Prodaneli, Concepcion, San Marcos, San Esteban, Annunciada*, and the *Trinidad (nao)* are worth full scale investigation. The remainder are either covered by sand, have disappeared, or their whereabouts are so uncertain as to make a proper search almost impossible. In the years ahead and as increasing archaeological attention focuses on the wrecks already named, much more is likely to be learned, not only of how the ships were wrecked and possibly their true identity, but also about their construction, armament and many other details of life at that time.

The manner of possible future investigation and excavation of Armada wrecks in Ireland is one which is causing growing concern to all those who seek to have such work based on recognized and disciplined methods and carried out by qualified personnel, with official approval at the highest level. In other words, what is required is a set of laws (long promised, incidentally) which will ensure that all Armada wrecks (and indeed all wrecks of historical or other importance) will be investigated only by those best qualified to do so, at the same time ensuring that the treasure hunting aspect which threatens to bedevil many wrecks is eliminated and that all items raised go into national or local museums.

Maritime law in Ireland is largely similar to that in England in relation to shipwrecks. International maritime law provides that every wreck, whatever its age, has a definite owner; thus all the wrecks of Armada vessels in Irish waters are technically owned by the present Spanish government and permission to remove anything must first be obtained through that source. In Irish law, the Receiver of Wrecks, a member of the Customs and Excise Department, must be notified by any potential salvor of the intention to salvage any wreck within Irish territorial waters. The salvor must have a licence from the Department of Transport and Power and must deliver any articles salvaged to the Receiver of Wrecks, who then determines their exact ownership. If the salvor has already entered into an agreement with the legal owners of the wreck and abides by this agreement, the Receiver of Wrecks (once he has received notification of any articles salvaged) bows out of the situation.

What this outdated set of laws means is that while there are safeguards to ensure that anyone diving illegally on a wreck in Irish waters (in other words, removing articles from it) can be punished, there is nothing whatsoever to prevent any diver from seeking out a wreck himself, as long as he leaves it alone. But the temptation is obviously there, especially in a remote place where transgressions might go unnoticed, to remove articles which could well be of almost incalculable historical value (if not of great monetary value). It is to be hoped that the present system of maritime law in relation to wrecks will be changed radically within a short time. It is vital, if the Armada and other wrecks are to be preserved for proper excavation, that a much more stringent and workable set of laws is brought in to replace the old and out of date legislation at present in force.

All three major excavations of Irish wrecks have had full official blessing and have followed proper legal procedures. The expedition members concerned have been trained to a very high standard and have observed to the full the guidelines normally followed in underwater archaeological research. In that they have set an example which it is hoped will be followed when the time comes for every accessible Armada wreck in Irish waters to be investigated.

The following gives brief details of the three major excavations on Armada wrecks around Ireland.

La Girona

On June 27, 1967, while diving off Port na Spaniagh near the Giant's Causeway, Co. Antrim, Robert Stenuit, the Belgian diver and marine archaeologist, discovered the remains of this vessel, wrecked on the night of October 28, 1588. The first items he found were a lead ingot and a bronze cannon, then a second cannon and many other items. Following this preliminary investigation, in the following two diving seasons and with a fully equipped expedition many items and artifacts were discovered on the ocean bed and brought to the surface. No significant remains were found of the ship itself. Stenuit's team excavated the site thoroughly and little if anything of real value from the wreck now remains on the bottom. The entire collection of recovered items is now housed in a permanent room of its own in the Ulster Museum, Belfast.

The list of items recovered includes: 1276 gold, silver and copper coins; thirty-five gold jewels, twelve gold rings, eight gold chains and two silver crucifixes (together with fragments of both); eight medallions; five nautical dividers, two astrolabes, three sounding leads; several fragments of hourglasses; two bronze cannon, fragments of muskets and flintlocks, fragments of swords or daggers, 188 iron and stone cannon balls, 1865 lead bullets; many items of lead, including ballast plates and ingots, pulley blocks, seals, a steelyard weight and some hull lining; debris and fragments of many silver forks, spoons, ladles, plates, dishes, sauceboats, spouts, phials, flasks, bowls, goblets, tankards, pots, candle snuffers, basins, inkwells, candlesticks and numerous other items. Also found were pewter vases, plates, bowls, dishes, soup plates, pots, candlesticks, jugs, etc. Many bronze items were recovered, including buckets, pestles, nails and pins; the copper artifacts included dishes, pots, hooks and various tools. Some pottery was also found, including pots, vases and decorated bowls. Among the many miscellaneous items were two anchors, an anvil, a knife and leather objects. The total number of artifacts salvaged was around twelve thousand.

The *Girona* is the first and most complete excavation of any Spanish Armada vessel around Ireland. The enormous wealth of material which the diving team took from the seabed – wealth in historical rather than monetary terms – has yielded an equally valuable mine of information on the period. However, it is doubtful if the galleass can continue to attract the attention hitherto given it by archaeologists and historians, since the other two major wrecks provide a much more valuable knowledge of shipbuilding methods and ship construction during the sixteenth century. No major remains of the *Girona* herself were discovered. She was wrecked in comparatively shallow water and the excavation was usually carried out in from twenty to thirty feet of water, in an area of strong currents where the sea bed was changed constantly by storms, and in extremely cold water.

La Trinidad Valencera

Members of the City of Derry Sub-Aqua Club were the first to find artifacts which could be identified as belonging to this Levantine vessel, which sank in Kinnagoe Bay (then Glenagivney or Glenganvey Bay) in the Inishowen Peninsula of Co. Donegal During a training dive in the bay in February 1971 the club's divers, swimming in about thirty feet of water, found bronze guns and other artifacts, thus ending a two-year search for the vessel. Showing a very responsible attitude, the club sought expert advice on the possible excavation of the wreck, recognizing its unique value as a site of archaeological interest. A clear claim of 'salvor in possession' was first established by the supervised lifting of bronze cannon from the sea bed, under the supervision of Colin Martin, Director of the Institute of Maritime Archaeology at St Andrews University, Scotland. Colin Martin is the most experienced figure in these islands connected with the excavation of Armada wrecks, having been involved with not only the *Valencera*, but also the *Santa Maria de la Rosa* in Blasket Sound, Kerry, and *El Gran Grifon* in Fair Isle, Scotland.

In May 1971 serious work began on the wreck. A metal detector survey was carried out together with systematic mapping of the site; preliminary excavations revealed other finds, such as iron, stone and lead shot, dividers, pottery, pewter, a brass bucket, powder ladle heads, a steelyard weight, hammers, guncarriage wheels, carriage fittings, animal bones, barrel hoops and staves, rope, canvas, leather (including a boy's leather boot), and a superbly preserved swivel mounted breech-loading cannon. The four bronze cannon include a matched pair of fifty-pounders, the largest shotted pieces used by either the Spanish or English fleets during the campaign, and each of which bear escutcheons and inscriptions showing that they were cast at Malines, Philip II's gun foundry in the Spanish Netherlands, by the *fondeur royal* Remigy de Halut. The other two bronze cannon were Italian made, one bearing the name of Zuanne Alberghetti, a gun founder who worked in the arsenal in Venice around 1560 (the *Valencera* was a Venetian ship).

Since then, further systematic work has been painstakingly carried out on the wreck by the Derry club members in conjunction with Colin Martin and the Institute at St Andrews. A conservation laboratory in Magee University College, Derry, helps with the preservation of the finds, and the project is being sponsored by the BBC archaeological programme 'Chronicle', Radio Telefis Eireann (the Irish television and radio service), and the Time-Life publishing group. Full salvage rights have been obtained by the City of Derry Sub-Aqua Club under stringent legal conditions and they retain sole rights of excavation, etc.

The *Trinidad* has not at the time of writing (spring, 1977) been fully excavated, but enough has been done to establish that her wreck is well worth the full scale scientific expedition which is now planned. Much of the ship's heavy timbers were pinned to the sea bottom by the massive weight of ballast, guns and anchors, together with thousands of smaller artifacts; they remain buried in silt on a flat sandy bottom at the base of a reef in thirty feet of water and some two hundred yards off the western end of the bay. It is with the careful and scientific excavation of these hull remains that the expedition must now concern itself.

Santa Maria de la Rosa

The finding of the remains of the wreck of the *Santa Maria* was a triumphant ending to the most exhaustive and largest underwater search by divers ever recorded anywhere in the world, a search which covered no less than fifteen million square yards of one of the roughest and most dangerous areas in the western ocean. It also marked the culmination of a long period of research by the leader of the expedition which found the wreck, Sidney Wignall. An experienced diver, he had started researching Irish wrecks of Armada ships in 1961, and at Easter 1963 a party of Irish divers associated with Sidney Wignall and led by Desmond Brannigan searched the main anchorage off the Great Blasket where the Spanish ships (but not the *Santa Maria*) had first anchored. This search was unsuccessful. Another party failed to find anything the following year, and in 1967 an English party of divers (not connected with Sidney Wignall) also dived and claimed to have found the wreck, a claim which was, however, later disproved, the alleged wreck turning out to be the 'two long pieces of heavy iron piping or pig iron lying in close proximity to a shallow heap of stones of natural origin.'

An intensive search was planned for 1968 and the services of a very experienced professional diver, Commander John Grattan of the Royal Navy, were recruited during a leave period to train and supervise the divers in a new underwater search system, known as the 'swim-line search', which he had perfected during diving work elsewhere. Working in rough conditions ('Force 4 gusting 5 was considered calm' says Wignall) the team of divers systematically and meticulously went over every inch of the sound, but without success. Finally on July 6, 1968 one of them located the wreck's remains.

The wreck of the *Santa Maria* lies some two hundred yards to the southeast of the underwater reef of Stromboli. It consists of a mound of packed limestone ballast one hundred feet long and forty feet wide at the widest portion of the mound, lying in some one hundred and ten feet of water on a flat shingle bottom. Later excavation was to show that the mound concealed much of the lower timbers, like those of the *Trinidad* pinned to the bottom by the weight of ballast and other articles, and preserved over the centuries by silting and concretion.

The remainder of the 1968 season was spent in survey and exploratory trenching around the wreck. In 1969 a metal detector survey was carried out by Jeremy Green of the Research Laboratory for Archaeology in Oxford (he had undertaken a similar job in the *Valencera* excavation), and later the hull structure itself was excavated. During this latter process, apart from the artifacts recovered much of the ship's structure was revealed, and from this a great deal of knowledge was accumulated on sixteenth century shipbuilding methods. Evidence was uncovered which confirmed a contemporary report that the *Santa Maria* had had her mainmast repaired at Corunna, reconstruction of the mainmast step being evident. Ground timbers were discovered, each second member being eight inches wide and twelve deep, spaced six inches apart, and the skin planking was four inches thick. In general, the most complete remains were those of the forward part of the vessel, together with most of the ballast. Colin Martin feels that the overall evidence suggests that the mast toppled towards the south soon after the wrecking on the reef and that the hull broke across aft of the mainmast, the stern section then pivoting 'to match the run of the ebbing tide'. It appears that the stern section has completely disappeared and with it much of the upper decks with their guns and other contents.

Among the items which were recovered from the wreck are remains of muskets, arquebuses, stone, iron and other shot; pewter plates (on which were the name 'Matute', signifying that they were the personal property of Captain Matute, an infantry captain known to have sailed with the *Santa Maria*); lead ingots, ballast, coins, and most grisly of all, some human remains. Of the ship itself there are parts of the keelson, stanchions, shifting boards, ground timbers, the stepping box for the mainmast, some skin planking and the mast truck.

The real value of the *Santa Maria* lies mostly in the information which a closely detailed examination of her hull structure reveals, contributing hitherto unknown knowledge of shipbuilding methods, particularly in relation to the Mediterranean or southern built ships, of which she was one. Her comparative lightness and frailty of construction confirms what has been written and said of southern built ships for many years – that they were quite simply not strong enough to withstand the rigours of war and long periods at sea in the rougher oceans off western Europe. Like the *Valencera*, the scattered and even pitiful remains of what was once a magnificent sailing vessel lying in a remote storm-lashed sound off western Ireland nevertheless house an incalculable treasure of archaeological and historical interest.

Appendix 4

IRISHMEN WITH THE ARMADA

Aspolle, Robert (survived wreck of *Gran Grifon* on Fair Isle)

Brenne*, Enrique (described as *capitan aleman*, possibly Henry Brennan)
Brewitt, Myles (seaman)
Browne, William (seaman)
Brown, John, of Clontarf, Dublin
Brun (Brown)*, Guillermo (described as *ingles* off *San Mateo*, which sank)
Brun*, Juan (perhaps John Brown, above)
Burley*, Ricardo

Car, Guillermo
Cler (O'Clery), Juan

Desmond, Gerald Fitz-James (died)
Desmond, Morris (Maurice) Fitz-John (died)
Desmond, Thomas, son of Sir John Desmond (died)
Dowrough, Friar James ne (survived *Duquesa* wreck)

Eustace, Edmond, claimant to Baltinglass title (reached Spain safely)
Fitzgerald, James Fitzmaurice (died aboard *Rata* off Mayo)
Fitzgerald, Maurice (survived wreck of *Gran Grifon* on Fair Isle)
Fitzgerald, Thomas (survived wreck of *Gran Grifon* on Fair Isle)

Galvan (Galvin)*, John (Juan)

Irlandes, Dionisio (of the Andalusian *Santiago*, returned to Spain)

Killaloe, Bishop of (wrecked in *Girona*)

Lario (O'Leary ?)*, Roberto
Lynch, Patrick, master-gunner

Machary, James (McGarry, McCarthy), of Tipperary (survived *Duquesa* wreck)
Mac-in-Persium, Andrew (drowned at Streedagh)
Mac-in-Persium, Brian (drowned at Streedagh)
Marley*, Pedro
M'Conor, Cahill (returned safely to Spain)
Moran*, Perucho or Pipochio (captain of galleass *Patrona*)

O'Brian, Guillermo (pilot)
O'Connor, Don Carlos
O'Dor*, Don Diego
O'Larit, Cormac (drowned at Streedagh)
O'Mullryane, Henry (returned safely to Spain)

Quinifort*, Patricio

Rice (Ruesse), John (Irish captain, died on *Santa Maria de la Rosa*)
Roche, Frances or Francis (died on *Santa Maria de la Rosa*)
Ronane (Ronayne), Patrick, of Limerick (died)

Vitres, Tomas (*clergio Irlandes*)

    *doubtful

Also with the Armada

An Irishman from Wexford survived the Clare Island massacre.
Three Irish pilots died aboard the *Girona*.
Bishop (probably Irish) wrecked with the *Santiago* (?) in north Mayo.

Many more Irishmen must have sailed with the fleet: exiled noblemen and local
chieftains; clergy including bishops; fishermen and sailors; soldiers and adventurers.
Forty-four are listed above; the full numbers will never be known, but it seems likely
that at least two hundred or so must have served with the Armada and possibly many
more.

THOSE IN IRELAND CONCERNED WITH THE ARMADA

English officials, including Irish officials in English government service

In Ireland
Sir William Fitzwilliam, Lord Deputy (member of Irish Council)
Sir Geoffrey Fenton, Secretary to Irish Council
Sir George Carew, Master of the Ordnance
Sir John Popham, Attorney General
Sir Henry Bagenal, Marshal of the Army
Sir Henry Wallop, Treasurer of the Council
All of the above were members of the governing Council of Ireland.

Munster
Thomas Norreys, Vice-President of province
Sir Edward Denny
James Trant, government agent in Dingle, Co. Kerry
David Gwynn, interpreter
Alexander Brywer, Mayor of Waterford
George Fanning, Mayor of Limeric

Connacht
Sir Richard Bingham, Governor of province
George Bingham, Sheriff of Sligo (Richard's brother)
Edward Whyte, Clerk to Connacht Council
Boetius Clancy, High Sheriff of Clare*
Nicholas Cahane, coroner of Clare*
Sir Turlough O'Brien of Clare*
Gerald Comerford, attorney in Connacht
    *Clare then formed part of Connacht

Ulster
Christopher Carleill, Governor of Province
Richard Hovenden
Henry Hovenden
Henry Duke

Irish chieftains and clans

Connacht
Sir Murrough ne Doe O'Flaherty (Galway)
Tadgh na Buile O'Flaherty (Galway)
Dowdarra Roe O'Malley (Mayo)
Richard Burke (Mayo)
William Burke (Mayo)
MacClancy (Leitrim)
Sir Brian O'Rourke (Breffni)

Ulster
The O'Donnell (Sir Hugh), (Tirconnell)
MacSweeney ne Doe (Tirconnell)
MacSweeney ne Bannagh (Tirconnell)
The O'Neill (Tirlagh Lynagh), (Tyrone)
Earl of Tyrone
Prince O'Cahan (Derry)
Sir John O'Doherty (east Donegal/Derry)
Sorley Boy McDonnell (Antrim)

Bibliography

Irish History: Nautical and Local

A Critical Examination of Irish History: T. Dunbar Egan, 1900

A Discovery of the True Causes Why Ireland was Never Entirely Subdued, etc: John Davies, 1784

Anglo-Irish Trade in the Sixteenth Century: A. K. Longfield, 1929

Annals of the Kingdom of Ireland: the Four Masters (ed. J. O'Donovan), 1856

Annals of Ireland: Sir James Ware, 1664

Annals of Ireland: Friar John Clyn and Thady Dowling (ed. R. Butler), 1849

Carndonagh Bell, The: W. O'Doherty (PRIA), 1891

Church and State in Tudor Ireland: R. D. Edwards, 1935

Course of Irish History, The: ed. T. W. Moody and F. X. Martin, 1967

Elizabethan Ireland: G. B. O'Connor (undated)

Elizabethans and the Irish, The: D. B. Quinn, 1966

Elizabeth's Irish Wars: Cyril Falls, 1950

English in Ireland, The: J. A. Froude, 1906

Gleanings from Irish History: W. F. T. Butler, 1925

The Great O'Neill: Sean O'Faolain, 1942

Hibernia Anglicana: Richard Cox

History and Topography of the County of Clare, The: James Frost, 1893

History of Clare: Rev. R. White (1973 ed.)

History of Galway: J. Hardiman (1974 ed.)

History of Ireland: E. A. D'Alton, 1912

History of the County of Mayo: H. T. Knox, 1908

History of the Diocese of Raphoe: Canon Maguire

Iar Chonnacht: Roderic O'Flaherty, 1846

Icon Antistitis: J. Lynch, 1660

Indestructible Nation, The: P. S. O'Hegarty, 1918

Ireland and Europe, 1559–1607: J. J. Silke, 1966

Ireland and Sixteenth Century Expansion: D. B. Quinn, 1958

Ireland under Elizabeth: P. O'S. Beare (tr. M. J. Byrne), 1903

Ireland under the Tudors: R. Bagwell, 1885–90

Ireland's English Question: P. O'Farrell, 1973

Irish Woods since Tudor Times, The: E. McCracken, 1971

Islandman, The: T. O'Crohan, 1937

Islands of Ireland, The: T. H. Mason, 1936

Life of Hugh Roe O'Donnell, The: L. O'Clery (ed. D. Murphy), 1895

Map of Ireland, 1300–1700, The: M. C. Andrew, 1924
Old Galway: M. D. O'Sullivan, 1942
Phases of Irish History: Eoin MacNeill, 1919
Reformation in Ireland Under Elizabeth, 1558–1580, The: Ronan Myles, 1930
Scots Mercenary Forces in Ireland: G. A. Hayes-McCoy, 1939
Social History of Ireland, A: P. W. Joyce, 1913
Strategy and Tactics in Irish Warfare, 1595–1601: G. A. Hayes-McCoy, 1941
Surnames of Ireland, The: E. MacLysaght, 1973
Tudor and Stuart Ireland: Margaret MacCurtain, 1972
Twenty Years A-Growing: Maurice O'Sullivan, 1953
Ulster Scot, The: J. B. Woodburn, 1915
Way that I Went, The: R. Lloyd Praeger, 1936
Wild Sports of the West: R. H. Maxwell, 1830

Contemporary Sources

Calendar of the Carew Manuscripts
Calendar of State Papers (Ireland)
Calendar of State Papers (Spanish)
Discourse Concerninge the Spanish Fleete Invadinge Englande in the yeare 1588, A: Petruccio Ubaldini (contemporary)
Pathway to Military Practice, A: Barnaby Rich (contemporary)
State Papers Relating to the Defeat of the Spanish Armada, 1588: ed. Sir John Laughton

Naval and General History

Age of Exploration: J. R. Hale, 1966
Drake and the Tudor Navy: J. Corbett, 1898
Europe Divided, 1559–1598: J. H. Elliott, 1968
Explorers' Maps: R. A. Skelton, 1958
Guns and Sails in the Early Phase of European Expansion: C. M. Cipolla, 1965
New Naval History, A: J. Entick
Queen Elizabeth I: J. E. Neale, 1934
Ship, The: Bjorn Landström, 1961
Spanish Seaborne Empire, The: J. H. Parry, 1966

Armada History

Armada Guns: M. Lewis. 1961
Armada Invencible, La: C. F. Duro, 1884
Armada Losses on the Irish Coast (I.S.): K. Danaher, 1956
Armada Ships on the Kerry Coast: W. Spotswood Green (PRIA), 1909
Captain Cuellar's Adventures in Connacht and Ulster, A.D. 1588: ed. H. Allingham and R. Crawford, 1897
Captain Cuellar's Narrative: ed. J. P. O'Reilly (PRIA), 1893

Defeat of the Spanish Armada, The: Garrett Mattingly, 1959
Elizabethan Navy and the Armada Campaign, The: D. W. Waters (MM), 1949
Full Fathom Five: Wrecks of the Spanish Armada: C. M. Martin, 1975
Graveyard of the Spanish Armada: T. P. Kilfeather, 1967
Ireland, the Armada, the Adriatic: J. de C. Ireland, 1974 (CP)
Some Survivors of the Armada in Ireland: M. Hume (RHS), 1897
Spanish Armada, The: M. Lewis, 1960
Spanish Armadas, The: Winston Graham, 1972
Spanish Armada Expedition, 1968–70; C. M. Martin (CP), 1971
Spanish Armada Salvage Expedition: S. Wignall (private)
Survivors of the Armada: Evelyn Hardy, 1966
Survivors of the Armada: review of same: J. de C. Ireland (IHS), 1966
Treasures of the Armada: Robert Stenuit, 1972
Wreck Detectives, The: Kendall MacDonald, 1972
Wrecks of the Spanish Armada on the Coast of Ireland, The: W. Spotswood Green (GJ), 1906

Miscellaneous

Archaeology Under Water: George F. Bass, 1966
Sailing Directions for the South and West Coasts of Ireland: Irish Cruising Club

Periodicals

I read many more periodicals than appear here; those omitted contained largely similar material to that in the works given here. The abbreviations contained in the bibliography refer to articles in various magazines and periodicals mentioned below, and are self-explanatory.

Irish Historical Studies (IHS)
Proceedings of Royal Irish Academy (PRIA)
The Irish Sword (IS)
Ulster Journal of Archaeology (UJA)
Journal of the Galway Archaeological and Historical Society (JGAHS)
English Historical Review (EHS)
Mariners' Mirror (MM)
Transactions of the Royal Historical Society (RHS[T])
Colston Papers (CP)
Geographical Journal (GJ)

Index

The Spanish Armada

Andalusia Squadron 43, 65, 179, 209, 210, 211, 213, 221
Armada ships, identification 179–80, 181, 216
Armament 112, 127, 146, 148, 151, 156, 167, 185, 196, 202, 211, 213, 216, 218
Biscay Squadron 43, 44, 46, 106–7, 197, 198, 200, 209, 210, 213
Biscayan personnel 162–3, 197
Carabelas Squadron 210
Castile Squadron 22, 43, 106–7, 112, 156, 167, 175, 197, 198, 209, 210, 211, 213
Castilian personnel 197
Clerics 136, 189–90, 202, 214, 222
Complements on board 88–90, 98, 100, 101, 106, 108, 112, 127, 128, 130, 145, 146, 148, 151, 156, 162–3, 167, 175, 185, 189, 190, 192–6, 198, 201–2, 206, 209–11, 214
Conditions of service 88, 108
Defeat by English fleet 18
Discipline 107, 108
Dutch in 55
Effects of geography on 76–8, 91–2
Effects on weather on 1, 18–19, 21–3, 57, 76–8, 88, 90–3, 99–100, 102, 104, 106, 109, 111, 113, 128, 146, 151–2, 213
Feluccas Squadron 210
First ships to reach Ireland 86, 87
Flemish personnel 162–3
Formation 1, 2, 209–10
Guipuzcoa Squadron 43, 145, 166, 167, 209, 210, 213
Imprisoned by Irish 189, 197
Irishmen with 23, 26, 33, 60–2, 64, 90, 95, 100, 221–2
Italian accounts 152
Italians with 67, 89
Land forces 59, 72, 100, 113, 117, 124, 131–3, 147–8, 207

Levant Squadron 20, 21, 43, 52–3, 59, 107, 108, 111–13, 127, 151, 185, 190, 195–6, 209, 210, 211, 213
Modern Yugoslav accounts of 152
Nationalities 89
Navigation 23–4, 94, 128
Navigators 128, 202, and see Juan, Capt. Marolin de
Neapolitan Squadron 202, 209, 210, 211, 213
Neapolitan tercio 127, 133; regiment of 127, 152
Netherlands personnel 55, 195
Numbers of vessels 1, 2, 21, 146, 154, 155, 209–10
Pataches and Zabras Squadron 198, 209, 210, 211, 213
Personnel captured by English 79–80
Pilots 26, 33, 94–5, 101, 107, 128, 157, 160, 163, 168, 170, 173
Portugal galleys 209, 210, 213
Portugal Squadron 43, 107, 148, 167, 209, 213–14
Portuguese personnel 89, 113, 162
Ragusan accounts 152–3
Ragusan personnel 89, 152–3, 196
Ragusan ships 20, 151–3, 195–6
Relics and remains 20, 87, 99, 100, 131, 132, 134, 159, 161, 171–3, 178, 184–6, 200–1, 216–20
Routes 18–19, 91, 92, 101, 106, 128, 212
Scots with 95, 160
Servants with 148, 164, 202, 214
Ship design and construction 148, 213, 216, 220
Ships captured by English 179, 190
Ships, repairs to 90, 91, 107, 151, 187, 204–5, 220
Ships, sizes of 20, 106, 108, 145–6, 148, 150–1, 156, 167,

169, 170, 175–6, 180, 184–6, 188–90, 193, 196–7, 199
Ships, speed of 100–2, 128
Ships, weaknesses of 18–21, 88, 92, 96–7, 128, 151–2, 167, 195, 213, 220
Sicilian galleys 58
Sicilian troops 127
Soldiers 2, 60, 65, 69, 106, 127, 148, 163, 174, 202
Spanish accounts 156, 180, and see Spanish State Papers
Squadrons, see also 209–10
Survivors, help given to 87–9, 103, 104, 116–17, 120, 125–6, 129–30, 132–3, 151, 180, 195, 203, 206
Survivors imprisoned by English 22, 139, 146–8, 164, 168, 175, 180, 188
Survivors, landing of 76, 83–9, 113
Survivors, murder/execution or sparing of 1, 30, 67, 114–17, 122–3, 124, 126, 131, 136–7, 145, 148, 160, 170, 178, 180, 185, 189, 197, 206, 207, 214, 215
Survivors, non-assistance to 149
Survivors, numbers of 130, 139, 180, 182, 185, 190–1, 214–15
Survivors remaining in Ireland 90, 112–13, 117, 139, 185–6, 203
Urcas Squadron 40, 43, 127, 128, 175, 190, 192, 209–11, 213
Venetian captains 127, 188
Venetian ships 127–8, 218
Wreck casualties 11, 98, 100, 117–18, 122, 130, 136, 139, 143, 145, 146, 151, 168, 170, 178, 180, 189, 214
Wreck, causes of 18–20, 22, 23–6, 104, 111, 113
Wreck, possible further identification of 216
Zabras 198, 209–11, 213

Ships of the Armada

Annunciada 150–3, 181, 190, 212, 213, 215, 216
Asunción 145
Barca de Amburg 127–8, 139, 190, 211, 212
Barca de Danzig (*urca*) 151, 152, 190
Casa de Paz Grande 190
Casa la Paz Chica 190
Castillo Negro 127–8, 190, 211, 212
Ciervo Volante 181, 190, 192, 211, 212
Concepcion 181, 216
Concepcion (*Delcano*) 41, 44, 47, 54, 212, 213
Concepcion (*Zubelzu*) 44
David (*urca*) 190, 210
Doncella 145
Duquesa Santa Ana 62, 65, 71–3, 76–83, 86–9, 91, 100, 104, 117–18, 181, 187, 194, 195, 212, 216
El Sanson 190
Esayas (*urca*) 190
Falco Blanco Mayor 190
Falco Blanco Mediano 36, 37, 40, 43, 47, 54, 181, 190, 212, 213
Florencia 188
Gato (*urca*) 190
Girona (Neapolitan galleass) 79–81, 87–92, 94–105, 111, 124, 181, 186, 187, 201, 202, 207, 211, 212, 216, 217
Gran Grifon, El 19, 127, 128, 139, 190, 218
Gran Grin, El 45–54, 57, 106–7, 181, 195, 212, 213
Isabella (Biscayan *patache*) 197
Juliana 52, 53, 181, 183, 185, 186, 211, 212, 216
La Lavia 108–13, 123, 127–8, 181, 185, 188, 211, 212
La Maria de Aguirre 197
Maria San Juan 146
Miguel de Suso 197
Napolitana 202
Nuestra Señora de Begona 72, 73
Nuestra Señora de la Rosa, see Santa Maria de la Rosa
Nuestra Señora de la Rosario 179
Nuestra Señora del Socorro 175, 197
Paloma Blanca 190
Patrona (galleass) 221
Perro Marino (*urca*) 190
Presveta Anuncijata, see Annunciada
Rata Encoronada, see Sancta Maria Rata Encoronada
Regazzona, La 20, 52, 59, 108, 127–8, 213
Santa Ana 104, 146 (and see *Duquesa*)
San Antonio de Padua 175

San Antonio de Padua (Castilian *patache*) 197
San Bernabe 145
San Buenaventura 146
San Esteban (Biscayan *patache*) 143–7, 149, 151, 179, 181, 197, 212, 213, 216
San Felipe (Portuguese galleon) 108, 148
San Gabriel (*urca*) 190
San Juan (Castile) 110–13, 115, 160, 181, 211, 212
San Juan (Portugal galleon) 158, 160, 162–4, 166–7, 172–3, 175, 177, 178, 202
San Juan (Ragusan) 174
San Juan Bautista (Castilian galleon) 22, 156–7, 164, 166–7, 171–5, 196, 198, 200
San Juan Bautista (*nao*) 174–7, 181, 212, 213, 215
San Juan de Sicilia (Levant) 111–12, 213
San Lorenzo 202, 204
San Marcos (galleon) 143, 144, 148, 149, 151, 153, 181, 212, 213, 214, 216
San Martin 18, 102, 107–8, 164, 169
San Mateo (Portuguese galleon) 108, 148
San Nicolas Prodaneli 45, 52, 54, 190, 195, 212, 213, 216
San Pedro (Castilian galleon) 106–9, 112
San Pedro Mayor (*urca*) 175–6, 190
San Salvador 146, 190
Sancta Maria Rata Encoronada (*Ratte* or *Rata* or *Rata Encoronada*) 47, 59, 60–2, 64–73, 76, 84, 88, 89, 100, 104, 117–18, 181, 194, 211, 212, 221
Santa Barbara 146
Santa Barbara (*urca*) 190
Santa Cruz 146
Santa Maria de la Rosa (*Nuestra Señora de la Rosa*) 20, 21, 28, 146, 156, 159, 161, 166, 167–73, 175–6, 178, 181, 186, 212, 213, 216, 218, 219
Santa Maria de (la) Vison 20, 110, 181, 188, 211, 212
Santa Maria 146
Santiago (Andalusian) 221
Santiago (*urca*) 62, 181, 190, 193–5, 211, 212, 216
Santo Andres 190
Sveti Jerolim 152
Trinidad 199, 200, 201
Trinidad (Castilian) 198, 201, 212, 213
Trinidad de Scala (Levant) 213
Trinidad (*nao*) 216
Trinidad Valencera, La (Levant) 20–1, 96, 103, 124, 126–31,

133–4, 138–9, 180, 182, 185, 211, 212, 215, 216, 218, 219
Trinidad (*zabra*) 213
Unidentified or doubtfully identified ships 37, 107, 109, 111–13, 117–18, 175, 181, 211, 212, 216
Ventura 190
Zuñiga 142–3, 201–5

General Index

Achill 45, 47, 64, 65, 195
Achillbeg Is. 45, 50
Achill Sound 47, 65
Adams, Robert 215
Adrian IV, Pope 4
Adriatic Sea 20, 151
Alberghetti, Zuanne 218
Alliagh (now Galliagh) Castle 129, 131, 133, 135, 207
Allingham, Hugh 118
Americas, the 6
Andalusia 208
Andalusia Squadron, see Armada
Anthony, John 168–9, 178
Antrim 7, 9, 11, 80, 94, 96–8, 102–3, 120, 124, 125, 130, 137, 141, 185, 187, 190, 207, 214, 216
Antwerp 110, 126
Aragon, Capt. 115
Aramburu, Marcos de 22, 156, 157–8, 160, 162, 154, 166, 167, 168, 171–8, 198–201
Aranda, Capt. Don Fernando de 211
Aranda, Don Martin de, Judge-Advocate 108, 112–14
Aran Is., Co. Galway 1, 41, 54, 142
Aranivar, Miguel de 174–6
Aranmor Is. 92
Ardara 80, 88
Ardnaree (Ardnearie) 189
Ards nr. Carna 40, 41, 213
Arechaga, Pedro de 40, 54, 55, 213
Argyll, Earl of 103
Arquillos, Alonso de 148
Arranmore Is. 184, 186, 211
Arranmore roads 184
Arthur, Christopher 11
Ascoli, Prince d' 163, 169, 170, 178, 213
Athlone 1, 53, 55, 66, 122, 154, 194
Auerede 163
Aughnanure (Fuathaidh) Castle 38
Avancini, Giovanni 65, 66, 67
Avila, Capt. Don Cristobal de 107–8
Ayamonte, Marquis de 40
Aybar, Capt. Hieronimo de 127,

135, 136, 139
Azores 58, 59, 155, 178

Bacia, Sgt. Antonio de 139
Baghuine (Bannagh) 83
Bagenal, Marshal 14, 62, 90, 187
Ballaghaline 147
Ballina, Co. Mayo 189, 192
Ballycastle, Co. Antrim 103
Ballyclogher Rock 161
Ballycroy, Co. Mayo 62, 66, 71, 208, 211
Ballymote, Co. Sligo 85, 86, 120
Ballynakill harbour 37, 38, 213
Ballyshannon 53, 120, 123, 184
Ballyshannon Castle 75
Baltic Sea 128
Bannagh, see Baghuine
Baptista, Petrus 142, 203
Baraona, Don Juan de 100
Barna 34
Barnagh Rock 172, 173
Bartolo, Capt. Juan de 188, 211
Bartolo, Nicolas de 188
Bazan, Diego de 174, 175, 176
Bazan, Don Alvaro de, Marquis of Santa Cruz 3, 4, 10, 20, 26, 58, 59, 105, 175
Beginish 160, 161, 167, 172–3, 177
Belderg harbour 192
Belmullet 64, 71, 192, 193, 195
Benbane Head 97–9
Ben Bulben Mt. 109
Benwee Head, Co. Mayo 62, 76, 191–3
Berdugo, Andres 202
Berte Castle 133
Bertendona, Don Martin de 20, 52, 59, 151, 210
Bilbao 163
Bingham family 72
Bingham, Francis 189
Bingham, George, Sheriff of Sligo 1, 55, 85–6, 109, 115, 119–20, 122, 138, 182, 187–90, 195
Bingham, Sir Richard, Governor of Connacht 1, 8, 12, 14, 22, 30–3, 35, 36, 38, 39–41, 44–9, 51–6, 66, 67, 69–73, 76, 85, 101, 119–20, 122, 138, 142, 149, 154, 182, 187, 189, 195, 203, 206–8, 215
Bingham's Castle 72
Biscay, Bay of 145
Biscay Squadron, see Armada
Black Rocks 76
Blacksod Bay, Co. Mayo 60, 62, 64, 65, 68, 71, 73, 76, 100, 192, 211
Blake, James 72
Blasket 130, 176
Blasket Is., Co. Kerry, 28, 157, 158, 160–2, 164–6, 170, 197,

199, 200, 201, 208, 213
Blasket Sound 23, 28, 146, 158–9, 161, 164, 165, 167, 168, 170, 172, 174, 175, 177, 180, 200, 201, 203, 208, 213, 218
Blasket, the 172
Bloody Foreland 92
Bobadilla, Don Francisco de 108
Bonner, Patrick 184–5
Borja, Francisco de 80, 94, 101, 102, 104, 139
Boyle 184
Braadillaun 37
Brandon Bay 158
Brandon, Mt. 157
Brandon Point 199
Brannigan, Desmond 219
Brehon laws 12
Brewitt, Myles 3
Bristol 155
Broadhaven Bay, Co. Mayo 25, 62, 64, 188, 191–5, 211
Brywer, Alexander 1, 22, 50, 154
Bull's Mouth, the 65
Bundouglas 37
Bundrowes 123
Burghley 50, 101, 150, 155, 162, 194, 203
Burke, Richard 66–7
Burke, William 189
Burkes of Mayo 31, 32, 46, 66, 76, 85, 119, 120, 189
Burrishoole (also Borreis, Borris, Burris), Co. Mayo 2, 50
Burtonport 183, 186
Byrte, John 54

Cadiz 17, 58
Cahan, Nicolas 143, 145–51
Calais 18, 19, 61, 65, 80, 81, 95, 104, 139, 152, 163, 164, 169, 202, 204
Calderon, Pedro Coco 22
Campbells, the 103
Canavera, Hernando de 139
Cape Clear 94, 109, 130
Cape, the 18
Cardenas, Don Garcia de 148
Carew Papers 187
Carew, Sir Peter 61
Carna 40, 41, 43, 213
Carricknaspania (Spaniards' Rock) 111
Carrick Rocks 64
Carrigada Is. 161
Carrigaholt (Carg-e-colle), Co. Clare 1, 9, 32, 150, 151
Carrigaholt Castle 149
Carrigan Head 91
Castile 115
Castile Squadron, see Armada
Castle Beste 133
Castlejordan 85
Castle M'Garratt, Co. Mayo 48, 73

Castleroe Castle 125
Catholic clerics 2, 3, 4, 6, 11, 57, 104, 116, 132, 136–7, 189–90, 203, 222
Cavan Co. 66
Challis, Capt. John 17
Clancy, Boetius (Sheriff of Clare) 1, 22, 142, 143, 147–8, 149, 151, 203
Clare Co. 142–5, 149, 151, 179, 180, 202, 206, 208, 214
Clare, Coroner of 180
Clare Is. 45–53, 195, 207, 213
Clear (Clare?) Island 35
Clew Bay, Co. Mayo 2, 35, 40, 43, 45–7, 50, 53, 65, 107, 180, 189, 196
Clifden, Co. Galway 37, 38
Clogher Head 161, 164, 165
Clonmel 51
Cloughglass 185, 186, 211
Cluidaniller 92
Coker, Robert 189
Coleraine 125
'Comerford' 73
Comerford, Gerald, Sheriff 51, 71–3, 85, 194
Connacht, Composition of 31, 32, 39
Connacht Council 34, 39, 48, 143
Connacht, Province of 1, 12, 14, 30–2, 53, 55, 56, 66, 119, 123, 142, 181, 206–8
Connelly, families 38
Connemara 30, 35, 38, 40, 45, 54, 190, 216
Conway, John 70
Cordoba, Don Diego de 148
Cordoba, Don Felipe de 148
Cordoba, Don Gonzalo de 39, 40, 54, 55, 56
Cordoba, Don Luis de 39, 40, 54, 55, 56
Cork 15, 22, 150, 155
Cork Co. 140, 141, 156
Cornelius, Bishop of Down and Connor, see Down and Connor
Cornwall 60, 155
Corrib, Loch 38
Corslieve 68
Corunna 11, 18, 19, 59, 61, 106–8, 146, 167, 168, 177, 180, 196, 198, 209, 210, 214, 220
'Cosgrave' 42, 43
Couenoole Strand 166, 168
Croaghacullion Mt. 78
Croaghnakeela Is. 42
Crofton, John 182
Cronagarn 92
Crown forces, see English forces in Ireland
Crows, the 177
Cruit Is. 186
Cuellar, Capt. Don Francisco de 106, 109–26, 188

Cuellar (town) 106
Cul Tra 186
Curraun (Corraun) Peninsula, Co. Mayo 35, 213
Cusack, George 147

Daly, Jack 70
Dartry (Dartraigh) Mts. 119
Dating x, 145
Davillaun Is. 36, 37
Dawros Head and Peninsula 78, 83, 187
Delcano, Capt. Juan 44, 213
Denny, Sir Edward and Lady 197
Derry 110, 124, 130–2
Derry, Bishop of 84, 120, 125, 137
Derry city 103, 129
Derry, City of, Sub-aqua Club 134, 218, 219
Derry Co. 74, 75, 94, 96, 120, 125, 129, 182
Desmond (region) 140–1, 200
Desmond, Gerald Fitzgerald, Earl of 61, 140–1
Desmond Rebellion 14, 15, 17, 30, 61, 140
Desmonds, the, see Fitzgeralds
De Suazo, see De Swasso
Devon 60, 155, 175, 190
'Diego, Don' 169
Dingle Bay, Co. Kerry 175, 200, 201
Dingle, Co. Kerry 1, 2, 10, 61, 162, 168
Dingle Peninsula, Co. Kerry 157, 159, 160, 167, 199
Dogherty, Richard 182
Dohooma 65
Donai, Capt. Horatio 127, 139
Donamona 32
Donegal 1, 8, 9, 22, 24, 25, 53, 62, 74, 77, 84–6, 89, 91, 93, 94, 96, 109, 113, 128, 129, 131, 139, 154, 156, 180, 182, 185–7, 190, 194, 214, 216
Donegal Bay 77, 78, 83, 86, 88, 89, 91, 92, 95, 109, 189, 192, 195
Donegal Castle 75
Donegal harbour 118
Donegal town 185, 187, 188, 190, 195
Doolin 147
Doona 65, 71, 72
Doona (Fahy) Castle, Co. Mayo 62, 65, 66, 68, 69, 70
Doonbeg 142, 143, 146, 149, 213
Doonbeg Bay 145–6
Doonbeg Beach, Co. Clare 145
Doulus 200
Dowgan, Henry 89
Down and Connor, Cornelius, Bishop of 132, 133, 136, 138

Dowrough, Fr. James ne 84, 90
Drake, Sir Francis 11, 58–9, 105, 169, 179
Drogheda, Co. Louth 131, 139
Dromoland Castle 149
Drumanoo Head 91
Dublin 4, 84, 122–3, 135, 137–8, 140, 154, 155, 197
Dublin, Bishop of 11
Dublin Castle 84, 86
Duirling Beag and Mor 42
Duirling na Spainneach 41, 44, 213
Duke, Henry 85, 87, 90, 101–3, 187
Dummore Head 82, 160, 166, 167, 170, 171
Dunaff 93
Dunanyme Castle 103
Dungannon 137, 139
Dungiven 125
Dungloe 182, 183
Dunkirk 126, 164
Dunluce 101, 102
Dunluce Castle 103, 124, 125
Dunmore 164
Dunpatrick Head 191, 192
Dunquin 161, 162, 165
Dunseverick 125
Duro, Capt. Fernandez 44, 53, 82, 146, 174–6, 209, 210
Dursey Is. 156, 157
Duvillauns, the 76

Eagle Is. 25
Edinburgh 138
Elizabeth I of England 2–8, 10–14, 15, 17, 18, 39, 46, 55, 61, 66, 73, 74, 86, 103, 104, 117, 118, 122, 126, 130, 135, 140–1, 152, 155, 185, 195, 197, 208 ·
Elly Bay, Co. Mayo 62, 64, 65, 72, 73
England, informers, spies and agents for 1, 8, 17, 66, 84, 85, 87, 90, 102, 104, 111–12, 120, 141, 166, 180, 194
England, naval forces of 3, 7, 18, 155, 225
England, proposed Spanish invasion of 3, 6, 7, 17
England, shores of 109; Armada wreck on 175, 190
English Channel 3, 52, 59, 60, 61, 94, 95, 128, 146, 148, 152, 162, 167–8, 175, 179, 190, 202, 204
English colonization of Ireland 4, 5, 6
English control in Ireland 4, 6–10, 12–15, 45–6, 74, 76, 84, 86, 87, 89, 90, 103, 104, 109, 115, 117, 118, 119–23, 125, 129, 130, 140–1, 149, 154–5,

162, 206–8
English forces in Ireland 3, 4, 7, 8–10, 14, 17, 18, 33, 38, 54, 69, 71, 74, 75, 116–18, 121–5, 133, 135, 140–1, 149, 154–5, 162, 203
English government structure in Ireland 8, 12, 141, 142, and see Irish Council
English ships in Ireland 75, 101
English State Papers 20, 22, 28, 34, 35, 43, 48, 53, 54, 88, 100–1, 125, 138, 150, 152, 176, 179, 182, 187, 189, 193–5, 203
Enriquez, Don Diego 11, 112, 113, 116
Erris (?Irris) 48
Erris, barony of 189
Erris, Lough 80
Erris Peninsula or Head 24, 25, 45, 60, 64, 66, 76–8, 109, 182, 192–5, 211
Escorial, the 104
Essex, Lord Lt. of Ireland 8, 12, 103
Eulane, Patrick 62, 90, 187

Fahy Castle, see Doona
Fahy Strand, Co. Mayo 62, 68, 69, 211
Fair Isle, see Scotland and Scottish Isles
Falls, Cyril 12, 176
Fanad 83
Fanad Head 93
Faranan, Salomon 89
Felipe, Capt. Andres 213
Feluccas Squadron, see Armada
Fenton, Sir Geoffrey 34–5, 44, 48, 49, 50, 52–3, 85, 120, 138, 180, 182, 189, 192, 194, 200, 201, 215
Fermanagh 85, 110, 118
Ferrol 18
Finistere, Cape 18, 102, 204
Fitzgerald family (see also Desmond) 140, 141, 200
FitzGerald (Fitzgerald), Maurice 60–2, 100
Fitzmaurice, James 61, 62, 90
Fitzwilliam, Sir William, Lord Deputy of Ireland 1, 2, 8, 12, 13, 15, 17, 18, 30–1, 48, 52, 54, 55, 66, 71–3, 84, 85, 89, 90, 101, 103–4, 120, 122–3, 129, 132–3, 135, 137–9, 141, 142, 154, 155, 195, 203, 206–8
Flanders 126, 143, 147, 149, 180
Fort Hill, Galway 54
Forreside-more 85
Fowley, Robert 54
Foxe, Patrick 84, 101, 137
Foze Rocks 161
France 4, 89, 94, 104, 138–9
France, ship stranded in 52

'Francisco, Don' 169
Francisco, Emmanuel 162, 178
Freaghillaun North and South 36–7, 39, 40
Fremoso, Emmanuel 162–4, 178
Frenchman's Hill 92
Fuathaidh (Aughnanure) Castle 38
Fynglasse (now Toorglass) 35, 45, 50, 51, 52, 53, 195–6

Galicia 11, 18, 190, 208
Gallagher, Raymond, see Derry, Bishop of
Galliagh Castle, see Alliagh
Gallowglasses 74, 83, 189
Gallows Hill (Cnoc na Crocaire) 148–9
Galway City and Bay 1, 10, 11, 32–6, 38–9, 41, 43, 44, 48, 51–6, 67, 71, 142, 180
Galway Co. 37, 38, 40, 56, 122, 206
Garvan Is. 93, 128
Giants' Causeway, Co. Antrim 125, 317
Gilbert, Sir Humphrey 11
Giron, Don Alonso Tellez 148
Glenagivney (now Kinnagoe) Bay 129–32, 211, 218
Glencar 117
Glennamong 68
Gloucestershire 155
Gnomore 38
Gola Is. 92
Goolamore 71
Grange 109, 110, 211
Granuaile, see O'Malley, Grace
Granvelle, Don Thomas de 60, 100, 124
Grattan, Cdr. John 161, 219
Gravelines 11, 18, 19, 61, 107–9, 148
Green, Jeremy 219
Green, Rev. William Spotswood 27–8, 37, 64, 176, 187, 196
Greenwich, National Maritime Museum at 200
Gregory, Pope 61
Grenada Wars 58
Grenville, Sir Richard 8, 59, 105, 155
Grey, Lord Leonard 74
Grey of Wilton, Lord and Lord Deputy of Ireland 10
Guadarrama Mts 104
Guevara, Don Alonso Ladron de 48, 52–5, 60
Guipuzcoa 146, 208
Guipuzcoa Squadron, see Armada
Gumarra, Miguel de 148
Guzman, Don Alonso Perez de, see Medina Sidonia
Guzman, Don Diego de 139

Guzman, Don Enrique Enriquez de 148
Guzman, Don Pedro de 60, 136
Gweebarra Bay 78, 92
Gweedore 182

Halut, Remigy de (gunfounder) 218
Hamburg 190
Harbour Lights 184
Havre de Grace 204
Hawkins, John 105
Heard, Richard 186
Hebrides, see Scotland and Scottish Isles
Hen Rock 177
Henry II of England 4
Henry VIII of England 74, 75
Herbert, Sir William 8
Herrera, Don Hieronimo de 100
Holycross, Co. Tipperary 80
Hontanares (Ontanar), Our Lady of 106, 114
Horra, Capt. Fernando 174, 176, 213
Hovenden, Richard and Henry 103, 133–9
Howard of Effingham, Lord 18, 19, 107
Hume 176
Hume, Maj. Martin 89

'Ibernia' 138
'I Breckana' 143
Iccoggy, Richard 72
Iceland 156
Igueldo, Pedro de 204
Illagh, see Alliagh
Illaunboy 161
Indian Guard of Galleons 115
Inver, Co. Mayo 62, 188, 191, 193–5, 211
Inishbiggle 65
Inishbofin 36
Inisheer 118
Inishfree Bay 184
Inishkea 62, 76
Inishkeith, see Scattery Is.
Inishmurray Is. 109
Inishnabro 160
Inishowen, Co. Donegal 2
Inishowen peninsula 129, 131, 133, 182, 185, 207, 218
Inishtearaght 157, 160
Inishtooskert 157, 160–2, 166, 167
Inishtrahull 94, 128
Inishvickillane 160
Iniskeen 120
Ireland, Dr. John de Courcy 151
Ireland, before Tudor conquest 3–5
Ireland, contemporary maps 24–5
Ireland, effects on war on 12–15

Ireland, Gaelic clan system in 5, 6, 10, 12, 15, 84, 140, 180, 208, 224
Ireland, invasion of England from 6, 7, 8, 17
Ireland, links with Spain 2–4, 6–11
Ireland, primitive conditions 7, 119, 120–2, 180
Ireland: titles of Lord Chancellor, Lord Deputy (Viceroy), Lord Lieutenant (Viceroy), Chief Justice, Treasurer at Wars, Marshal of the Army; see Irish Council, 12
Irish administrators in English pay 142–3, 147, 150
Irish Council 12, 14, 22, 50, 154, 207
Irish exiles in Lisbon 2, 3, 26
Irish exiles in Rome 2
Irish pilots, see Armada
Irish Sea 96
Irish soldiers in English pay 131, 133–8
Irish spies for Spain 3
Irish State Papers 20, 22, 28, 34–5, 43, 48, 53, 54, 88, 100–1, 125, 138, 150, 152, 176, 179, 182, 187, 189, 193–5, 203
Islandes, Dionisio 221
Islands of Ireland, The 165
Italian accounts, see Armada
'Italian deserters' in Ireland 67
Italians in Armada, see Armada
Iveglia, Ohmucevic 152–3, 213
Ivelja, Peter 196
Ivella, Doliste de, see Iveglia

James VI of Scotland 66, 73, 126, 138, 141
John, Don, of Austria 58
Juan, Capt. Marolin de 81, 104, 139

Kahane, Nicholas, see Cahan
Kelly, Maj. 133, 135, 136, 138
Kenmare Bay 157
Kenmare River 156
Kerry 1, 2, 4, 9, 21–3, 25, 28, 61, 94, 128, 140, 154, 156–7, 163, 198, 200–1, 206, 214, 216, 218
Kerry Head 199
Kid Island, Co. Mayo 62, 191–3
Kilbreedagh Rock 177
Kildare, Bishop of 11, 203
Kilkenny 51
Killala Bay 25, 45, 77
Killaloe, Bishop of 11, 64, 100
Killybegs (Calebeg) 1, 11, 25, 77, 79, 86–8, 90–2, 95, 99–102, 180, 185–6, 211
Kilmurray Ibrickane 142, 146
Kilrush 150, 151
Kiltoorish Lake 79, 82, 83, 86, 87

Kincasslagh 183, 184
King's Mt 109
Kinnagoe Bay, formerly
  Glenagivney, q.v.
Kinrovar 65
Kinsale, Battle of 6, 10, 86, 208
Knockalina 193
Knocklettercus 68
Knockmore Mt 45
Knockmoyleen 68

Lacada Point 98–102, 208, 211
Lara, Don Rodrigo Manrique de
  60, 100
Lasso, Don Rodrigo 139
Laughton 176
Leahan Mt 78
Lee family 42–4
Leenane 35, 36
Leinster, Province of 14, 140
Leitrim Co. 66, 85, 110, 116, 118
Leiva, Antonio Luis de, see
  Ascoli, Prince d'
Leiva, Don Alonso Martinez de
  57–60, 62, 64–8, 70–7, 79, 81,
  82, 84–7, 89, 91, 94, 95–6, 100,
  101, 104–5, 124, 187, 188, 195,
  206–8, 210, 211
Leiva, Don Diego de 100
Leiva, Don Santo de 57–8
Leon 115
Leon, Don Luis Ponce de 60,
  100
Leon, Rodrigo Ponce de 139
Lepanto, Battle of 30, 58
Levant Squadron, see Armada
Licornio, John de 162, 163, 178
Limavady, Co. Derry 125 .
Limerick 1, 8, 11, 30, 53, 154
Limerick, Bishop of 30
Limerick Co. 140, 149
Limerick, Mayor of 143, 151
Lisbon 2, 3, 11, 17, 19–22, 40,
  46, 58–61, 72, 102, 106, 108,
  127, 146, 148, 152, 164, 180,
  196, 198, 201, 202, 208, 209,
  210, 214
Liscannor 142, 143, 151, 202, 203
Liscannor Bay 143
Loaysa, Juan Perez de 202
Loch Corrib 38
Loch Gill 117
Loch Glenade 117
London 139, 154, 186
London, Tower of 18
Loop Head 1, 149, 150
'Loughesullemore' 84
Lough Foyle 129–32, 182
Lough Mask 32
Lough Melvin 118–20, 122, 124
Loughros 79, 80
Loughros Beg Bay 78
Loughros More Bay 77–80, 91,
  211
Loughros Point 78

Lough Swilly 74, 93, 131, 182
Lund, Capt. Juan Hernandez de
  211
Lure, the (rock) 171
Lurga Point 144, 146, 213
Luzon, Capt. Don Diego de
  136–7, 139
Luzon, Don Alonso de 57, 127,
  130–6, 139, 152, 211

Maam 38
McCabb, Melaghlen 189, 192,
  206
'McClancy' 85, 119, 120, 123–4
MacClancy, Dartry 118, 121, 122
MacClancy, sister of 124
MacClancy, son of 124
McClancys, the 85, 118, 119,
  120–1
McDonagh family 42, 44
MacDonald, James (of the Isles)
  89, 103
MacDonald, Lady Agnes 89, 103
MacDonalds (Scots clan) 103, and
  see McDonnell
'McDonnell' 138, 139
McDonnell clan 80, 103, 104,
  120, 130, 136, 141, 207
McDonnell, James (son of Sorley
  Boy) 103
Mace Head 41, 42
Machary, James (also Mettarg,
  McGarry, McCarthy) 80, 81,
  90, 95, 105, 194
Mac-in-Persium, Andrew 221
Mac-in-Persium, Brian 221
McMahon 85
MacQuillan clan 103
McSweeney Bannagh (Baghuine)
  83, 87, 89, 90
McSweeney (official) 150
'MacSweeny' 75, 137, 187
MacSweenys (MacSweeney) clan
  75, 76, 83, 84, 88, 103, 120,
  207
Madrid 61, 104
Magee University College, Derry
  219
Magno, Jeronimo 60, 100
Maguire, chieftain 85, 120
Maguire, Hugh (son of above)
  85
Malbay 144, 150
Maldonado, Antonio 148
Malin 76
Malines, Netherlands
  gunfoundry 218
Malin Head 93–4, 128, 129, 202,
  211, 212 (map)
'Manglana' 179
Manona, Francisco de 168, 173
Manrique, Capt. Don Garcia
  127, 136
Manrique, Don Antonio 139
Marco, Capt. 164

Mares, Capt. Don Pedro 72, 73,
  100, 211
Marholm church 13
Marine archaeology 216–19
Marley, Pedro 221
Martin, Colin 218–20
Martinez, Juan 171, 174
Mason Is. 42
Mason, T. H. 165
Mattingly, Garrett 175, 176
Matute, Capt. 220
Maxwell, William Hamilton 65,
  69
Mayo Co. 9, 24, 25, 30–2, 35, 45,
  46, 54, 55, 62, 64, 66, 76, 77,
  84, 91, 122, 182, 188–9, 191–3,
  214
M'Donnell, Sorley Boy
  (Somhairle Buidhe) 101, 103,
  104
Medina, Don Juan Gomez de
  127, 210
Medina Sidonia, Duchess of 72
Medina Sidonia, Duke of (Duke
  Alonso Perez de Guzman)
  18–22, 24, 26, 40, 51, 53, 57,
  59, 60, 72, 102, 106–8, 127,
  148, 160, 163, 164, 169, 198,
  202, 210
Medrano, Don Diego 210
Melendez, Gonzalo (Gregorio)
  174, 176
Mendoza, Don Alvaro de 139
Mendoza, Don Antonio Hurtado
  de 198, 210
Mendoza, Don Bernardino de,
  Ambassador to France 104
Mendoza, Don Pedro de 48, 50,
  51, 52, 57, 106–7, 213
Mercator 24
Merryman, Capt. Nicholas 101,
  102
'M'Glanchie' (MacClancy) 120,
  and see MacClancy
M'Hugh Duff, Hugh Oge 120
Mieres, Don Diego de 48, 52–5
Milan 58
Milanese Cavalry 58
Miltown-Malbay, Co. Clare 142
M'Inabbe, Thomas Burke 72
M'Manus, Brian 90
Moher, Cliffs of, Co. Clare 142,
  143, 202
Monaghan Co. 85
Moncado, Hugo de 202, 204, 210
Moirs, the 58
Mordaunt, Capt. 148
'Morton, Mr.' 148
Mostion (Mostyn?), Thomas 182
Mostyn, Capt. William 84
Mountjoy, Baron 8, 10
Moy River, Co. Mayo 32
M'Ranyll, Moilmory 72
M'Sweeny ne Doe (na dTuath)
  62, 80, 83–91, 101

M'Sweeny ne Doffe, *see* M'Sweeny ne Doe
M'Tyriell, Marcus Roe 72
M'Tyrrell, Ferreigh 72
Muckross Head 91
Mullaghderg 184, 185, 186, 211
Mullet Peninsula, Co. Mayo 62, 64, 72, 76, 77, 194
Mulmosog 88
Mulrany (Mallaranny) 45, 50, 195
Munster, Province of 8, 11, 14, 15, 30, 61, 140–2, 146, 147, 200, 206, 207
Murad, Sultan of 152
Mutton Is., Co. Clare 143, 144, 146–9, 213
Mweenish Is. 42

Naghten, Philip, Bishop od Ross 11
Naples, Regiment of, *see* Armada
Naran 92
National Maritime Museum, Greenwich 200
Navas, Marquis of 148
Neapolitan Squadron, *see* Armada
Neapolitan Tercio, *see* Armada
Nephin Beg 68
Netherlands, the 3, 6–8, 32, 58, 61, 126, 148, 218
Newmarket-on-Fergus, Co. Clare 149
Newport 145
Newtown 117
Normans, the 3
Norris brothers 8
Norris (Norreys), Sir Thomas 8, 141, 154, 197
North Channel 103
North Sea 18, 21, 53, 60
Nova, Francisco de 137
Nova, Jean de 80, 94, 101, 102, 104, 137, 139
Nowe, Monsieur de 139; son of 'Tyllyny' 139

O'Bayll, Conor, Bishop of Limerick 11, 30
O'Boyle Is. 79, 82
'O'Boyle's country' 187
O'Brien, Donough 31
O'Brien, Mahon 32
O'Brien, Sir Turlough 146, 148, 203
O'Byrne clan 14
O'Cahan clan 120, 138
O'Cahan (head of clan) 125, 130, 136
O'Carr, Peter, 162, 163, 178
O'Conor clan 38, 115
O'Conor, Rory 38
O'Dogherty, *see* O'Doherty, Sir John
O'Doherty clan 129

O'Doherty, Sir John 2, 129, 130, 132, 133, 135
O'Donnell, Calvagh 75
O'Donnell clan 15, 74–6, 89, 119, 120, 129
O'Donnell, Hugh Dubh 75
O'Donnell, Hugh Manus (abb. to O'Donnell) 75–6, 83–6, 89, 113, 117, 120, 122–3, 137, 138, 141, 185, 207; daughter of 75, 103
O'Donnell, Ineen Dubh (*see* MacDonald) 89, 103
O'Donnell, Red Hugh 75, 76, 84, 86, 89, 137, 208
O'Donnell, 'Sir Hugh' 103
O'Fflaertie (O'Flaherty) 35, 44
O'Flaherty clan 36, 38, 39, 40, 46
O'Flaherty, Sir Murrough (ne Doe) 38–40
O'Flaherty, Tadgh (na Buile) 40–2, 44, 56
Ohmucevic-Grguric, Capt. 152
O'Lasit, Cormac 221
Olisti-Tasovic, Nikola 152
Olmedo, Hernando de 148
O'Male (O'Malley?) 35
O'Malley clan 45–8, 50
O'Malley, Dowdarra Roe 48–53
O'Malley, Grace 45–8, 70
Ommanney, Adm. Sir Erasmus 186
O'Molloy, Capt. Greene 189
O'Mullryana, Henry 221
O'Mulryan, Conor, Bishop of Kildare 11, 203
O'Neill clan 15, 75, 103, 119, 125, 129, 138
O'Neill, Hugh, *see* Tyrone, Earl of
O'Neill, Shane 75, 103
O'Neill, Tirlach Lynagh 85, 86, 89, 113, 117, 138, 141, 207
Oquendo, Don Miguel de 145, 146, 208, 210
Oria, Herrera 176
Orkneys, *see* Scotland and Scottish Isles
Orlando, Manuel 112–13, 188
Ormond, Earl of 50, 51, 53, 141
O'Rourke 85, 90, 119, 120
O'Rourke, Sir Brian of Breffni 66, 84, 117, 118
O'Rourkes, the 89, 117
Ortelius 24
Ossory, Bishop of 11
Osuna, Duke of 148
O'Sullivan, Maurice 165
Ottoman naval forces 58
Oughterard, Co. Galway 38
Oveden, *see* Hovenden
Owenduff River 71
Owenmore River 71
Owey Is. 92
Owle, barony of 50, 51

Owles 189
Ox and Cow (Bull and Cow) Is. 156, 157

Paleologo, Don Manuel 60
Pale, the 4, 7
Pallavicini (Palavicino), Sir Horatio 139
Papal forces in Ireland (*see also* Smerwick) 4, 10
Paredes, Count of 60, 100, 124
Pares, Sergeant Alonso de 152
Paris 104
Parma, Duke of 61, 126, 162, 164
Pataches and *Zabras* Squadron, *see* Armada
Patent Rolls 40
'Patt' 70
'Pedro, Don' 169
Pelham (?) 8
Penafiel, Marquis of 148, 213
Peramato, Capt. Juan de 211
Perlines, Francisco 148
Perrott, Sir John, Lord Deputy of Ireland 8, 12–15, 17, 18, 30–2, 39, 55, 75, 76, 86, 142
Philip II of Spain 2, 3, 4, 6–8, 10, 11, 17, 20, 22, 26, 57–9, 61, 73, 81, 85, 89, 104, 105, 115, 128, 142, 163, 164, 169, 170, 178, 203, 206, 208, 218
Plate fleet 115
Plantations 5, 6, 185
Plymouth 18
'Pollilly' (Elly Bay, Co. Mayo) 64, 73, 180, 194
Popham, Sir John, Attorney General 150, 162
Port Hill 78
Port na Spaniagh (Port na Spainneach or Portnaspania) 98, 99, 103, 211, 217
Portnoo 92
Portrush 87, 130
Portugal 11, 58, 146
Portugal Squadron, *see* Armada
Privy Council 123, 154, 155, 207
Prodanelic, Marin 196, 213; brother of 196
Protestantism, *see* Religion
Pueblo, Count of 148

Ragusa (Dubrovnik) 53, 151–2, 196
Ragusan ships and personnel, *see* Armada
Raleigh, Sir Walter 8, 105, 141, 155
Ranjina, Marin 196
Rathlin Is. 103
Rathlin O'Birne Is. 78, 91
Recalde, Juan Martinez de 44, 46, 57, 105, 107, 148, 158, 160ff, 172ff, 197, 200ff, 208, 210

Religious considerations 2, 3, 4, 6, 11, 57, 104, 132, 136–7, 189–90, 203
Religious personnel and foundations in Ireland 116, 118, 222
Renvyle, Connemara 37
Requeses, Don Luis de 58
Revenge 59, 155, 178
Reyes, Capt. Gaspar de los 48, 52–5
Ridge Point, Achill 65
Rockall 57, 62, 156
Rome 2, 58
Rosbeg 79–82, 88, 187, 208, 211
Roskeeragh Point 109
Rossan Point 78
Ross, Bishop of (Philip Naghten) 11
Rossclogher Castle 118–20, 122–5
Rosses, the (Co. Donegal) 92, 182, 183, 185, 208, 216
Ruiz, Alonso 148
Russell, Sir William 203
Rutland Is. 186

Saavedra, Capt. Juan de 202, 204
St Augustine's Monastery, Galway 54
St John's Point 91
St Leger 74, 75
St Leger, Sir Warham 141
St MacDara's Is. 42
St Quentin, Battle of 30
Salto, Capt. Beltran del 135, 136, 139
Salto, Don Pedor de 139
San Lucar 208
San Martin, Capt. Juan de 211
San Sebastian 143, 145, 179, 180
Santa Cruz, Marquis of, see Bazan, Don Alvaro de
Santander 177, 208
Santiago 11
Scattery Is. (Inishkeith) 150, 203
Scattery roads 150, 190, 213
Scotland and Scottish Isles 18, 19, 21, 22, 60, 62, 66, 68, 73, 76, 80, 85, 90–6, 98–101, 104, 107, 109, 110–12, 117, 124, 130, 131, 136, 138, 139, 152, 156, 164, 187, 190, 202, 213, 218; Fair Isle 19, 128, 190, 202, 218; Hebrides 111–12; 'Ibernia', prob. Scottish isle 138; Orkneys 19, 109, 127–8, 202; Shetlands 19, 109, 125, 127–8
Scots with Armada, see Armada
Scottish merchants in Flanders 126; settlers, soldiers et al in Ireland 7, 32, 74, 83, 89, 103, 130, 207
Segovia 106

Severn River 155
Seville 11
Shannon River 1, 30, 61, 141, 143, 149, 150–3, 190, 203, 213, 214
Shee, Henry 51
Shraghnamanagh Bridge 71
Sicilian galleys and troops, see Armada
Sidney, Sir Henry 8, 57
Silva, Antonio de 100
Silva, Capt. Bartoleme Lopez de 100
Skelligs, the 157
Skerries Rocks 97
Slea Head 168
Slieve Car 68
Slieve League 25, 77, 78, 91
Slieve Tooey 78, 80
Sligo 1, 9, 24, 25, 66, 85–9, 109, 110, 113, 117–18, 120, 122, 123, 174, 180, 185, 188
Sligo Castle 85
Sligo town 109, 115, 214
Smerwick harbour 158, 160, 163
Smerwick, Papal force at 4, 10, 30, 160
Smythe, Capt. Nathaniel 54
Somersetshire 155
Spain, agents in Ireland 11
Spain, contact with England 2, 3, 6, 7, 10–11, 26, 33, 42
Spain, invasion of England by 3, 4, 7, 17
Spain, State Papers 44, 82, 95, 100–1, 185, 190, 192, 193, 195, 197, 201, 204
Spaniard Cave 98, 99
Spaniards' Rock (Carricknaspania) 111
Spanish Graveyard 148–9
Spanish Point 145, 148, 149, 213
Spanish Rock 98
'Spanish Sea, The' 94
Spenser, Edmund 141
Spenser, William 15
Spinola, Capt. Fabricio 100, 211
Staad, Abbey of 116, 122
State Papers, see English/Irish and Spanish
Stenuit, Robert 87, 98, 100, 101, 217
Stooken 177
Strabane 85, 124
Stragar River 88
Streedagh Point, Co. Sligo 111, 115
Streedagh Strand, Co. Sligo 109–16, 122–3, 126, 174, 188, 208, 211, 215
Stromboli, H.M.S. 171
Stromboli Rock and Reef 28, 159, 170–1, 173, 213, 219
Strype, John 215
Stukeley, Thomas 61

Sussex, 3rd Earl of, Lord Deputy 8, 12
Swasso, Don Graveillo de 55, 195, 196
Sweeney 83, and see McSweeney
Swilly, Lough 74
Synge, John Millington 64

Taaffe, William 85, 120, 138, 182
Tagus River 3, 20, 21, 22
Taranto 152
Terceira, Battle of 58
'Tellez', see Enriquez, Don Diego
Tello, Don Rodrigo 100
Thomond 1, 9, 122, 142–4, 146, 149
Thomond, Earl of 31
Tipperary Co. 141
Tirconnell 15, 74–6, 83–6, 89, 101, 103, 113, 207
Tiraun, Co. Mayo, see Torane
Tirawley, Co. Mayo 55, 180, 182, 189–92, 206, 211
Tobermory Bay, Hebrides 111–12, 213
Toorglass, see Fynglasse
Torane (Tiraun), Co. Mayo 62–4, 71–3, 194, 195
Tormore 78
Tory Is. 92
Traditions in Ireland of Armada wrecks, vii, 28, 145, 149, 181, 184–5, 186, 188, 191, 192–4, 198, 200
Tralee, Co. Kerry 1, 22, 43, 180, 196–8, 200, 213
Trant, James 162, 166, 170, 173, 175–6
Trinity College, Dublin 188
Tromra Castle 146
Truskmore Mt 109
Tuama na Spainneach (Spaniards' Graveyard) 148–9
Tullaghan Bay, Co. Mayo 62, 65
Tully Mt 37
Tuscany, Grand Duke of 188
Twenty Years a-Growing 65
Tyburn 66
'Tyllyny', son of M. de Nowe, see de Nowe
Tyrone, Earl of (Hugh O'Neill) 75, 85, 86, 133, 138, 141, 185, 207, 208

Ulster Museum, Belfast 206, 207, 217
Ulster, Province of 14, 15, 32, 74–6, 103, 123, 125, 138, 141, 181, 185
United Service Inst., London 186
Urcas Squadron, see Armada

Valdes, Don Pedro de 210
Valdes, Gen. Diego Flores do

106, 156, 174, 179, 210
Valentia Is., Co. Kerry 200, 201, 213
Vayell, Murrough Oge M'Murrough I 90
Venetian ships and personnel, *see* Armada
Vicey, Port of 160
Vidal, Capt. Francisco 100
Villa Franca, son of Count of 113
Vizconde, Federico 60, 100

Wales 7
Wallop, Sir Henry 22, 155, 173, 206
Walsingham, Sir Francis 17, 50,

51, 84, 155, 194, 197
Waterford 51, 155, 197
Waterford Co. 11, 140, 141
Waterford, Mayor of 1, 22, 50
Westport, Co. Mayo 45
Wexford Co. 53
White Strand 145, 165
Whyte, Alderman Stephen 53, 72, 143, 151, 189
Whyte, Edward 34, 35, 39, 48, 49, 51, 52, 53, 62, 67, 72, 143, 175, 189, 192, 194, 198
Wicklow Co. 14, 140
Wight, Isle of 18, 60
Wignall, Sidney 28, 161–2, 172, 219

Wig Rock 161
Wild Sports of the West 65, 69
William I of England 4
Wilton, Lord Grey de 141, 160
Winds, prevailing 7
Wodloke, George 50, 51

Young Is. 167, 177
Yugoslavia, *see* Ragusa

Zabras and *Pataches* Squadron, *see* Armada
Zapata, Capt. Don Sebastian 136, 139
Zealand, ships of 26